About Island Press

Since 1984, the nonprofit organization Island Press has been stimulating, shaping, and communicating ideas that are essential for solving environmental problems worldwide. With more than 1,000 titles in print and some 30 new releases each year, we are the nation's leading publisher on environmental issues. We identify innovative thinkers and emerging trends in the environmental field. We work with world-renowned experts and authors to develop cross-disciplinary solutions to environmental challenges.

Island Press designs and executes educational campaigns in conjunction with our authors to communicate their critical messages in print, in person, and online using the latest technologies, innovative programs, and the media. Our goal is to reach targeted audiences—scientists, policymakers, environmental advocates, urban planners, the media, and concerned citizens—with information that can be used to create the framework for long-term ecological health and human well-being.

Island Press gratefully acknowledges major support from The Bobolink Foundation, Caldera Foundation, The Curtis and Edith Munson Foundation, The Forrest C. and Frances H. Lattner Foundation, The JPB Foundation, The Kresge Foundation, The Summit Charitable Foundation, Inc., and many other generous organizations and individuals.

Generous support for the publication of this book was provided by Margot and John Ernst.

The opinions expressed in this book are those of the author(s) and do not necessarily reflect the views of our supporters.

LIFE AFTER CARBON

LIFE AFTER CARBON

*The Next Global
Transformation of Cities*

PETER PLASTRIK
JOHN CLEVELAND

ISLANDPRESS   Washington | Covelo | London

Library of Congress Control Number: 2018946757

All Island Press books are printed on environmentally responsible materials.

Manufactured in the United States of America
10 9 8 7 6 5 4 3 2 1

Keywords
Austin, Berlin, biophilic urbanism, Boston, Boulder, C40, Cape Town, Carbon Neutral Cities Alliance, climate change, Copenhagen, London, Melbourne, Mexico City, Minneapolis, New York City, Oslo, Paris, Portland (OR), renewable energy, Rio de Janeiro, Rotterdam, San Francisco, Seattle, Shanghai, Singapore, Stockholm, sustainable cities, Sydney, Toronto, transit, urban resilience, Urban Sustainability Directors Network (USDN), Vancouver, Washington, DC

FOR URBAN CLIMATE REBELS

—

our friends, tribe, and inspiration

You take delight not in a city's seven or seventy wonders,
but in the answer it gives to a question of yours.

—ITALO CALVINO

Gaia is a tough bitch.

—LYNN MARGULIS

People are unlikely to jettison an unworkable paradigm,
despite many indications it is not functioning properly,
until a better paradigm can be presented.

—THOMAS KUHN

CONTENTS

—

PROLOGUE

—

Creation Stories

Our blue planet has become an urban world. Thousands of cities cover the surface of the earth, housing most of humanity and its economic activities. These are modern cities—developed in much the same mold since the early 1800s, when the world turned to fossil-fuel energy to drive the Industrial Revolution's technologies and globalized markets, urbanization, and pollution.

But the modern city model has outlived its usefulness. It cannot solve the very problems it has helped create, especially global warming. In response, cities worldwide have developed waves of innovations—new policies, programs, tools, business models, and more—to prevent long-term climate damage. Cities that are leading the way—those most fully committed, ambitious, and inventive—are rejecting and replacing basic ideas upon which the modern city was built.

This is not the first time cities have reinvented themselves. It is the next time.

Our story starts in a sacred place in a pioneering city where the arc of the modern urban paradigm is revealed, from its origin before living memory to the beginning of its replacement in our time.

On a riverbank in Australia, our Aboriginal guide sings the birth of a modern city.

"Where all the skyscrapers are right now was a eucalyptus farm," recounts Dean Stewart, of Wemba Wemba-Wergaia heritage, motioning toward the glass-and-steel buildings framing the river's west side. "You'd have bullrushes and water reeds all around this area," as well as mangrove and red gum trees, kangaroos, koalas, pelicans, blackfish, dolphins, and thousands of indigenous people.

At this very spot, he says, "an ancient waterfall a meter-and-a-half tall completely cut this river in half," separating freshwater upstream from the ocean's salty water.

Stewart sways rhythmically, his eyelids fluttering under a New York Yankees baseball cap, as he points into the dark waters. There, he says, the cascade's stones provided a passage across the river: "This waterfall was like an umbilical cord that physically connected the entire traditional population of this region for thousands of years." It was more than a place to walk over: "It had profound spiritual significance for the entire humanity of this area. Every single one of us would know the ancient creation story of the waterfall. We'd know the music of this ancient river system in front of us. We'd know the songs of the mountain ranges, the music of the landscape, of the animals, of the plants. Everything was animated and bound through songs and stories."

Stewart's voice competes with the swelling noises of traffic, pedestrians, and construction. "Listen," he instructs his audience of about forty people from cities on five continents. "These are exactly the same sounds you hear in any major city around the world. These modern city sounds can drown out our ability to connect with country, to connect with place. One of the biggest challenges for us, as city slickers, living our urban lifestyle, is to make some of those connections. Two hundred years ago, you'd be hearing the sound of this ancient river tumbling over the waterfall right here."

Not anymore. In 1835, white settlers arrived on the scene for the first time, rowing up to the waterfall. They founded Melbourne, laid out a street grid alongside the river they called the Yarra, and brought in thousands of sheep, cows, and horses. "Right here, literally, travelers from another world with unimaginable technology and a completely different skin color landed and changed everything forever," Stewart says. "For the Aboriginal civilization that had been here for 50,000 years, this is ground zero." When gold was discovered inland, tens of thousands of fortune seekers from around the world descended on Melbourne, turning a sleepy village into a boomtown. The city dynamited the waterfall to allow boat traffic to get up and down the river and to reduce periodic flooding. "By blowing up the waterfall," Steward says, "they blew up the ancient creation story and the song of this region as well."

The Melbourne that arose embraced a radically different creation story, a tale of industry, commerce, and economic wealth, development, consumption, and growth driven by fossil-fuel energy. This is the story of the modern city, emerging in the nineteenth century with the Industrial Revolution, first in London, and spreading worldwide ever since, now the common habitat for half of humanity. Today more than 4.6 million people live in greater Melbourne, which consists of thirty-one municipalities along the Yarra River and nearby coast. During the week, hundreds of thousands of people commute into the central city, whose buildings ascend from the street grid laid out more than 180 years ago. Like many twenty-first-century cities, Melbourne's population is growing fast, and the city is firmly embedded at the high end of the global economy, with direct flights to Beijing, Los Angeles, Shanghai, and Vancouver. The benefits produced by modern Melbourne are evident: the city's systems house, feed, protect, transport, and employ people at an enormous scale probably never imagined by the place's indigenous people or feasible under their social and economic structures.

Stewart leads the group along a bridge where the waterfall once stood and walks over to a river-wall. "Look over the edge and down," he instructs. "The tide is out a bit so you can see that, for whatever reason, some of the big ancient rocks that made up those waterfalls—incredibly—are still here today. Guys, those rocks are an ancient human culture site. They were used by Aboriginal families in their bare feet before Jesus Christ, Moses, Mohammad, and Abraham were even born." He motions toward nearby pedestrians on the sidewalk and crowds of people in riverside restaurants: "Most Melbournians wouldn't even know those rocks are there."

Wrapping up the walk, Stewart takes the group to a small grassy area surrounded by concrete walkways. Imagine, he says, that this is still the wetland it was two hundred years ago, and we're going to cross it—but not as a crowd: "We're going to go traditional—walking single file, many people with a single footprint." Otherwise, he says, "When you walk, you've just crushed every egg, every nest, destroyed every plant, scared all the bird life and fish away. You've scared away your lunch and your dinner, not just for yourself, but for your whole community."

Yet it is in the very swarms of people moving unsustainably and unaware through this most modern of places that Stewart finds hope for the future. For hundreds of years, he says, people have been eating and socializing at this riverside spot: "It might be craft beer and red wine now, but what we're doing is something absolutely ancient. I find this an inspiration. In our modern, capitalistic world, we are still drawn to exactly the same place. We're still doing exactly the same thing without even realizing it. The land is still calling us to it."

Many other modern cities appear in the pages that follow. To find ideas that respond to the existential dangers of climate change, they are looking back in history to indigenous ways of working with nature and to forgotten ways of consuming resources without producing waste. They are also looking forward to using advanced technologies that tap the earth's renewable bounty and "smart" technologies that efficiently manage a city's metabolism, its use of materials and energy. And to sustain the benefits of modern city living, they are learning how to prepare for a future rendered uncertain by Gaia's response to the industrialization and urbanization that built Melbourne and other modern cities across the globe.

INTRODUCTION

—

The key task now is to tell a new story; of what it is to be a human in the 21st Century.

—GEORGE MONBIOT

A new urban model is emerging worldwide—transforming the ways cities design and use physical space, generate economic wealth, consume and dispose of resources, exploit and sustain the natural ecosystems they need, and prepare for the future.

The model is upending the pillars on which our modern cities were built. It is most evident in several dozen cities, half of them in the United States, that are widely regarded as leaders in making extraordinary efforts to prevent global warming and protect themselves from climate turbulence. These pioneering cities—we call them *urban climate innovation laboratories*—are trying, in just a few decades, to eliminate fossil fuels from their immense, complex systems of energy supply, transportation, buildings, and waste management. Just as systematically and rapidly, they are preparing their built infrastructures, ecosystems, economies, and residents to handle the grave impacts of extreme storms, rainfall, heat, drought, and rising seas—conditions already experienced by many cities and projected to get much, much worse.

A city innovation lab isn't a facility with highly controlled conditions, high-tech equipment, and scientists in white coats. It's not a loft full of computer-savvy urban pioneers holding all-night hack-a-thons. The laboratory is the *entire city*, the complex, real urban world with its messy swarms of businesses, governments, and organizations; urban systems; ideas, interests, and politics; built infrastructure, natural ecosystems, economic sectors; and, of course, all

1

manner of people and groupings. These city labs exist on every populated continent but are concentrated mostly in the US, Canada, China, western and northern Europe, Australia, and Japan. Most are well-known global cities, including Austin, Berlin, Boston, Copenhagen, London, Minneapolis, New York City, Oslo, Paris, Portland, Rotterdam, San Francisco, Seattle, Shanghai, Singapore, Stockholm, Sydney, Toronto, Vancouver, and Washington, DC. Some are smaller, high-spirited cities like Boulder and Melbourne. Several—Cape Town, Mexico City, and Rio de Janeiro—are stepping energetically onto the world climate stage.

These cities are innovating aggressively and radically—by developing and implementing experimental projects, tackling entire urban systems, and reweaving the physical and cultural fabrics of their entire respective cities. Their numerous innovations contain a set of profound ideas that are changing each city's wealth, metabolism, ecology, and identity. These ideas contain the seeds of a new urban paradigm that is reshaping what people think a city can and should become. They introduce new ways for cities to compete successfully in a global twenty-first-century economy that is shifting to renewable energy. They herald new ways for cities to more efficiently use the vast quantities of energy and materials they need. They announce new ways for cities to value and obtain the benefits their wetlands, forestlands, open spaces, and other ecosystems provide. They signal new ways for cities to develop the social and physical adaptability needed to anticipate and prepare for uncertain future conditions.

Many of these ideas have been hovering offstage, even for decades, looking for traction in cities. They were incubated within conceptual frameworks for sustainable development, environmental services, eco-efficiency, urban metabolism, and New Urbanism; or the urban agendas of UN-Habitat and the Club of Rome's Earth Charter; or thought-leader formulations such as the "economy of cities" revealed by Jane Jacobs, the Cradle to Cradle™ principles of designer William McDonough, the "biophilic urbanism" of professor Timothy Beatley, and Jeremy Rifkin's economic vision of the third Industrial Revolution. Now they are being moved onto the world's urban stage by leading cities responding to the imperatives of climate change. They are spreading to other cities, carried through robust global networks that share information, support innovation adoption, and collaborate on further experimentation. At the same time, the mounting "climate-smart" requirements of consumers, corporations, investors, professions, and state and national levels of government are forming enabling conditions that accelerate and globalize the trajectory of this urban evolution.

Since cities were invented some six thousand years ago, they have often evolved fundamentally in response to war and conquest, trade and technologies, earthquakes and other natural disasters, as well as demographic shifts, social reforms, and political revolutions. This time, climate change is driving a full-scale evolution.

The earth's climate has changed drastically many times throughout the planet's long lifespan, but not in the relatively short epoch of city building. "During our entire 6,000-year history as a civilized society, we humans have lived in warm stable climatic conditions," notes Will Travis, former executive director of the San Francisco Bay Conservation and Development Commission. "No great amount of ice was freezing or melting so, except for waves and tides, sea level wasn't going up or down." Most cities arose near water, especially along seacoasts—where an estimated one-hundred-million-plus Americans and six hundred million Chinese live today, most of them in cities. Now these and inland cities face unprecedented climate dangers.

The new urban model is still in an early stage of emergence. Its elements have not yet been fully defined and assembled into a coherent practice by cities. It has not yet locked in as the comprehensive new way of doing business in cities, and it faces considerable obstacles. The fossil-fuel sector continues strenuous political resistance to sweeping changes, and many national and state-level governments have failed to pursue sensible policies. Cities have limited control over many factors needed to implement radical innovations. Many city residents are reluctant to embrace changes that alter their lifestyles or cost them more money. Even the most forward-looking and capable cities sometimes struggle to develop the technical competencies, financial capital, and community constituencies needed to move forward aggressively.

Life after Carbon is an exercise in future mapping. It starts at the edge of the known world of urban climate action—the profusion of innovations that cities are developing using technical know-how, robust information sharing, and full-throated advocacy for change. Then it looks down the road these cities are traveling on and offers a framework for the ideas and applications that are propelling them toward a new urban future. The map we offer is not a picture of what should be happening; we leave that advocacy to others. Nor is it a prediction about what will happen; on most days, the world seems too turbulent to tell with any confidence whether it will ascend to a new order or descend into chaos. Instead, the map is a projection of possibilities grounded in what is already happening in cities.

We bring together what many urban innovators in numerous cities are thinking and doing and propose that they have begun to invent a different way for a city to be a city. We describe this future destination and illuminate a pathway, still being constructed, for getting there.

In coming years, cities around the world will need to undertake far more radical decarbonization and climate adaptation strategies than they have tried so far. Our hope is that the framework we provide supports their pursuit of this next generation of changes. It serves as a benchmark against which to assess whether a city's plans and decisions can have maximum beneficial impact for the city or whether opportunities are being missed. It can help cities recast the purpose of their climate-change efforts into the broader goal of creating a better city for current and future generations of residents. Presented in this light, a city's climate strategies can resonate more with the public and stakeholders. Innovation lab cities have already recognized that their climate innovations are generating positive side effects such as the creation of "green" jobs and the reduction of air pollution, waste, and energy costs. But only a few cities have offered their residents a tangible and comprehensive picture of their city's future in an era driven by the energy revolution and climate turbulence. The story we tell in *Life after Carbon* can arm cities with a compelling narrative about themselves and their futures.

Since 2009, we have worked with many of the cities best known for designing and implementing climate innovations. We have helped these cities' leaders team up across the United States and globally to advance their innovation processes. As advisors and enablers, we've gotten to know hundreds of city climate innovators across greatly different contexts—all part of a new international community of urban climate practitioners. We've shared firsthand in their many successes and frustrations and have admired their tenacity in the face of difficulties and setbacks.

We joined representatives of seventeen leading cities inside the Dome of Visions, a temporary geodesic structure erected along Copenhagen's waterfront, and helped them form the Carbon Neutral Cities Alliance (CNCA), a global research-and-development network pursuing innovations for radical decarbonization in cities. We guided climate-change leaders from thirty-three cities worldwide—from Cape Town to Paris, Rio de Janeiro to Shanghai—through study tours of four US cities (Austin, Boston, San Francisco, and Washington, DC) whose content we developed and delivered. We've advised some of the leading US philanthropic investors in urban climate action, helping shape the granting of tens of millions of dollars. We've debriefed city climate innovators around the world to produce reports about the edge of urban innovation for reducing greenhouse gas emissions and preparing for climate disruptions. Especially important to the development of our insights has been John Cleveland's "deep dive" into Boston's carbon reduction and climate preparedness as executive director of its Green Ribbon Commission, a world-class group of business, institutional, and civic leaders.

We know many of the questions that cities are asking about the various challenges involved in climate innovation, including: How can we obtain even bigger reductions in greenhouse gas (GHG) emissions? How can we decide how much sea-level rise to plan for? How can we pay for innovations? How can we develop more and sustained local political support for change? How can we ensure that the costs and benefits of climate action are distributed fairly in the community? How can we enlist other governments in the metropolitan region to the cause?

This book's starting question is different from these questions. In what way, it asks, is the remarkable proliferation of urban climate innovation, with all its creativity, successes, and challenges, changing the fundamental nature of cities?

Innovation by cities is an age-old phenomenon. The experiments of ancient cities produced profound and enduring advancements: markets, democracy, libraries, bureaucracy, universities, and writing. Cities "have been engines of innovation since Plato and Socrates bickered in an Athenian marketplace," notes urban economist Edward Glaeser. "The streets of Florence gave us the Renaissance, and the streets of Birmingham gave us the Industrial Revolution."

But cities are more than platforms for innovation; they, themselves, are an innovation. Born out of experimentation thousands of years ago, they are a great and sustained invention that reveals, realizes, and refines the collaborative potential of our species. "At the brink of recorded history," explains Lewis Mumford in his masterwork, *The City in History*, "a great urban transformation took place." It was an implosion of human power: "The many diverse elements of the community hitherto scattered over a great valley system and occasionally into regions far beyond, were mobilized and packed together under pressure, behind the massive walls of the city."

This innovation, "the city," keeps changing, in a continuous evolution from its origin in the simple Neolithic village to its manifestation as the complex modern metropolis. But the urban essence remains: the city is a dense collective of human energy and talent that in a defined geography and governance boundary develops a thickly built living environment, exploits natural ecosystems near and far, spatially organizes social distinctions and cohesion, and generates economic wealth.

The city is more important than ever. When the modern city began to develop around 1800, there were few large cities. Demographers say that only about 3 percent of the world's one billion people lived in cities. Just a few cities—London, Beijing, Tokyo (known then as Edo), Baghdad, and Istanbul among them—had ever contained as many as one million residents. In North America, only Philadelphia held more than forty thousand people. When Britain invaded New York City in 1776, its force of thirty-two thousand soldiers outnumbered the city's inhabitants.

Now, though, 3.9 billion people live in cities—more than half the world's population—and millions more arrive every month by birth or migration from rural areas and small towns, in search of economic advancement or personal development. In the US, about three hundred cities each have one hundred thousand or more residents. Worldwide, more than five hundred cities contain at least one million people, and there are thirty-one "megacities" with more than ten million people each. A single megacity, the Greater Tokyo Area, is home to more people than lived in all cities in the world just four lifetimes ago. In this century, the majority of the next generations' children will be born and raised in cities. By 2050, the United Nations projects, population growth could add two billion people to cities. Two of every three human beings will dwell in cities.

As we became an urban-dwelling species, we made cities in the same basic modern image. Whatever a city's age, history, or location, affluence and stage of development, economic niche or governance model, it has developed and manages massive, complex systems for buildings, transportation, energy supply, waste, water, and more. And these systems use pretty much the same technologies and processes and are professionally managed in much the same way everywhere. In all but the world's poorest nations, 90 to 100 percent of urban populations have access to electricity. In most big cities, driving is the way to get around; between 50 and 90 percent of urban travel to and from work is done in privately owned vehicles rather than on public transit or by walking or bicycling. In China, the astonishing surge of urbanization that occurred during the past twenty years—hundreds of new cities for hundreds of millions of people—adhered to familiar elements of modern-city design: huge "superblocks" of massive energy-devouring buildings; wide streets, highways, and ring roads for cars; separated residential areas and office districts; and sprawl. These cities, explains international journalist Wade Shepard in *Ghost Cities of China*, are "centralized, 'downtown,' urban areas that consist of a commercial core and, often times a CBD (central business district), which are surrounded by residential areas, schools, hospitals, and green space."

Even in Rio de Janeiro, Mexico City, and other megacities where huge populations live in informal settlements, much of the standard urban model prevails. It's just swamped by slum dwellings and stymied by poor transportation infrastructure, inadequate waste and sewage systems, and ineffective land use. "Rio de Janeiro is actually two very distinct cities," explains Larry Rohter, former South American bureau chief for the *New York Times*. "Some five million people live at or near sea level in what Brazilians describe as 'the asphalt,' supplied with the usual public services: subways, electricity, garbage collection, and at least a semblance of the rule of law. But another million or more Cariocas, as Rio residents call themselves, have been consigned to 'the hillside,' a world of squatter settlements known as favelas, most of them indeed on hills, in which normal urban amenities like sewers and running water are scarce and a strikingly different system of laws, values, and conduct prevails."

It was no accident that the development and spread of modern cities coincided with the development and spread of the Industrial Revolution and the fossil-fuel economy. Starting in Britain, cities became the places where investors in new coal-burning factories could most profitably organize and obtain the necessary mass labor and consumer markets they needed, as Andreas Malm explains in his award-winning *Fossil Capital*. As cities grew into centers of population and economic activity, they also became the locales from which as much as 70 percent of all greenhouse gases are emitted.

The urban evolution triggered by climate change is a story of coevolution: modern cities are changing the planet's climate; the climate is changing modern cities. Cities are where the climate challenge and opportunities reside and where responses must work.

Life after Carbon unfolds in three parts.

It starts in the urban climate innovation laboratories we know. We show what makes them tick and describe the many innovations that put them at the leading edge of urban transformation. The twenty-five innovation labs we draw inspiration from—our main database—are located in fifteen different countries and six continents. They are in several different climatic zones, with about two-thirds on seacoasts. They generate varying amounts of per capita GHG emissions. They are relatively wealthy cities, in either global or national contexts.

FEATURED URBAN CLIMATE INNOVATION LABORATORIES

Austin, US

Berlin, Germany

Boston, US

Boulder, US

Cape Town, South Africa

Copenhagen, Denmark

London, UK

Melbourne, Australia

Mexico City, Mexico

Minneapolis, US

New York City, US

Oslo, Norway

Paris, France

Portland, US

Rio de Janeiro, Brazil

Rotterdam, Netherlands

San Francisco, US

Seattle, US

Singapore, Republic of Singapore

Stockholm, Sweden

Sydney, Australia

Toronto, Canada

Vancouver, Canada

Washington, DC, US

Other cities probably deserve the title of climate innovation lab. Adelaide, Auckland, Bogotá, Bristol, Buenos Aires, Curitiba, Hamburg, Helsinki, Milan, Oakland, Shenzhen, Tokyo, and Yokohama come to mind. We draw on some of their efforts in the chapters that follow but do not know them well enough to feature them more fully.

Leading innovation cities serve as key hubs in the numerous organizations and networks of urban climate innovation practitioners that have emerged worldwide in just a few decades. This is an extraordinary and unprecedented urban capacity: countless city officials, community activists, professionals, corporate leaders, scholars, and others collaborating to develop and share policies and practices that work.

In the book's second part, we closely examine four transformative ideas that are contained in lab cities' climate innovations and are replacing ideas from which the modern city model developed. We show how new ideas in the eighteenth and nineteenth centuries reshaped the physical, economic, environmental, and social characteristics of urban settlements, making them into the cities in which we live. We describe the similar evolutionary process that is occurring today, touched off by the innovative urban response to climate change and unleashing ideas that amount to a new model for the development of future cities.

Finally, we depict the work that lies ahead on the road to urban transformation. Cities cannot complete the journey by themselves, even as they support each other and band together. They simply don't control or strongly influence enough of the factors for success. It turns out, though, that cities are not alone in their struggle. The same transformational ideas are becoming broadly held and applied by businesses, professionals, consumers, citizens, and policymakers at other levels of government. They are emerging as a widespread way of thinking, a *gestalt*, which guides decisions in realms where cities have little control. This unmistakable trend promises to carry change beyond the world's most innovative cities and into cities everywhere.

Even as radical change gains traction in these ways, we must recognize that the work of urban climate innovation is still in an early stage of development. There is much more to do not just to spread and accelerate innovation but also to boost its effectiveness and deepen its impact. We close the story of the next global transformation of cities, the one we see all around, by surveying the landscape of crucial work ahead. This work is already under way in innovation lab cities.

The potential urban transformation we describe has decades to go before it can become the new normal for cities. Climate change is not the only driver of urban disruption and innovation, but it has several momentous characteristics. Its threat is planetary; every city must pay attention and the sooner the better. Its causes and effects are comprehensive and systemic; nearly every core urban system's performance and viability are at stake. It impacts the private, public, professional, and nonprofit sectors, as well as the individual, family, neighborhood, city, metropolitan region, state, national, and international levels.

Because of climate change, cities around the world will be different at the end of the twenty-first century. Whether they will be prosperous, healthy, safe, and better places for everyone to live remains to be seen. There's no guarantee that a climate-driven transformation will occur fully in all cities or many cities or even just a few cities. But a possible future city, a radically different city than the modern one we know, is coming into view. It is emerging in cities all around us, in the cities that have decided to turn the climate disaster into an opportunity, in cities that are making the urban future now.

*L*ife after Carbon depicts a global urban dynamic but converts financial amounts, distances, weights, temperatures, land mass, and other quantities into American-used units of measurement. As much as possible, conversion of non-US financial amounts is based on exchange rates at the time. In the case of Chinese names, we have employed the Chinese practice of putting the family name before the given name.

PART I

—

On the Innovation Pathway

01 INNOVATION PROLIFERATION

—

Cities are standing up, taking action and using one single, unified voice to combat the effects of climate change.

—PARIS MAYOR ANNE HIDALGO

When you spend time in some of the world's most prominent urban climate innovation laboratories, as we have, you can see the future of cities in the making. A whirlwind world tour of the labs would provide a set of unique urban experiences.

In San Francisco, we would visit a huge facility on a pier on the city's famous bay. We'd put on white plastic hardhats and roam through the noisy, solar-powered Recology building, around machines that sort 1.5 million pounds of urban waste every day— garbage, paper, food scraps, bottles and cans, computers, batteries, furniture, and much more—all destined for recycling, composting, and reuse. "A world without waste" is the plant's mantra.

In Copenhagen, we would take a bicycle ride during the evening rush hour that sends tens of thousands of bicyclists streaming home from work and school along a specially designed 242-mile street-and-road network that is a route of choice for commuters. It's a constant flow of people, young and old, managers in suits, women in high heels, parents hauling children—in a city that has more bikes than cars.

Alongside Boston's sparkling harbor on a clear morning, we would visit an eight-story, 132-bed hospital built on a waterfront site raised more than three feet above the existing ground level, with critical electrical equipment located on the roof instead of in the basement to avoid flooding from rising seas and storm surges. We'd walk around the building's exterior to see landscape walls that will serve as artificial reefs to buffer rising waters.

In Mexico City, we would ride one of the hundreds of red, articulated Metrobúses that move along bus-only corridors in the city's extensive bus rapid transit (BRT) system. Every day, nearly one million passengers, including many car owners, take the fast, reliable service, which didn't exist just ten years ago.

In Shanghai, inside a building on North Zhongshan Road, we would eyeball a huge, wall-mounted computerized board that displays trading prices for the city's cap-and-trade market for CO_2 emissions of more than three hundred companies. You can monitor market activity on a smartphone, if you read Chinese.

One afternoon, in Vancouver's Southeast False Creek neighborhood, under the Cambie Street Bridge, we would tour the first pump station in Canada that mines sewage for heat to warm water that circulates into nearby buildings and heats thousands of residences.

In New York City, we would head offshore to see where the $60 million Living Breakwaters project is installing a half-mile-long underwater "necklace" of stone and bioenhancing concrete mounds and restoring oyster beds to protect a community and beaches destroyed by Hurricane Sandy. "Rather than cutting communities off from the water with a levee or wall," proclaim project designers, "our approach embraces the water."

In Rotterdam, we'd walk through the Zoho "climate-proof" district and into Benthemplein Water Square while it is dry—a large public space for mingling, events, and recreation that also serves as a giant rainwater collector, with a water wall, a rain well designed to visibly gush rainwater onto the square, and three basins that collect water and slowly release it into the ground.

We could show you much more of the climate-driven urban future.

In Oslo, we could visit the city hall where the Nobel Peace Prize is awarded, then have a beer in a café on nearby, treelined Karl Johans Gate, the city's main street, in a historic business and office downtown area from which cars will be banned starting in 2019.

In Seattle, we could climb the wood-and-steel steps of the six-story Bullitt Center, described by owners as the "greenest commercial building in the world." The center is designed to function "like a forest of Douglas fir trees," explains Bullitt Foundation president Denis Hayes, a cofounder of Earth Day, "getting its energy from the sun, soaking up the rainwater, and serving as an incredible public amenity."

In Sydney, we could enjoy views of the iconic opera house and busy harbor from one of the downtown office buildings that have reduced GHG emissions by more than 45 percent, saving $21.6 million a year on electricity costs, and have cut annual water consumption by 36 percent, the equivalent of nearly two thousand Olympic-sized swimming pools.

In Minneapolis, we could ride on the eleven-mile-long electric light-rail, Green Line, opened in 2014 with eighteen stations, operating twenty-four hours a day through bustling neighborhoods and corridors and carrying an average of nearly forty thousand riders each weekday. Initial plans for the $1 billion line changed after community groups protested that low-income neighborhoods with majority African American and immigrant populations would be bypassed.

In Portland, Oregon, sixty miles from the Pacific Ocean, we could jog over the Willamette River on Tilikum Crossing, the first major bridge in America for pedestrians, bicyclists, and public transit only—no cars or trucks. The $135-million span's design was raised three feet to accommodate future tidal surges on the river.

In Stockholm, we could peddle an electric bicycle through the Royal Seaport, a completely new low-carbon-emissions district that is just minutes from the city center and will have nearly fifty thousand housing and office units powered by renewable energy. Developers have had no problem selling apartments, and there was a waiting list for rentals.

The urban future lives online, too, in case you want to trek there without leaving home.

You can send emails to any of Melbourne's seventy-seven thousand publicly owned trees. Since 2013, many of them have received love letters from around the world. One tree got an email asking it how to solve Greece's financial crisis. The golden elm at Punt Road and Alexandra Avenue was saved from being removed to widen a road because it had received so many adoring emails from locals.

At the website for Cape Town, the first African city to adopt a climate-change strategy, you can listen to a catchy tune, "Get Your Piece of the Sun," a mix of traditional South African music and other music genres that was commissioned by the city government to promote the use of solar water heaters—a campaign that contributed to the installation of forty-six thousand of the devices.

Each of these examples is a city innovation in response to climate change. Promoting bicycling and walking, speeding up bus movement through a city, and banning cars from central districts are ways to reduce the urban flow of gas-powered cars and their GHG emissions. Cutting energy consumption in buildings and by industries, recycling waste, mining wastewater for heat instead of burning fossil fuels, and promoting solar water heaters also lessen damaging emissions. Redesigning buildings, public squares, and coastlines and raising bridge heights reduce a city's vulnerability to flooding and sea-level rise due to climate change, while caring for a city's trees soaks up excess storm water and helps cool streets subject to increasingly hot weather.

Many of these city innovations have received recognition and awards from organizations pushing for climate action. Many are being adopted by other cities. Taken together they amount to just a small fraction of the vast portfolio of innovations under way in these climate-lab and other cities worldwide. They are the leading edge of a rising wave of urban change.

When global warming appeared on the world's radar screen in the late 1980s, few people worried about what cities would do about it. Cities were widely regarded as environmental villains, not saviors. Even two decades later, says Sadhu Johnston, then Chicago's chief environmental officer, "Most environmental groups were not seeing cities as playing a role when it came to climate change and environmental benefits. Cities were still viewed as 'the evil city,' with pollution coming out and resources going in to be consumed."

It was widely assumed that a serious response to climate change was up to national governments cooperating internationally, as well as private investors and professionals like engineers and architects. Those who did think about a role for cities weren't sure how much cities could do or would be willing to do to reduce GHG emissions. These types of concerns hindered advocates of city climate innovation for many years. Steve Nicholas recalls the first cabinet meeting of Seattle's newly elected mayor in January 2001, when he was the city's director of sustainability: "We were developing the mayor's first 100-day agenda. The mayor asked what should be in the agenda, what should he try to accomplish? I raised my hand and said, 'Mr. Mayor, what we need is a climate action plan.'" The suggestion got a vigorous reaction. "The idea drew more than a few chuckles from some of the mayor's other advisers," says Nicholas, now working at a nonprofit that helps cities develop and implement climate strategies. "They said things like, 'This is a 100-*day* agenda, Steve, not a 100-*year* agenda' and 'They call it *global* warning for a reason, Steve.' Even in a politically progressive city like Seattle, the feeling was that we don't have a dog in the climate fight, it is not our issue, and that there is not enough that we can do to make it worthwhile to invest the political and financial capital."

In 2009, mayors showed up in force in Copenhagen to influence national leaders negotiating at the United Nations conference to reduce greenhouse gas emissions, but they were kept on the sidelines. "We had a tent in the middle of the town square," recalls Michael Bloomberg, then-mayor of New York City. "Mayors couldn't even get into the main conference hall." The talks failed, but six years later, when national leaders met in Paris to try again to reach an agreement, cities were in the spotlight. By then the UN had reported that as much as 70 percent of global GHG emissions was produced in cities: "Urban centres have become the real battleground in the fight against climate change." Its top executive, Ban Ki-moon, had told his bosses, the world's nation-states, that the "struggle for global sustainability will be won or lost" in cities.

When the Paris talks opened, leaders from more than four hundred cities assembled at the Renaissance-era Hôtel de Ville (city hall) to press national leaders and pledge collective support for ambitious climate-change efforts. A year and a half later, when President Donald Trump announced his intention to withdraw the US from the Paris climate accord to reduce GHG emissions, nearly three hundred American mayors rose up in defiance and pledged publicly to uphold the agreement. By then, membership in the Global Covenant of Mayors for Climate and Energy exceeded seven thousand cities committed to achieve a carbon-neutral world this century. Meanwhile, a global network with a focus on the climate risks of urban areas, the 100 Resilient Cities, had expanded to cities that contained a total of five hundred million people.

The mounting urban uproar has helped turn up the heat on national governments to take climate action. More significant, though, has been the outpouring of urban climate innovations, which shows national leaders and everyone else that cities are doing a great deal in response to climate change—and could do even more.

Cities determined to take ambitious climate action have had to invent nearly all of what they've done. "When we did the first global warming analyses, realizing how huge the issue was, we wondered how we could ever reduce our emissions," recalls Susan Anderson, director of the Bureau of Planning and Sustainability in Portland, Oregon. She participated in one of the earliest efforts to figure out what cities could do, the 1991 Urban CO_2 Reduction Project: "I used to live on the ocean. Huge ships would go through the channel between the coast and an island. If they wanted to shift the direction of these gigantic tankers, they had to start doing it a mile ahead of time. That's how we city people felt: we have this huge world running on fossil fuels and we see this end point to get to. But how do we move the tanker?"

Even traditional responses to climatic risks, such as building bigger barriers to prevent flooding, won't work in cities threatened by seas rising many feet and a sharp increase in intense downpours. "We can't just keep building higher levees, because we will end up living behind 10-meter [30-foot] walls," explains Henk Ovink, a globe-trotting Dutch urban planner who serves as his nation's Special Envoy for International Water Affairs. "Big gates and dams at the sea" will not be enough to protect cities from the climate turbulence that is coming, he says.

Despite the challenges, a great surge of climate innovations designed, tested, and implemented by cities is sweeping through the world. Mayors assemble several times a year to share and promote the thousands of actions their administrations have taken. Nearly every day, clusters of city-government staffers worldwide meet online, by phone, or in person to exchange information and advice about climate policies and practices that no city worried about just a few years ago. An online stream of city climate news from *Daily Climate*, *Citiscope*, *CityMetric*, and other sources regularly surfaces inspiring stories about what cities are doing.

C40 Cities, a global network of megacities, reported in 2015 that sixty-six member cities had taken more than 9,831 actions to reduce emissions or adapt to climate change since 2009—half of them implemented citywide and a quarter of them costing more than $10 million each. Researchers looking at a mix of ten large cities in different regions and climates, and with different socioeconomic conditions, calculated that in 2014–2015 alone they spent more than $6 billion to adapt to climate changes. In 2017, the 100 Resilient Cities announced its member cities had taken more than 1,600 actions, many of them aimed at climate adaptation. A year earlier, the Urban Sustainability Directors Network found that about ninety of its members, all North American cities, were planning or had implemented projects to protect bicycle lanes on streets, switch municipal fleets to low-carbon fuels, help commercial buildings improve their energy efficiency, and install LED streetlights. That same year, in China, twenty-three cities that altogether contain nearly a fifth of the nation's population committed to achieve long-term reduction of GHG emissions by pioneering green and low-carbon development. And 189 cities around the world—more than fifty of them in the US—measured and publicly disclosed their GHG emissions using the Carbon Disclosure Project (CDP) system.

The content of this city-driven profusion is incredibly broad. In December 2016, C40 Cities recognized leading climate actions by more than thirty cities. When the Carbon Neutral Cities Alliance's twenty cities met in July 2017, it had to limit each member's update on accomplishments to just a few minutes or risk spending hours just sharing news.

- Berlin was phasing out use of coal in the city.
- Copenhagen was developing one hundred megawatts of wind power and will be using electric public buses.
- New York City had installed one hundred megawatts of solar power and wanted to increase that amount by tenfold.

- Rio de Janeiro had built a ten-mile metro line and added a fifteen-mile bus rapid transit line.
- Stockholm had decided to phase out its last coal-burning plant by 2022, years earlier than planned.
- Toronto had adopted a ten-year plan for its bicycle network, dedicating about $12 million a year to implementation.
- Washington, DC, has designed a city Green Bank to finance local renewable energy and energy-efficiency projects.

As eye-opening and impressive as the variety, inventiveness, and global volume of city climate projects may be, it only begins to reveal the deeper pattern of urban transformation that's occurring. To see more, you have to study the world's urban climate innovation laboratories.

02 URBAN CLIMATE INNOVATION LABORATORIES

—

In the course of the past 2,500 years, a small number of relatively large cities have functioned as hotbeds of revolutionary creativity.

—ÅKE ANDERSSON

Urban climate innovation labs are cities that have come to understand themselves, their place in the world, in a new way and act boldly on their changed awareness. They take to heart the challenge of climate change. They publicly commit to do more about it than many national governments have pledged. They immerse themselves in figuring out what they can do. And they start doing it, despite the many technical, political, economic, and social difficulties involved.

They are changing just about everything in "the city"—the buildings, streets, neighborhoods, and other physical infrastructure; the supply and use of energy, water, transportation, green spaces, and other land; as well as the consumption of resources and the disposal of waste. They are changing the economic opportunities and the costs of doing business and living in the city. They are changing the minds and habits of their residents. They are changing the identities of their cities.

These labs originate from decisions by city government and civic leaders, especially mayors. Without a mayor's leadership and blessing, a city rarely becomes a climate innovation laboratory. Whether mayors are elected locally or appointed by national governments, they command important local assets and the power to mobilize others.

"Mayors define cities," observes scholar Benjamin Barber in *If Mayors Ruled the World*. "A mayor can incarnate the courage of a city." When climate-ambitious mayors rule for several terms—for instance, New York's Michael Bloomberg, Boston's late Thomas Menino, Sydney's Clover Moore, and Vancouver's Gregor Robertson—they can shape much of the city's lasting response to climate change.

Some mayors (and city managers) act because they feel a compelling moral obligation to participate in reducing global warming to save the planet and society. "Climate action is not something to be undertaken somewhere else in another time by someone else," says Oslo's Governing Mayor Raymond Johansen, who trained as a plumber and became a longtime local and national politician. "We have to take responsibility."

Some feel a deep love of place, of their particular city, and a desire to protect its people and treasures from harm. "Doing nothing is not an option," says Ahmed Aboutaleb, appointed mayor of Rotterdam after working in public relations and as director of a nonprofit institute for multiculturalism. "The proper functioning of the city is much too important to be left to chance." Vancouver Mayor Gregor Robertson, an organic-juice entrepreneur turned politician, sees positive impacts in taking climate action. "It just makes good sense for the health of the city," he says. "Whether it's economic opportunity or quality of life, these changes are benefits. They're not easy. People have to change their lifestyle and the city has to change how it operates. But that's life—and if we don't change, there are dire consequences."

Some mayors have experienced climate-induced devastation in their cities and pledge not to let it happen again. And some envision opportunities to make their cities into better places for their people. "Climate action will not only keep us safer in the face of higher tides, more intense storms, and more extreme heat," explains Boston Mayor Martin Walsh, a former local union official and representative in state government. "It will also create jobs, improve public spaces and public health, and make our energy supply more efficient and resilient." In Cape Town, where about half of the 3.7 million residents live in extreme poverty, Executive Mayor Patricia de Lille also strikes an upbeat note: "A city that pays attention to the source of its power, its energy, food and livelihoods, a connected, integrated city of neighbourhoods and communities, is the kind of city of which we all dream," says the former laboratory technician, trade-union leader, and political-party founder. "Only the courageous pursuit of low-carbon living will get us there."

But the development of urban climate innovation laboratories depends on more than the decisions of a few individuals. City labs are much bigger social platforms than that. In these cities, there has been enough convergence of thought and vision to permit each city to step off its business-as-usual path. The convergence occurs within and across the basic layers of a city's people. Some leaders of local government, civic institutions, and the business and academic communities—whether elected, appointed, or self-anointed—decide to do something about climate change. A share of the city's skilled professional class—city planners, architects, engineers, real estate developers, government and corporate managers, financiers, environmental and social-change advocates, community organizers, philanthropists, and university researchers—integrate climate realities into their assumptions and practices. And a portion of the city's populace, *the people*, comes to value having ways to live, work, play, and consume that take climate change into account. These layers of society interact constantly in any city, stimulating and constraining each other's evolution in thought and action. In innovation lab cities, they align around the need to act boldly on climate change.

For climate innovation to occur, says Debbie Raphael, director of the San Francisco Department of the Environment, "You have to have courageous elected officials. Their careers are on the line." But there's much more to the equation, she continues: "You also have to have a willing public. The public can be the fierce champion or put up a lot of resistance. And you have to have innovative businesses with a desire to be at their own cutting edge of change." When these characteristics join with the existence of highly skilled government bureaucrats, Raphael says, San Francisco and other cities develop "a culture of risk taking that permeates everything."

In the city climate labs we know, as more and more people in each social layer comprehend climate change and commit to action, the city's convergence around taking climate action reaches a critical mass. Something new begins to emerge: a citywide "ecology" of connected, interacting people, institutions, and sectors that align their knowledge, skills, and assets to develop responses to climate change. This alters the culture and politics of the city, introducing a way of being that rejects business as usual, expects the city to be as "climate smart" as possible, and supports taking risks—trying things—to make it so.

This new urban culture is not monolithic. Many people in a city innovation lab may be unconvinced of the new direction or may support a change in concept but not when it directly affects their lives. Some may contend that changes will disproportionately burden or benefit certain economic, social, ethnic, racial, or religious groups and areas in the city and perpetuate historical inequities. Nearly any city climate innovation will encounter skeptics and opponents, and sometimes the concerns slow or even halt the pace of change. But in an urban climate innovation lab, the ecology of climate-change agents generally prevails over inertia and opposition.

A Global Mosaic

You have to know more than one city lab to get a feel for what they are and what they mean for the evolution of cities. Although these cities draw inspiration and innovations from each other, they vary in ways that shape their climate-change priorities and the innovations they produce.

Their climates and geographies differ, and therefore so do the biggest climate threats they face. Boston, Stockholm, and Vancouver are cold-weather cities that require enormous amounts of energy to heat buildings, while Austin, Mexico City, Rio de Janeiro, and Singapore use energy mostly to cool buildings. Copenhagen has been damaged by torrential cloudbursts, while Washington, DC, and Melbourne face extreme heat in summer, and London anticipates droughts. Nearly half of coastal Rotterdam's inner city lies below sea level, Boston's harbor district stands on low-lying fill that could be inundated by rising seas, and land in Shanghai is slowly sinking while the city contends with rising oceans and river flooding.

The cities differ in their relevant historical legacies: population density, type of energy supply, housing stock, public transit, economic opportunities, and more. Some—Shanghai, London, Paris,

──────────── AWAKENING

*B*efore climate change arrived in the headlines in the late 1980s, the groundwork for climate leadership had been laid. The creators of urban climate innovation labs span three overlapping generations, each of which experienced its own jolt of awakening and urgent call to action.

Those who are in their sixties, seventies, or eighties were present when the environmental movement came to life, assembling for the first Earth Day in 1970, spurred by biologist Rachel Carson's 1962 book, *Silent Spring*, which warned of the dire impact of pesticides, and by the mounting visible crises caused by hazardous and toxic industrial processes.

City innovators in their forties and fifties, many of whom are entering positions of substantial authority in government, business, and the civil sector, were coming of age when a 1987 United Nations report "Our Common Future"—known as the Brundtland Report after its chair, Gro Harlem Brundtland, Norway's first female prime minister—put a new idea onto society's radar screen. It offered "sustainable development" as an overarching concept in which the use of physical ecosystems and renewable resources would occur "within the limits of regeneration and natural growth." Brundtland called for action by all nations but also signaled the importance of cities: "The most immediate environmental concerns of most people will be urban ones."

These two generations were joined by a third generation of innovators that arrived after the dawn of climate-change awareness. The commitment of countless numbers of twenty- and thirty-year-old innovators, many of whom are raising young children, was sparked by Al Gore's 2006 documentary film *An Inconvenient Truth*, which detailed the advent of global warming, argued that the means were available to reverse the trend if only there was the political will to act, and called on viewers to take personal responsibility for solving the problem.

Singapore, and New York City—are among the densest cities in the world. Boston, Boulder, Cape Town, London, and Sydney have relied heavily on burning coal, natural gas, and fuel oil for electricity and heating, while Oslo, Seattle, and Vancouver depend mostly on hydropower that produces relatively low GHG emissions. Copenhagen's highly efficient district heating system, set up in the 1980s, warms 97 percent of the city. Few cities outside of Europe have anything like this.

The cities' building stocks have different characteristics that affect their energy efficiency. In Sydney, for instance, 70 percent of residents live in apartment buildings, not single-family houses. In Paris, nearly 80 percent of buildings were built pre-1974, before any regulatory standards for heating efficiency were in place. In London, 60 percent of housing has solid exterior walls, instead of cavity walls that can be filled with extra insulation to reduce energy consumption.

How people move around also varies from city to city. In Copenhagen, 29 percent of all trips are taken on bicycles, a percentage far greater than in any North American city. Shanghai Metro opened its first line in 1993—more than a century after London built the first underground—and quickly became the world's largest rapid transit system by length of route.

Lab cities have histories of economic and social disparity and injustice based on race, ethnicity, or class. In Cape Town, the nation's apartheid policies left behind spatial patterns of residential segregation that located poorer communities far from employment opportunities, making the cost of providing and using public transport unsustainable. Boston, New York City, Washington, DC, and other US cities have long histories of racial discrimination in housing and labor markets.

Another critical distinction among city labs is their governance and political contexts. Some cities exercise direct control over taxation, building codes, and other important policies as well as essential assets like utilities. Voters in Boulder and San Francisco have supported local tax increases that pay for climate action. Portland has tightly limited urban sprawl for decades to make the city more compact and dense. Seattle and Austin own their electric utilities. Stockholm and Austin control large expanses of land that are being developed into low-carbon residential and commercial districts.

Other cities don't have sufficient authority over building codes, mass-transit and road systems, and other important drivers of change and must depend heavily on state or provincial and national governments to adopt climate-smart policies.

In some cases, the cities exist in highly supportive policy contexts: San Francisco innovates within California's cap-and-trade market for carbon emissions, and Stockholm functions under Sweden's carbon tax, the highest in the world. Shanghai serves as a pilot site for climate innovations that China's central government wants to design and spread, including development of a cap-and-trade market for carbon emissions. Singapore is a city-state in which the same political party has won every election for the last seventy years.

Many climate-innovation cities have to skirmish endlessly with hostile higher-level administrations. Cape Town went to court to force the national energy regulator to allow the city to purchase solar and wind energy from independent producers instead of relying on the national energy utility's fossil-fuel electricity. Copenhagen's mayor pressed the nation's prime minister to support affordable-housing requirements for urban developments to help ensure future cities are not just for affluent residents. Many US cities, of course, have denounced the federal government's hostility toward climate-change policies.

The variations among city labs mean that climate innovation is more of a ragged edge of change than a solid wall advancing uniformly across the world's urban landscape. Although city labs tackle climate change comprehensively, they tend to focus attention on different problems in different ways and develop different strengths, or strong suits, for innovation.

Nonetheless, the set of city labs we know share three characteristics that put them at the front end of urban climate innovation. They commit to achieving audacious long-term goals for responding to climate change. They focus on urban systems as the targets for achieving the large-scale change they seek. They initiate experiments—risking failure—to see what will work. Year after year, they design, test, revise, and implement a profusion of innovations.

03 GOALS, SYSTEMS, CLUSTERS, AND WAVES

—

Build the city of your dreams and watch as the choices you make shape your city. . . . Every decision, big or small, right or wrong, has real consequences.

—SIMCITY

City laboratories around the world pursue radical goals for climate change. They want to eliminate the use of fossil fuels in the production of electricity, heating and cooling of buildings, and powering of vehicles—replacing it with renewable energy sources. They want to end the dominance of automobiles and trucks over city streets—replacing them with flows of pedestrians, bicyclists, buses, trams, and light rails that invigorate city life. They want to ensure that every new and existing building, from single-family houses to office and apartment towers and industrial facilities, uses only a small fraction of the energy and water that is currently consumed or produces surplus energy for sale. They want to eliminate the vast amount of solid waste that cities bury in landfills, dump into waterways, or ship to other places—replacing waste management with a *circular economy* that reduces consumption of materials while reusing and recycling nearly everything.

These cities know that climate science suggests that by 2050 at the latest, it is crucial to reduce annual GHG emissions worldwide by at least 80 percent, or else global warming will exceed two degrees Celsius above preindustrial levels, and that increase risks climate disruption at a scale, frequency, and intensity that threatens human civilization. In response, innovation lab cities have committed to accomplish an "80 by 50" reduction, their share of the world's required effort. Several innovation cities have gone further. Vancouver, a Pacific Rim city of about 650,000 people, committed to derive 100 percent of the energy used in the city—for electricity, heating, and transport—from renewable sources by 2050. Stockholm, with a population of nine hundred thousand, also aims to become fossil-fuel-free—by 2040.

Other city climate labs have established dramatic goals consistent with their particular contexts. Cape Town, facing a predicted doubling of energy consumption and emissions by 2040, committed to reverse its business-as-usual course and, instead, reduce emissions by 37 percent. Rio de Janeiro, with six million people, became the first city in the Global South, the world's many developing nations, to pursue the goal of *carbon neutrality*, a commitment to offset emissions the city doesn't eliminate by funding GHG-reducing projects elsewhere in the world.

The same type of bold goal setting prevails in the climate-adaptation efforts of innovation lab cities. Boston's adaptation plan recognizes the city's substantial vulnerability to climate changes and embraces the goal of not just coping with the changes but "increasing the city's ability to thrive in the face of intensifying climate hazards, leading to stronger neighborhoods and improved quality of life for all residents." Rotterdam, a city of 623,000, dedicated itself to "create a climate-proof city for all the people . . . both now and for future generations."

When a city's goals offer a desirable vision for the future, it can attract local backing. "When I ran for mayor the first time," says Vancouver Mayor Gregor Robertson, "one of my key goals was to make Vancouver the greenest city in the world by 2020. I was in a situation where I thought I'm going to be very clear about my goals if I'm elected. There was lots of support and interest in that big, audacious goal." A few years later, the city adopted the 100 percent renewables goal and, Robertson says, "The uptake has been huge. People in Vancouver get it and support it. We have citizens and businesses helping to drive it."

The beauty of establishing an ambitious, seemingly unreachable destination is that it helps people recognize that business as usual won't get the city there. "Stretch goals," when taken seriously, force a city's elected officials, civic leaders, skilled bureaucrats, residents, and businesses to consider and create new ways to reach their desired future. Contemplating the stretch opens the city up to the need for climate innovation. Something different has to happen, but what is it?

Urban Systems

Many cities around the world are implementing climate-action projects. They install LEDs on streetlights, put solar panels on municipal buildings, build a light-rail line, collect and compost food waste, plant more trees, raise streets and roads to prevent flooding, and so on. These projects matter—every little bit helps—and many require impressive effort. But a project will almost never have the big impact a city needs to achieve ambitious climate goals. At best, it's a first step toward the much more challenging work of transforming a city's core systems.

A focus on changing urban systems is a defining feature of innovation lab cities. It's only by transforming the performance of city-wide systems that a city can become carbon-free and strongly climate resilient. This still involves doing projects, of course, but each project is part of a plan that targets the entire system for radical changes and envisions what the reinvented system should look like. Change at system scale requires numerous projects.

Urban analysts have various ways of describing a city's many systems: built and natural systems; governance, social, and economic systems; education, human-service, and entertainment systems; and market and regulatory systems, for example. But cities striving for high-impact climate action tend to target what we call *delivery* and *spatial systems*. Delivery systems supply a city with energy, transportation, shelter, waste disposal, water, health care, and other essential services—a handful of which produce the bulk of a city's GHG emissions. Spatial systems organize a city physically—regulating the use of land—into individual building sites and blocks of buildings; neighborhoods; shopping, industrial, and other districts; campuses (usually for universities, hospitals, and corporations); parks, forests, rivers, and other natural features; and networks of streets, roads, sewers, electricity distribution, communications, and other physical infrastructure. These spaces are at the front line of a city's exposure to extreme precipitation, sea-level rise, and other climate impacts.

Cities can calculate the amount of GHG emissions produced by each delivery system and can assess the vulnerability of their spatial systems to different types of climate changes. Boston's storm-water drainage system, for instance, is designed to handle 4.8 inches of rain in twenty-four hours, but more rain than that can produce substantial flooding in parts of the city.

An innovation lab city's general climate goals, such as an "80 by 50" reduction in GHG emissions, cascade down into its delivery systems. San Francisco turned its 80 by 50 overarching goal into measurable targets—0-50-100—for three delivery systems: zero waste (send nothing to the landfill); 50 percent clean transportation (take half your trips by bus or bike); and 100 percent renewable energy (choose power from renewable resources). New York City targeted a 30 percent reduction in the energy used by its system of buildings by 2025, on the way to deeper reductions in the longer run. Adaptation plans in Boston, Copenhagen, and Rotterdam describe climate-resilience goals for specific at-risk neighborhoods in the cities' spatial systems.

These urban systems are massive and operate with enormous throughput:

- San Francisco sorts through more than forty-five million pounds of solid waste a month, a weight equivalent to about 12,500 compacted Tesla Model 3s.
- Shanghai's metro—fourteen lines, 340 miles long, and still expanding—transports more than ten million riders on a weekday.
- Paris draws its water supply from two rivers and 102 different groundwater sources.
- London contains ten thousand miles of water pipes.
- Boston's downtown waterfront district has more than three thousand buildings with thirty thousand residents and twelve thousand workers.
- Mexico City's bus rapid transit system has sixty-five miles of corridors, more than 141 stations, and three-hundred-plus buses.

- In New York City, Uber and other ride-hailing services, with a total of fifty thousand vehicles on the streets, served sixteen million passengers in one peak month.
- In Washington, DC, the city's waste treatment plant, the world's largest, covers 150 acres, handles more than one billion gallons per day, and is fed by some 1,800 miles of sewers.
- Even "little" Boulder, with about 108,000 residents, contains forty-six thousand buildings, sixty-three thousand registered vehicles, and 650,000 trees.

The systems also involve large sums of money—user payments, tax revenues, long-term debt, private investment and assets, and business revenues, for example. San Francisco's regional transit authority costs more than $1 billion a year to run, while DC Water obtains about $600 million a year in revenue. Boston's harbor area generates $2 billion a year in economic activity. Shanghai's port, the world's busiest, makes a profit of more than $1 billion a year handling more than thirty-five million containers. New York City's property is worth more than $1 trillion, nearly as much as the annual gross domestic product of Mexico.

As ambitious as climate innovators may be, they have to be careful when intervening in their city's core systems. They can't disrupt the performance of these indispensable urban systems too much; breakdowns are not an option. The systems must meet multiple performance requirements, such as for service availability and reliability, not just climate-related standards. Changing the systems is likely to have impacts on the city's social and economic systems, generating financial gains for some people and new costs for others, which may generate political conflicts.

With boldness necessarily tempered by caution, the systemic changes innovators pursue usually play out over multiple years or decades. And there are plenty of other complicating factors, even in lab cities.

Bumps in the Road

Climate innovators face a gauntlet of intimidating technical and institutional challenges when it comes to designing and implementing innovations.

Cities' core systems are technically complex and often have not been analyzed before to determine how they can be decarbonized or made more climate resilient. New York City brought together fifty experts from real estate, engineering, architecture, labor unions, and affordable housing, as well as environmental advocates, to work with city staff to conduct the most thorough analysis ever of energy use in the city's buildings. They collaborated for more than a year before issuing a 185-page report. That's about how long it took a working group in Boston to put together, with help from consultants, an in-depth analysis of the city's vulnerability to climate changes. The project cost about $1 million. It also took a year or so for London officials, working with the private sector, to develop a comprehensive database about the city's energy supply and to produce four scenarios about potential future supply that users could apply to a digital, street-level map of the city.

As cities work on understanding individual systems, they find that the systems are interconnected—forming a *system of systems*. Working on one may affect others. The system of buildings, for instance, consumes energy, but it also consumes water and produces wastewater and runoff, while the building's parking spaces for cars and bicycles, as well as proximity to mass transit, may affect residents' mobility choices. But the governance of any city's multiple urban systems is fragmented—within departments and agencies of local government, among the vertical layers of local, state or provincial, and national governments, and between the public and private sectors. This patchwork of control often impedes cross-system collaboration and coordination of budgets. "It's a huge challenge for big cities," says Sarah Ward, head of energy and climate change in Cape Town. "The bigger the city, the less integrated its systems. You have to break down the siloed way of doing things, but there are such turf battles and resistance." Keeping infrastructure resilient is "a multiorganizational endeavor," notes Peter Williams, chief technology officer of IBM's Big Green Innovations, adding that this "necessary level of collaboration" happens in very few cities.

Nearly every city has complaints about the limits of its control over innovations. A 2015 report by C40 Cities and Arup found that two-thirds of the nearly ten thousand climate actions taken by sixty-six cities worldwide involved partnering "with other actors to leverage their respective powers" or focusing "on creating an attractive environment for others to act," because the city had limited power to act directly on its own.

The development of technologies relevant to climate innovation presents additional challenges for cities. Although the performance and reliability of green infrastructure, green buildings, and renewable-energy infrastructure have improved substantially in the last decade, some uncertainties or inadequacies linger—and are the subject of ongoing experimentation and design improvements. Meanwhile, technological advances such as autonomous vehicles and storage batteries are entering the marketplace and disrupting systems and plans. Today, cities are considering how the emergence of autonomous vehicles will affect urban mobility systems. These vehicles "could decrease traffic fatalities, increase the adoption of electric vehicles, and provide mobility services to disadvantaged communities," notes an assessment by Portland. But "they also have potential to significantly increase transportation carbon pollution." Developments in batteries will impact the design and performance of urban electricity systems, and the spread of "smart" technologies has numerous potential implications for cities. But how might they enable or hinder cites' climate-change efforts?

Cities also find a range of difficulties in implementing the plans they have developed. Many of them, for instance, don't have the local private-sector expertise to design and install large amounts of green infrastructure. "Melbourne doesn't have a highly evolved green roof sector yet," notes Ian Shears, the city's sustainability manager. "If we want to get green roofs here, we need to have the industry to support it." To help that sector develop, the city worked with a local university and businesses to produce a guide to going green in the Melbourne context—part of a larger strategy of incentives and regulations for private-sector greening. Vancouver is developing a Zero Emissions Building Centre of Excellence, with public, private, and philanthropic funding, to help the local building sector figure out how to meet the city's new standard for zero-emissions buildings.

Political Headwinds

In every lab city, innovators have countless tales about the difficulties of mustering and sustaining the political will needed to advance climate innovation.

Money is at the heart of many local political tangles driven by potential economic wins and losses. Who locally should pay for changes, and who should reap financial benefits? When fossil fuels are to be phased out, what about the economic impacts on local fuel distributors of natural gas or gasoline? When investments are needed in physical infrastructure, how much of it should the private sector or the government pay? Will new costs make city living less affordable for low-income households? Will public investments in green and transit infrastructure result in the gentrification of neighborhoods and the displacement of low-income residents?

Even cities with robust economies, like Copenhagen, worry about whether there will be enough private investment for climate innovation. "If we look at the total investment behind the city's climate plan," says Jørgen Abildgaard, the city's executive climate project director, "more than 90 percent is based on private investment. So we have to be in a dialogue with the private companies and investors. Otherwise we will never get there." Many cities fear that increasing the cost of real estate development to pay for climate actions may diminish investment in new construction.

San Francisco's Debbie Raphael notes that the city's elected officials often want to put aggressive climate policies in place, but without causing big financial impacts, especially for housing, for which costs are already sky high. These "competing virtues" appeared when her team was developing a city ordinance to require new buildings to provide parking spaces with "readily available" capacity for charging electric vehicles (EVs). "I knew the elected officials didn't just want to cover 10 or 20 percent of new buildings," Raphael says. "They expect us to push the envelope." But she adds, "They were very, very, *very* concerned about affordability, about making things too expensive. That's a risk for them." The proposed ordinance targeted 100 percent of parking spaces in new buildings with more than nine units. But it also took into account likely changes in the technology for charging electric vehicles and the increased cost to building owners (and occupants) for meeting the requirements. Under the ordinance that was adopted, every targeted new building must upgrade the design of its electricity service to support the additional demand for *all* of its parking spaces. But only 10 percent of a building's spaces have to be ready to go, meaning that electricity conduits and wiring are in place so users can install their own charging equipment. Another 10 percent have to have conduits installed but no wiring. "We understood that EV charging technology is likely to change and the type of wiring needed will likely change as well," Raphael notes. The remaining 80 percent of a new building's parking spaces have to have conduit laid, but only in areas that are inaccessible or hard to reach, which will reduce the future cost of installing the charging infrastructure. These modifications hold down the required costs while applying to all parking spaces.

Climate innovation may also upend the business models of city systems, raising anxiety about how they will generate revenue. Electricity and water utilities, for instance, were designed to succeed financially when consumption of their commodities increases. Pushes to boost efficiency threaten to reduce utilities' revenues and may leave customers feeling that they are paying more for less. Other government revenue models may also be at risk. Melbourne relies substantially on parking revenues, with the average parking meter generating more than $10,000 a year in income, Shears explains, so greening projects that will remove many parking spaces raise fiscal concerns.

Core urban systems may face other financial pressures. They may have failed to keep up with maintenance of equipment and infrastructure or to invest in expansion to accommodate population growth in the city. These types of financial practices erode the performance and appeal of mass-transit systems, even as they necessitate even more costly investments.

Local economic interests shape political constituencies for and against changes, and often a *constituency for change* has not yet formed—electric vehicle owners, for instance—while opponents to change are fully present. In San Francisco and other cities, groups of local residents have vigorously opposed city plans to increase the density of buildings and number of residents in their neighborhoods—but the beneficiaries of expanded housing don't exist yet.

Even in innovation lab cities, not everything goes the way that innovators might want. Mexico City, with a population of nine million, embraced swift development of what is now the world's sixth-largest bus rapid transit system, with traffic lanes used exclusively by buses and other features that make buses a preferred mode by ensuring faster travel and few delays due to traffic. But the city continues to accommodate cars by building highways and only slowly curbing its large number of parking spaces, says Bernardo Baranda Sepúlveda, regional director of Latin America for the Institute for Transportation and Development Policy, which has helped spread the BRT model worldwide. Shanghai's innovative cap-and-trade market to reduce GHG emissions doesn't include seven large, polluting, state-owned companies operating in the city—a decision made by the national government.

There's no one best way to build political will in a city. Much depends on complex factors of local politics and also on the city's governance model, which determines who has power to decide what. Some local political aspirants raise the banner of becoming a green, climate-smart city and win office. Some get elected with a campaign focus on other local issues and then decide to push climate action and broader changes in the city. Some build active constituencies for climate action by emphasizing the ways it will improve life in the city. "Many mayors still struggle to win political and popular support for climate action," notes a C40 Cities report, adding that they should promote the idea that "low carbon development will raise living standards faster." In some cities, local business leaders, advocacy groups, or community-based groups may organize demand for city policies and programs that advance climate actions. Some local officials ask voters to approve of plans, a way of both testing and building constituencies for change. In 2011, Boulder's voters narrowly adopted a Utility Occupation Tax to fuel city efforts to gain control over its electricity generation—rejecting a nearly $1 million campaign funded by the investor-owned utility serving the city. Voters renewed the tax in 2017.

Newly elected officials often build on their predecessors' ambitious efforts, and sometimes they go even further. Oslo's new city council, in 2015, speeded up by ten years the city's commitment to GHG reductions. To sustain local political momentum, some climate-active mayors who are leaving office try to anoint their successors, but this doesn't always work. Eduardo Paes, former mayor of Rio de Janeiro, says that setting and publicizing ambitious and measurable goals for climate action helps keep the pressure on successive city leaders over the long run: "You get the next mayor, the guy or lady that's going to come after you, to be ashamed if he doesn't reach certain targets."

Transitions between local government leaders often slow down climate-action momentum for months, as innovators wait to see what the new leaders want to do. Without strong, positive signals from committed elected officials and their cabinets—not just pronouncements of aspirational goals—innovators can become worn down by the sheer difficulty of advancing changes through government's bureaucratic and political mazes. Bill Updike worked under three mayors during his seven years in Washington, DC, government driving climate-action innovations: "It takes so long to get something moving—with the research, the requests for proposals, the contracting, approval, and implementation—and if you're changing elected officials and agency heads, there's the potential of losing all the work you've done."

Much of the success that urban climate innovators report seems to boil down to situational improvisation. They invent solutions to the political clashes that arise, fashioning a compromise here—a tradeoff there.

Perhaps there are two rules for urban climate innovators to live by. First, expect snags no matter what the innovation may be. When Sidewalk Labs, an urban technology that is part of Alphabet, Google's parent company, announced in 2017 that it would spend $50 million to plan a green, high-tech neighborhood in Toronto's derelict waterfront, the project was promoted by Prime Minister Justin Trudeau and heralded internationally. But that didn't prevent a variety of concerns from arising locally. With plans to have the neighborhood filled with sensors and cameras inside buildings and outside, autonomous vehicles on the streets, and robots collecting garbage, what data would be gathered about what people were doing? How would it be used and who would own it? The head of Sidewalk Labs, Daniel L. Doctoroff, a former New York City deputy mayor, anticipated criticism and held public meetings as part of a yearlong planning process. Sidewalk Labs, he says, is "very sensitive to the fact that there's going to have to be an intense community conversation."

In Melbourne, Ian Shears has championed ambitious efforts to green the city for nearly ten years. But how cities use their physical space, he says, "is an area of constant tension." He offers the example of planting trees alongside roads to help reduce the heat emanating from the pavement: "It will make more of a difference if we plant trees along roads than putting more trees in Fitzroy Gardens. But the drainage people want to use the road. The engineers want to use it for traffic. Pedestrians want to use it. Cyclists want to use it. Public transport wants to use it. And I want to plant trees and absorb water and create permeability."

The second rule: persist in spite of setbacks. Shears and other leading city climate innovators have as many stories about this as they do about the political difficulties they've faced. Although there is an undeniable urgency to take climate actions, you have to play a long game too. In New York City, for instance, Mayor Bloomberg's 2008 proposal for congestion fees on vehicles to reduce traffic and pollution was shot down in the state legislature. Nine years later, though, a version of the idea was resurrected with a good chance of adoption— this time as a way to also generate funding to help fix the city's subway system that politicians had long neglected. We've also seen some city-government innovators take another approach to being persistent. After they leave their city jobs, they press from the outside, with political allies, for elected officials to take climate actions.

As if the maze of systemic complications wasn't enough, climate-innovation cities tackle most of their climate challenges and the related systems all at the same time. San Francisco, a coastal city of nearly nine hundred thousand, has been working to decarbonize the delivery systems that emit GHGs and is recognized worldwide for its achievements in approaching *zero waste*. Now the city is also tackling green and gray infrastructure systems—helping restore wetlands in the San Francisco Bay and designing ways to strengthen the city's seawall while winning voter approval to pay for the fix.

Like every innovation lab city, San Francisco has many climate-action balls in the air—and it has to keep them in motion, not crashing to the ground, for a long time.

Innovation Clusters and Waves

In city labs, each climate innovation is part of a cluster of innovations needed to radically change the performance of an urban system. Copenhagen has a world-class bicycle network, but it is also upgrading its public transit system and supporting the use of electric and hydrogen vehicles. Shanghai, with twenty-five million people and China's largest urban economy, has a cap-and-trade market for reducing carbon emissions, but it also offers incentives for the purchase of electric vehicles and promotes increased energy efficiency in buildings.

Developing these clusters of system-changing innovations involves substantial experimentation. Cities have to design and test innovations to see what will work within the city's particular context. They have to figure out what combination of innovations might have the greatest impact on the system and how innovations will fit together when implemented. Experimentation also helps cities to identify pathways for putting innovations to use in a system. What will the *system owners*—directors, managers, and investors with decision-making power—agree to do? How will it be embedded into the system's plans and operations? How will it be paid for?

Innovation clusters in a system usually come into existence in waves that roll out over the years. A city may start with low-hanging fruit, changes that appear to be easier for the system and community to accept, before initiating innovations that are more difficult to advance because, for example, they cost more money, impose unpopular regulations, or disrupt everyday processes. A city may learn from its first innovations what might be most impactful to do next. Or it may realize that the innovations it has put in place won't produce the desired results and that it needs another, bolder, wave of innovation.

Innovation in One Core System

The cluster and wave patterns of urban climate innovation are evident, for instance, in the way that San Francisco and other lab cities have tried to get carbon out of their transportation systems. They have organized innovation along two approaches: *Fuel switching* replaces fossil-fuel vehicles with renewable-energy vehicles powered by electricity, hydrogen, or biofuels. *Mode shifting* gets people to walk, bicycle, and use public transit instead of driving.

Cars and trucks powered by fossil fuels are tightly woven into the fabric of modern-city mobility. Since 1888, when Bertha Benz packed her two children into the car built by her engineer husband and drove sixty-four miles along wagon tracks to see her mother, automobiles have been emitting greenhouse gases. Today, nearly all of the world's more than 1.2 billion automobiles and trucks run on gasoline and diesel, and most of the roughly seventy million new vehicles sold annually also burn fossil fuels. Worldwide, transportation systems—vehicles, along with rail, air, and marine transport—produce about 14 percent of all GHG emissions.

SWITCHING TO ALTERNATIVE FUELS

In the 1970s, San Francisco adopted a transit-first approach and opened its BART (Bay Area Rapid Transit) subway, now a 107-mile system with forty-five stations. But at the beginning of the twenty-first century, the city found that its transportation system generated 40 percent of the city's GHG emissions. Since then, it has worked to reduce transportation emissions, starting with a focus on using alternative fuels.

City-driven fuel switching mostly involves purchasing new alternative-fuel vehicles or, to a lesser extent, retrofitting older vehicles to use green fuels. A key to this approach is the cleanness of the new fuel source. In San Francisco, Oslo, Vancouver, and other cities leading the charge on electric-vehicle adoption, much of the electricity is generated from hydropower, but in cities that burn fossil fuels for power, conversion to EVs still relies on GHG-resulting electricity. City governments typically start fuel switching with vehicle purchases they control. San Francisco has been converting its public-transit fleet of more than one thousand buses, trolleys, light-rail vehicles, streetcars, and cable cars into zero-emissions transports. London had the largest electric bus fleet in Europe in 2016 and targeted its famous double-decker buses—three thousand of them operate in central London—for conversion to hybrid-electric technology.

Cities have to make sure the new vehicles will be able to provide reliable transport for many years. In 2015, San Francisco tested in fire trucks the use of renewable diesel fuel produced from fats and vegetable oils, with the potential to reduce emissions by 50–60 percent. Then, Mayor Ed Lee announced the city's entire diesel-powered fleet of nearly two thousand vehicles would use the renewable fuel. The city also started, with federal funding, to promote the use of hydrogen-fuel-cell electric vehicles, a technology that is only beginning to reach the market. Oslo, a world leader in fuel switching, tested five hydrogen-fuel-cell buses on city routes to see how they would perform.

Innovation cities also invest in the development of publicly available fueling infrastructure to assure potential owners of alternative-energy vehicles that they will be able to obtain renewable fuel when they need it. The fastest-growing alternative infrastructure is being built for electric vehicles, with cities setting up thousands of EV charging stations, often located at parking spaces reserved for electric vehicles only. San Francisco began to build its EV charging infrastructure in 2009, and in 2015, the city experimented with three off-the-electricity-grid solar-powered charging stations. In the US, cities and other areas contained more than thirty-five thousand public charging stations by 2016. Shanghai had about 3,500 publicly available charging points in 2017 and planned to add twenty-eight thousand more by 2020. Infrastructure is also needed for other types of fuel. San Francisco opened its first biodiesel fueling station in 2016 for commercially licensed diesel vehicles. Oslo piloted an "energy station" that provides multiple types of vehicle fuels, including gasoline.

Since city-owned fleets make up only a small fraction of all vehicles on the road, innovation lab cities extend their fuel-switching approach to influence the vehicle-purchasing decisions of their residents and businesses. Half of the world's fourteen top EV-selling metropolitan areas contain innovation lab cities. The cities provide financial incentives—reduced or waived registration, toll road, and parking fees—that augment whatever subsidies national and state or provincial governments offer. Oslo, a coastal city of about 640,000, dubbed the "electric vehicle capital of the world," with more than twenty thousand electric vehicles registered locally, offers EV owners a batch of benefits on top of the national government tax breaks that make the EVs cost competitive. The city provides free parking, free access to toll roads, and free transport on ferries, as well as the EV owners' favorite enticement: access to the less-busy traffic lanes reserved for buses and taxis. Shanghai, the city with the largest number of EV sales globally, subsidizes about $4,000 of the purchase price, on top of national government subsidies, and exempts EVs from the city's cap-and-auction system for new car license plates.

SHIFTING TRANSPORTATION MODES TO REDUCE DRIVING

Climate-innovation cities also try to reduce driving. In San Francisco's 2004 climate action plan, then-mayor Gavin Newsome stressed the city's commitment to promote "alternatives to automobile transportation." To enhance the attractiveness of San Francisco's mobility choices, the city would increase the frequency of transit service, construct new rail lines, add bus routes, and extend service hours. It would expand the city's network of bike lanes, paths, and routes, and install bike racks and stations throughout the city. To "discourage driving," it would cap or reduce the number of parking spaces in the city.

San Francisco enhanced this initial strategy to reduce driving by focusing more on changing land uses. It redesigned streets and sidewalks to help speed up bus and trolley service, make bicycling and walking safer, and improve walking conditions. It expanded its regional bicycle network into 431 miles of lanes and routes, designating bike lanes on streets with green paint containing slip-resistant materials for greater traction in wet conditions. The city required new residential and commercial developments to provide long-term parking for bicycles. It developed plazas and other public spaces with landscaping for pedestrians, connected the downtown street grid to the waterfront, and designated lanes on streets for the exclusive use of public transit vehicles.

Along with Portland and several other cities, San Francisco promoted "transit-oriented development": high-density development projects that mix residential, retail, and commercial uses next to existing public transit lines, creating walkable, compact communities near public transportation. The city is also developing "complete neighborhoods"—compact residential places with nearby stores, markets, groceries, health clinics, day care centers, libraries, parks, schools, and public gathering places—so people have less need to travel to other parts of the city. And it has been investing billions of dollars to expand and upgrade its public transit system, while also promoting expansion of a bike-sharing service in the region.

END OF AN URBAN HIGHWAY

Standing in a single place in San Francisco, you can see the past and future of urban transportation systems. The Embarcadero is a broad boulevard and pedestrian promenade built alongside a three-mile-long, one-hundred-year-old seawall, with piers extending into the vast San Francisco Bay. For tourists and locals, this spot provides panoramic views of bridges, islands, ferries, ships, and shores. It is a mecca of restaurants, shopping, historic buildings, hotels, and palm trees, adjacent to a busy financial district.

This is where Debbie Raphael, director of the city's Department of Environment, brings us to learn about the city's climate situation. A plant biologist, she turned to work in government to "use science to change the world." Before the city's mayor appointed her, Raphael worked for California's Governor Jerry Brown, running the state's Department of Toxic Substances Control. Some twenty years in the environmental protection business, she's an experienced leader—a troubleshooter and innovator.

"When you are standing on the Embarcadero and look out across the water, you become very aware that you are on a peninsula," Raphael says. "This fact of our geography steers the direction of the city when it comes to climate innovation." With a limited amount of land available for development, San Francisco has become the second-densest urban core in the US, behind only New York City. The city's population nearly doubles with commuters during the day, Raphael adds.

The city's density impacts its mobility system. "Because we are on a peninsula and we are a robust financial and business hub, there is tremendous pressure on the transportation system. That pressure has been both a blessing and a curse. A curse, meaning it is very dense here and hard to get around," says Raphael. San Francisco had the nation's second most congested roadways in 2015, behind only Los Angeles. Its extensive regional public transit system is heavily used; subway stations in the city are often overcrowded.

San Francisco . . . second-densest urban core in the US: Mike Maciag, "Mapping the Nation's Most Densely Populated Cities," *Governing*, October 2, 2013, http://www.governing.com/blogs/by-the-numbers/most-densely-populated-cities-data-map.html. San Francisco . . . second most congested roads in 2015: Lauren Parvizi, "San Francisco's Traffic Congestion Is 2nd Worst in the U.S.," *SF Gate*, April 3, 2015, http://www.sfgate.com/cars/article/San-Francisco-s-traffic-congestion-is-2nd-worst-6172993.php.

The blessing in all of this, Raphael continues, is that due to the difficulty of moving around the city, "there is tremendous support for public transit, for getting people out of cars, for giving people a different way to get in and out of the city." In the 1950s and 1960s, she notes, "the solution to moving people around was more freeways, bigger, bigger highways." A concrete, elevated, two-deck freeway was built along the city's waterfront, right next to where we stand looking over the bay. "It was a fateful decision," Raphael says. "The Embarcadero Freeway completely cut off the financial center, these beautiful skyscrapers and old buildings, from the water." Every day about seventy thousand vehicles barreled along the roadway: "It created a dead zone in perhaps the most beautiful part of the city."

That freeway is not here anymore. The busy waterfront expanse is a living symbol of what can happen when a city changes its mind about the reign of cars.

In San Francisco's 2004 climate action plan, the city's approach was to "promote walking, biking, and public transit," Raphael says. The strategy was foreshadowed more than a decade earlier, when the Embarcadero Freeway figured in a dramatic, politically tense decision. In October 1989, an earthquake caused more than $5 billion in damage in San Francisco and killed sixty-three people. A fifty-foot section of the San Francisco–Oakland Bay Bridge fell. "I was on the bridge when it collapsed," Raphael recalls. "It was very, very emotional."

The quake damaged and closed the Embarcadero Freeway. "Mother Nature gave us the opportunity to rethink the fateful decision made nearly four decades earlier," says Raphael. Longstanding opposition to the freeway rekindled and, in 1991, after a political battle, elected officials decided to demolish the structure and invested $50 million in creating the new Embarcadero. The bold decision, Raphael says, provided a new way to address the city's mobility pressures: "It created the ability to have multimodal

---

Every day about seventy thousand vehicles barreled along the roadway: Wikipedia contributors, "California State Route 480," *Wikipedia*, accessed January 21, 2018, https://en.wikipedia.org/wiki/California_State_Route_480.
Longstanding opposition . . . the new Embarcadero: "Removing Freeways—Restoring Cities," Preservation Institute, accessed February 6, 2018, http://www.preservenet.com/freeways/FreewaysEmbarcadero.html.

transport downtown. It allowed for bike lanes and trolley cars. The F Line—old trolleys that have been rescued from all over the world and lovingly restored—is a treasured piece of public transit in the city."

The highway's demolition was not intended to reduce GHG emissions; in 1991, that goal was not yet on the radar screen of most cities. But it signaled that San Francisco was willing to take a difficult step to diminish its dependence on the automobile, a goal other innovation lab cities have embraced.

Cities around the world have substantial control over local land use, and to reduce driving and improve quality of life, they are rethinking a century of land-use decisions that enabled automobiles. Vancouver, for instance, decided in 2015 to remove two elevated, forty-five-year-old viaducts that convey traffic between its downtown and eastside neighborhoods. The action fit the city's strategy to reduce the motor-vehicle share of all residents' trips to 33 percent in 2040 from 60 percent in 2008.

Other climate-innovation cities have pursued similar land-use innovations to shift mobility modes. Oslo links new and more-compact developments—"higher and tighter," as Mayor Raymond Johansen puts it—with access to public transport "so the CO_2 footprint will be as light as possible." The city is also reducing the number of on-street parking spaces in the central city and cutting the number of parking spaces new developments must have. The Xinzhuang Metro Station in Shanghai's southern suburbs was the first site in China to expand an existing station into a "minicity" of new, mixed-use developments with a transportation hub, an office tower, a hotel, multiple residential buildings, and a shopping mall. In 2016, transit-oriented development became Cape Town's primary approach to spatial development, partly to reverse the discriminatory structure that is a legacy of apartheid: the city center has a low population density because black residents were forced to live on the city's outskirts in high-density, low-income settlements, a long way from jobs in the city. "We need spatial integration and connections to address this inequity," explains the city's Sarah Ward. "It's the city's biggest challenge. That's why we're obsessed with using transit-oriented development."

Some innovation labs have employed additional approaches to discourage driving. Mexico City officials report that because of the BRT system, some 170,000 people left their cars at home and rode buses, a 15 percent shift in travel mode from vehicles to public transit. And the bus system could be expanded. "We have a proposal for 29 BRT lines," says Bernardo Baranda Sepúlveda of the Institute for Transportation and Development Policy. "We've modeled how many passengers each line would carry, the emissions reduction, and costs."

Plans for connecting overcrowded Shanghai and nearby cities into a megacity of fifty million residents hinge on the creation of high-speed rail and subway networks to move millions of commuters between and within cities every day.

Bike sharing—thousands of rentable bicycles in docking stations throughout a city—was originally launched in Copenhagen in 1995 and has become a fixture in most innovation cities. Minneapolis initiated the first US bike-sharing system in 2010 with seven hundred bicycles at sixty-five stations, and in 2017, the city started planning to phase "dockless" bicycles into the fleet.

Singapore, a city of 5.7 million, established as a British trading post in 1819, plans to increase its bus fleet, double its rail network, expand bicycle paths, and quadruple the distance of covered walkways, which are essential during the city's tropical downpours.

In efforts to reduce driving by increasing its cost, Stockholm, London, and Singapore charge congestion fees for vehicles entering the central city. Stockholm's fee of up to $4 is highest during rush hour. London's daytime fee is about $16 daily and could be boosted in 2019 by a $15 surcharge on vehicles that don't meet strict emissions standards. Singapore's system targets segments of roads that are heavily congested with prices that vary by time of day. These three systems raise a total of $485 million in annual fees.

Some cities have been experimenting with a more radical approach to reducing driving: they prohibit it.

GOING CAR-FREE

Swedish bloggers called it "the Obama effect," and one of them issued a distress call: "Help us, Barack Obama. You're our only hope."

Days earlier, in September 2013, the president of the United States had arrived in Stockholm for a two-day visit. Security-minded local officials closed the road from the airport to the city for Obama's motorcade and kept cars and buses out of much of the downtown area. After Obama left, the city returned to normal; its peak-hour traffic congestion is ranked worse than that of Los Angeles and London. Then city officials noticed something unexpected. During the presidential visit, the level of nitric oxide in the air, emitted when transportation fuels are burned, had decreased an average of 30 percent in the inner city. A commenter on a Swedish website asked, "Can we make Obama stay, to keep our city clean?"

Two years later, Stockholm conducted its first-ever car-free day, joining fifteen other Swedish towns and cities in closing off streets as part of European Mobility Week. The initiative, called *I stan utan min bil* (in town without my car), closed all roads in the city's Old Town, many of the busy shopping streets around the central railway station, and several of the city's major bridges.

Other cities worldwide have resorted to temporary bans to clean their air. On February 24, 2000, the capital of Colombia, Bogotá— not one of our innovation lab cities but a world leader in transportation innovation—barred the city's eight hundred thousand privately owned cars from using city streets for the day. The results were spectacular. "The toxic haze over the city thinned," writes Charles Montgomery in *Happy City: Transforming Our Lives through Urban Design*. "People still got to work, and schools reported normal attendance." In 2014, the city held a car-free week, and in 2015, it also banned motorcycles.

When Paris, a city for more than 1,500 years, now with 2.2 million people, decreed a car-free day in September 2015, city officials reported that pollution levels dropped 33 percent on the Champs Elysées and 40 percent along the Seine River.

San Francisco made a stretch of Market Street, a main thoroughfare that starts at the Embarcadero, into a car-free zone, and New York City barred cars from Times Square, one of the world's most visited urban areas. "You can see the energy on the street that is there now, that used to be filled with just a sea of traffic," says the city's former commissioner of transportation Janette Sadik-Khan, who proposed the action to Mayor Bloomberg in 2009. "All of the mayor's deputy mayors were gathered around the table to see whether we would close Times Square. The mayor went around the table and asked everyone what they thought," she recalls. "This was in the middle of an election year. Let's just say not everybody thought this was such a great idea. But the mayor turned to me after the presentation and said, 'I don't ask my commissioners to do the right thing according to the political calendar. I ask my commissioners to do the right thing, period.' And he shook my hand and said, 'Let's do it.'"

These cities didn't need a visit from President Obama to reveal the benefits of keeping fossil-fuel-burning cars off their streets. They just needed the political will to impose a short-term ban. But if a temporary prohibition produced such desirable results, why not go further?

Enter Oslo, whose city council announced in 2016 that it would ban cars from the central city by 2019, the first comprehensive and permanent ban by a European capital. The designated forbidden zone is not just a street or small district but 444 acres of streets and buildings with about ninety thousand workers, one thousand residents, eleven shopping centers, and roughly one thousand parking spaces on the streets. At the same time, Oslo committed to expand the city's bicycle-lane network and to substantially increase investment in public transportation, since people no longer allowed to use their cars will need other ways to get into and move around the central city.

The pattern of innovation clusters and waves that we've seen in the transportation systems of San Francisco, Oslo, and other innovation lab cities also occurs in the other core urban systems. As these cities push climate-driven innovations into their systems, they have noticed that it's not just air-pollution levels that are changing for the better.

04 MAKING A BETTER CITY

—

A city is more than a place in space, it is a drama in time.

—PATRICK GEDDES

Urban climate innovations for transportation and other city systems generate what innovators call *cobenefits*—positive effects that go beyond carbon reduction.

You can see this in Mexico City's Zócalo, a central district of narrow streets, one of the largest city squares in the world, the seat of the city and national governments, as well as an important political, commercial, and tourist area. The district had lost nearly all of its residential population, was notorious for traffic congestion, and couldn't be reached easily on public transportation. But the city's transportation innovations have had a big impact, reports Mary Skelton Roberts, codirector of the climate program at the Barr Foundation in Boston, who has visited the city's bus rapid transit system three times with delegations from Boston: "They put a BRT station not far from there, made the area completely walkable, widened the sidewalks, and created parklets for people to just sit and congregate. It is one of the most vibrant sections of Mexico City today."

A big change in the use of city space is what Vancouver was hoping for when two auto-carrying viaducts were removed and replaced with parks and a new neighborhood. "It's a step that creates opportunities," says Mayor Gregor Robertson. The highways, he explains, have "a lot of wasted space underneath" that will be used instead for more green space and to increase density, with projected new housing for as many as eight thousand residents, plus shops and businesses.

Oslo expects this sort of improvement when its ban on driving in downtown takes effect. The city center, says Anja Bakken Riise, a former political advisor to Oslo's vice mayor for environment and transport, will be "more attractive and more accessible without car traffic. We want to make the city come more alive. We have very few playgrounds for children. There is not enough emphasis on how to develop an attractive city for elderly people. How do we create spaces where people can enjoy themselves without necessarily having to buy something?"

It's also what Chinese cities are seeking as they dismantle a legacy of oversized highways and "superblocks" of residential high-rises isolated from the rest of the city—in favor of walkable, mixed-use, transit-oriented urban models. Guidelines for "green and smart urban development," issued in 2016 by the China Development Bank, promote complete neighborhoods, public green space, walking, biking, public transit, energy efficiency, and renewable energy.

A shift toward "zero-emission mobility," declared mayors of seven innovation lab cities in 2017, "will result in less congestion and less pollution, while making our roads quieter and the air we breathe cleaner." It also means fewer deaths from traffic accidents, while more walking and bicycling make people healthier.

Cobenefits also result from a city's other climate actions, analysts report. C40 Cities identified these as increased healthiness, economic efficiency, innovation, productivity, growth in the technology sector, and quality of life. "A well-designed city can reduce congestion, improve air quality, reduce noise pollution, and decrease energy use," state the China Development Bank guidelines. "It can create enjoyable spaces for everyone, from children to the elderly, and increases options for daily life. It makes neighborhoods more attractive and livable, and creates cities with more vitality and economic prosperity." These benefits sound much like those extolled in the GHG-reduction plan of Seattle, a city of more than seven hundred thousand: "Residents who can meet many of their daily needs by walking, bicycling, or riding transit also benefit from lower overall household costs, improved health, thriving local business districts, and increased opportunities for housing and jobs."

Cobenefits from climate action are so evident and compelling that they have become a key way that leading-edge cities frame the purpose of climate action when they seek support of residents. They want to make the cities better, not just carbon-free or climate ready.

Getting Better All the Time

No lab city we know has more explicitly and fully embraced the risk taking and discipline of climate innovation than Copenhagen. This nine-hundred-year-old city of 760,000 souls, a longtime trading center on an island commanding an approach to the Baltic Sea, isn't just innovating in the era of climate change. It serves as a climate-innovation supplier to cities worldwide. The city is intentionally using—benefiting from—climate innovations to make itself into a better city.

"We are a city in a hurry, because of the circumstance of climate change," says Jørgen Abildgaard, who shepherds implementation of the city's climate-action plans. A former energy planner for the Danish government and business consultant, Abildgaard, like so many city residents, travels by bicycle to work and anywhere else in Copenhagen.

Like other innovation lab cities, Copenhagen has set radical goals, taken a systemic approach, and aggressively tackled both GHG reduction and climate adaptation. Its most immediate target is to be "carbon neutral" by 2025—to reduce GHG emissions and off-set those that remain by producing more clean energy than the city needs and selling it to others. The city's outpouring of innovations has attracted worldwide attention: offshore wind farms, district-scale heating systems for nearly every building, bicycling as a pre-ferred in-city travel mode, and citywide storm-water management through green infrastructure. "We can show visitors that a small city can make big changes," Abildgaard says.

Copenhagen has built a strong reputation for linking environmental and economic performance. It is "one of the greenest and most economically productive metropolitan regions in the world," concluded a 2014 London School of Economics study. The city's global positioning is enviable: a highly skilled workforce with nearly half of all adults holding a university degree, a high rate of entrepreneurial activity and relatively low unemployment, a world-class clean-technology cluster of businesses and research assets, and strong flows of private investment and public funding for research. Copenhagen's population has been growing, and the city's density is similar to Boston's and San Francisco's. Consumption of energy, electricity, and water has declined, and so has waste production. The city's per-capita GHG emissions fell 40 percent between 1991 and 2012.

Copenhagen's flow of climate innovations doesn't just happen; it has to be planned and managed. "We have more than 60 GHG-reduction projects running," says Abildgaard, "and when I set up the city's implementation plan I told the city council it would be a step-by-step learning process. We would test solutions and see if they work, and then take the next step. There would be mistakes and failures." The city's climate roadmap classifies each of these projects by its stage of innovation development: "analysis and strategy," "tests and demonstrations," and "implementation." Among the thirty tests and demonstrations are ways to reduce energy consumption in existing buildings, use large-scale heat pumps in the district heating system, reduce driving needed to deliver freight to large businesses in the city center, sort and recycle more plastic waste, and design and build a transit station for bicycle- and car-sharing along with trains. Meanwhile, the city is researching what to do with organic solvents that emit GHGs and the development of biogas from waste. The city budgeted nearly $150 million for the three-year plan, while city-owned utilities were expected to invest almost $1.8 billion, mostly for wind turbines and a biomass-burning plant for the district heating system. And the city's cloudburst plan is implementing three hundred projects in neighborhoods—fifteen a year—to keep rainwater out of low-lying areas and sewer pipes.

Abildgaard takes us on an afternoon bicycle ride to experience the city's world-renowned passion for bike riding. Traffic lights on some stretches of the specially designed bicycle network, which extends into the suburbs, are timed so cyclists moving at twelve miles per hour never hit a red light. Bicyclists have their own lanes, separated from other street traffic. At intersections, they get a head start over cars when traffic lights turn green. The city has about fifty-four thousand parking stands for bicycles. In winter, it removes snow from bicycle paths before clearing it from most car lanes.

"We have a lot of bikers, and it is the preferred mode," says Abildgaard. "The biking culture is really all kinds of people—the

CEO from the big bank, the mayor, the worker in the factory, the students—because it is the most convenient way to go." Nearly everyone says it's the easiest and quickest way to get around, and 29 percent of *all trips* are taken on bicycles. "For the last two to three decades there's been support for developing biking from the city council," says Abildgaard. The city constantly adds to and tweaks the bicycle system. Since 2014, it has built ten bridges in the harbor area for use only by bicycles and pedestrians.

We cycle around new low-carbon developments and cloudburst projects in neighborhoods and through pedestrian-only streets overflowing with shoppers. Along the way, we watch teenagers swim in the harbor's clean water and catch glimpses of offshore wind turbines in the distance. Finally, we take a breather on a bridge, from which we can look across the harbor at the city's blend of historical and contemporary architecture.

"For me," Abildgaard says, "this bridge is about the city's focused priority on the way I move around in the city. The bridge and the marked bicycle lanes show me that biking is a priority. There are no cars behind me or on the side of me. The noise is completely different. On the way here, we took a street that was closed to cars. The priority is for biking, walking, and public transport, and that changes the street a lot. It changes the feel of the city. The city's space is used differently now. There are many more people out in the space than there were 20 years ago. Instead of sitting at home looking at TV, people are outside. We do the counting and we can see that the time that people are using urban space is increasing."

As we head back toward the city center, Jørgen Abildgaard shares a final thought that captures Copenhagen's spirit of climate innovation: "We want to make a better city." In spite of all the attention paid to the city's leading green performance, he adds, "We are well aware that we also have to learn to do better."

To learn how to do better, Copenhagen eagerly connects with other cities around the world.

05 THE REBEL ALLIANCE

—

Do. Or do not. There is no try.

—MASTER YODA
The Empire Strikes Back

Cities learn from and teach each other. They naturally "connect, interact, and network," points out Benjamin Barber in *If Mayors Ruled the World*.

For more than two decades, growing numbers of cities have been doing what comes naturally: engaging with each other worldwide in formal and informal networks to share what they've learned about urban climate innovations and collaborate on developing and refining new innovations. These cities recognize that, for perhaps the first time in history, the success of any individual city depends, to a large degree, on the success of cities collectively. In meetings, conference calls, and online chats just about every day of the year, mayors and city managers, community activists and nonprofit leaders, architects and other professionals, and business owners and bankers enthusiastically share their know-how and war stories. Within this multitude, innovation lab cities function as generative hubs, producing innovations and connecting with and inspiring other cities to make climate innovation come alive.

We call this global mesh the *Rebel Alliance*, after the band of insurgents in *Star Wars* and *Rogue One* that pitted its meager resources against those of the Galactic Empire and plotted to destroy the planet-obliterating Death Star. The emergence of this dense web of connections among urban climate innovators and early adopters of innovations has been spurred by visionary mayors, like London's Ken Livingston and New York's Michael Bloomberg, and funded in large part by philanthropies as well as governments.

It's a self-organizing, tireless swarm with no commander-in-chief, following the "North Star" of climate action. Its participants apply what they learn back in their cities, where they engage with elected officials, community organizations, business leaders, and others to refine the world's growing, tested knowledge into workable local actions.

Gregor Robertson, mayor of Vancouver, went to the Vatican with a group of mayors to meet with Pope Francis after the pontiff's 2015 encyclical on climate change. He returned home remembering something the mayor of Stockholm, Karin Wanngård, had said: "She told us about this port redevelopment project, the Royal Seaport." The new residential neighborhood, just minutes from the city's center, will be a "climate-smart" area with no carbon-dioxide emissions from fossil fuels when completed in 2030. "It's 'carbon positive' with 12,000 homes, affordable housing—it's got everything," says Robertson. Hearing about the project got his competitive spirit going: "Right away I think, okay, we've got to do better. When you see examples of other people doing well and making smart moves, you realize you haven't figured it all out. We won't have the same type of solution as Stockholm, but it shakes us up."

Mary Skelton Roberts, of the Barr Foundation, visited Mexico City to study the use of bus rapid transit (BRT) there. A native Spanish speaker with a master's degree in city planning, she thought Mexico City might have valuable lessons for her city, Boston: "It had to change policy to prioritize a new hierarchy of transportation modes: it's walking, then biking, then public transit, shared vehicles, and then it's single-occupancy vehicles. They flipped the 'transportation pyramid' on its head. We thought some of those same policies and the leadership that was needed in Mexico City could be really inspirational for our leaders."

Clover Moore, a teacher elected as an independent to the state legislature and then four terms as Sydney's lord mayor, recalls a meeting of mayors during which then-mayor of London Boris Johnson pocketed her city's plan for increasing bicycle use. "Boris and I were sitting on a bus and I pulled out our bike plan," she told a mayors gathering while onstage with Johnson. "And I said, 'This is what we're doing,' and you took it from me and you put it in your bag and said, 'I'm going to do that.' Not only did you do it," she finished, "but you've now got 'Boris Bikes'"—the nickname for the more than ten thousand rentable bicycles at 750 stations around London.

Call it borrowing, copying, or stealing—when cities want to know what they might do next, they look to other cities and their innovations. "I've seen firsthand what works when one city holds valuable lessons for many others," Bloomberg told mayors and staff from thirty cities around the world at the end of a 2015 study tour of American climate-innovation cities bankrolled by Bloomberg Philanthropies. "Each city has its own unique culture and its own unique needs. But the principal nuts and bolts of mass transit, parks, sanitation, and the power grid tend to be pretty similar. So the more we help mayors and city officials innovate and collaborate, the more progress we can all make."

The Barr Foundation supports Boston's extensive participation in a set of regional, national, and international networks. "We back smart, aggressive, focused leaders of cities," says cofounder Amos Hostetter. He participated in, and Barr funded, a trip to Rotterdam by Boston and Massachusetts leaders to study climate-adaptation innovations.

Cities find inspiration in each other's decisions. Rodrigo Rosa, a former business journalist and special aide to the mayor of Rio de Janeiro, was on the Bloomberg Philanthropies–supported study tour when he heard about the commitments of San Francisco, Stockholm, and Vancouver to entirely eliminate fossil fuels from their cities' energy supplies. He was so impressed with the cities' ambitions that he decided that such a sweeping goal should be part of the fifty-year plan his city was developing: "I brought that back to Rio and we discussed it internally as part of our vision for the next decades."

Copenhagen's Lord Mayor Frank Jensen was pleased when a deputy mayor of Beijing asked about forging a sister-city agreement between the cities. But he had a particular type of relationship in mind: "I said, 'We don't want to have protocol business with other cities—drinking champagne and wishing each other happy new years. We want to make concrete business with other cities.' And she said, 'That's what my mayor wants to do. We want to learn from you.' And that was the start of a beautiful friendship between our cities."

Cities find confirmation and confidence when they gather with each other. While San Francisco's Debbie Raphael was in Paris for a United Nations meeting on climate change, she wandered into the "Green Zone," a huge building set aside for city people and others to congregate. "It was packed," she recalls. "Everywhere I turned every person I met was in that building because they thought it was the most important place to be at that moment. To be surrounded by that kind of energy and commitment and creativity was phenomenal. We were so diverse in terms of geography and perspective, but the unifying theme was that climate change was the most important thing for us to think about and that Paris was the most important place to be."

Many of the world's linked urban climate rebels come from the ranks of professions and business. For years now, Ed Mazria, an American architect in his midseventies, has zigzagged among cities across the world, pushing for big gains in the energy efficiency and emissions reductions of the built environment. Mazria realized more than a decade ago that it was crucial to transform the architecture of buildings if cities were going to make sizeable reductions in GHG emissions. He founded Architecture 2030, a nonprofit concentrating on climate solutions through the design of the built environment, and has focused in recent years on the urban building boom in North America, China, and India. It will amount, he says, to about 52 percent of the world's building growth during the next fifteen years—a potential source of enormous amounts of GHG emissions unless new buildings are much more energy efficient than existing ones.

In 2013, Mazria traveled to China for the first time to meet with government officials, researchers, and architects: "I presented at a meeting where building efficiency and emissions reductions were becoming a big issue. China, like most of the world, was building out new infrastructure along the lines of 20th century Modernism—sealed high-rise and glass wall buildings, automobile-oriented development with super blocks and wide boulevards"—an energy-intensive approach the US was beginning to question. Mazria worked with Chinese colleagues to illustrate that pedestrian- and transit-oriented development and high-performance green-building alternatives would not necessarily be more expensive and would lead to significantly lower emissions and air pollution. Two years later, he was in Shenyang, a large industrial city in the nation's northeast, to sign the China Accord with Chen Zhen, secretary-general of the Architecture Branch of the China Exploration and

Design Association, and fifty-two Chinese and international architecture and planning firms committed to phase out GHG emissions in built environments. A year after that, he was back in China with Chinese colleagues, cohosting a historic two-day workshop, "China: Towards a Zero Carbon Built Environment," for professionals and government officials. In September 2017, the first follow-up training program was held in Shanghai, with about two hundred Chinese building-sector professionals participating.

Woven into the fabric of this global mesh of urban climate innovators is a set of hubs—networks and member organizations, mainly—that facilitate the connections and collaborations of hundreds, even thousands, of urban rebels. One of these, the nine-year-old Urban Sustainability Directors Network (USDN), has 170 member-cities in North America with a total of more than seven hundred active participants, and has raised more than $17 million from twenty-four foundations and their members for its work. Nils Moe was a founding member of USDN while he served as Berkeley's sustainability director, before he became the network's managing director. The role has thrust him into an endless whirlwind of activities. In three months of 2017, for instance, he lived mostly out of his suitcase, traveling to meetings, conferences, and planning sessions to engage with members, partners, and funders in Denver, Sydney, Melbourne, Hawai'i, New York City, and San Francisco, while also guiding the intense preparations for USDN's annual meeting, a five-day event in San Diego.

As few as twenty years ago, this energetic global uprising barely existed. It had no standing in world affairs. Today, though, it reaches deep into and connects hundreds of cities, the private and nonprofit sectors, key professions, and community-based organizations. It enables innumerable enthusiastic and effective exchanges about climate innovations—a new "world knowledge" in the making.

In *Star Wars*, the heroic Rebel Alliance defeats the evil Empire by stealing the Death Star's engineering diagrams and firing a missile into the weak spot they reveal. Our urban climate rebels are clever and courageous too. They share a cause, and they eagerly exchange and build resources for change.

But it will take more than this to transform the world's modern cities.

PART II

—

Toward Global Transformation of Cities

06 THE POWER OF TRANSFORMATIONAL IDEAS

—

Daring ideas are like chessmen moved forward. They may be beaten, but they may start a winning game.

—JOHANN WOLFGANG VON GOETHE

As climate innovations proliferate in cities, it has become common to hear urban innovators talk about the "transformation" of urban systems, neighborhoods, the economy, and the entire city. But what exactly about the city is being transformed, and how does transformation happen? The answers lie in our understanding of the essence of both cities and innovation.

Cities arrange their built and natural space in ways that establish the fundamental elements of urban life—the underlying economic activities, life-maintaining metabolism, use of natural systems, and inhabitants' capacity to shape a shared future. For instance, when Boston created more and more land during the last centuries by filling in its harbor, it generated enormous new economic activity and value. When newer Chinese cities erected "superblocks" of apartment buildings distant from workplaces and shopping, they ensured high rates of energy consumption by people who had to travel by car to meet their needs. When cities the world over dedicated space for roads to accommodate vast numbers of automobiles, they enabled levels of air pollution that damage natural ecosystems and people's health. When cities in the US located infrastructure, such as highways and roads, and used zoning to concentrate and isolate poor, minority, and immigrant populations in less desirable areas, they marginalized entire social groups.

When the design and use of urban space changes, so may a city's fundamentals. "Space can change people's lives," says Bryan Koop, senior vice president of Boston Properties, one of the biggest developers of green-certified office properties in the US. This was the effect in Copenhagen, as Jørgen Abildgaard points out, when that city built harbor-crossing bridges for bikers and pedestrians only: the way people move around the city and what they experience changed.

It wasn't the first time that designing and constructing a new bridge has altered a city's fundamentals. When Pont Neuf opened for traffic in 1604, spanning the Seine River in Paris, it was unlike other bridges: Much wider than city streets, built of stone, not wood, its entire surface was paved. No houses lined its sides, so anyone crossing could take in the urban river landscape. Its raised spaces, such as sidewalks, were reserved for pedestrians. The bridge "had a direct and profound impact on the daily life of Parisians. It introduced them to a new kind of street life, and it transformed their relation to the Seine," observes professor Joan DeJean. "Parisians rich and poor came out of their houses and began to enjoy themselves in public again after decades of religious violence. The Pont Neuf became the first truly commercial entertainment space in the city: since access cost nothing, it was open to all."

A city's broad plans for the use of space may also have transformational impacts, which can endure for centuries. About three thousand years ago, China's Shang dynasty placed temples at the center of its cities and, reports Joel Kotkin in *The City*, "great cities throughout most of classical Chinese history would be dominated by adherence to the 'cosmic pattern.'" When William Penn drew up plans in 1682 for a 1,200-acre city in the New World—Philadelphia—he envisioned "a greene country town" with wide main streets arranged in a rectangular grid, a central square of ten acres, and four squares of several acres each providing additional open space. More than three hundred years later, Philadelphia has grown into a city of 1.5 million residents, but its underlying spatial design remains. "The Penn grid is a gift from the past," says architect Alan Greenberger, chairman of the city planning commission. "It created a rational, highly dense fabric of streets that facilitate the movement of people, goods, and ideas."

In the following chapters, we show that the climate innovations of pioneering cities are changing underlying fundamentals of cities. The cities are still cities, of course—densely populated and thickly built environments within distinct geographic and governance boundaries. But as their underlying elements change, the cities will not be the same as they were before. They are being transformed.

But what are they being transformed into by innovations?

In the Heart of Innovation

Every urban climate innovation is a method wrapped around an idea.

In the case of city climate innovations, the methods are designed to affect people's decisions and actions in four ways.

THEY ENCOURAGE VOLUNTARY ACTION

Innovations engage and stir people with information and encouragement, using why-to and how-to campaigns to provide details about how to, for instance, cut energy consumption at home or floodproof a building, and sometimes describing other people who are doing the same.

THEY SEND PRICE SIGNALS

Innovations motivate people with financial incentives or deter them with increased expenses—subsidizing the cost of, say, purchasing and operating electric vehicles or, for instance, levying congestion fees.

THEY OFFER CHOICES

Innovations entice people with new and more appealing options—faster bus service, expanded subway service, attractive green infrastructure for streets, and more.

THEY ISSUE REQUIREMENTS

Innovations command people with mandates—for example, policies limiting the amount of energy a building may consume, requiring restaurants and households to separate food waste so it can be composted, or banning vehicles from parts of the city.

These methods reflect an understanding of human nature and strategies for influencing decisions and behavior. When people are told what to do, for instance, they may instinctively come up with counterarguments. "People are wired to refute imperatives," explains climate-change communications strategist Lisa Bennett. "Passing a law that requires people to change their behavior is one effective way around this." But, she adds, "efforts to attract people to a cause are much more likely to yield a positive response than those that threaten or make demands."

The climate innovations surging out of city labs are not distinguished by their motivational methods. You can use these methods to shape people's behaviors for most any purpose, not just climate action. What distinguishes climate innovations are the particular ideas that they contain. These ideas address more than climate change. They are new ideas about the essence of cities—their economies, metabolism, nature, and social capacities. As the climate innovations that contain them gain traction in cities, they are replacing the ideas from which the modern city developed.

The Premodern City

A little more than a century ago, few cities in the world had electricity, cars, or skyscrapers.

When the first central power station went online in New York City in 1882, thanks to inventor Thomas Edison, it lit up four hundred lightbulbs in nearby buildings, and Edison had no way of measuring the energy supplied or of billing his customers. Today, New Yorkers spend $15 billion a year on electricity—to do a lot more than just keep the lights on.

When five European-made cars arrived in Beijing in 1907 for the start of the first "Peking-to-Paris" race, they were the only cars in the city. Local officials didn't want them to be driven in the streets; they were supposed to be pulled by mules. Today, Beijing contains five million cars, which contribute so much exhaust emissions to the city's hazardous air pollution that they are sometimes banned from the roads.

In the early 1900s, few buildings stood more than ten floors high. But the use of reinforced steel frames and other construction techniques produced the skyscrapers that now form signature sky-lines in most major cities worldwide. Today, Shanghai's stunning twenty-first-century skyline contains more freestanding buildings above 1,200 feet than any city other than Chicago, where some of the first skyscrapers rose more than a century ago.

Time-travel back a little further, to the seventeenth and eigh-teenth centuries. You would easily recognize the cities of those times as cities: dense hives of energized humanity; massive infrastruc-tures of streets, roads, alleys, buildings, bridges, plazas, and more; swarms of people, vehicles (mostly horse drawn), and ships in con-stant motion; lighting and noise everywhere; ceaseless economic and cultural activity. But they were not the *modern* cities we live in today, with electricity, cars, and skyscrapers.

Zoom in on London during the early 1700s and the details reveal arduous conditions for most of its several hundred thousand inhab-itants. The narrow, cobblestone streets, alleys, and bridges are con-gested with pedestrians, vendors and their carts, and horse-drawn transports. Roads become muddy and flooded in winter, impassable, and unpleasantly dusty in summer. Dirt and pollution fill the air so much that candles are sometimes needed at midday in busy shops, and travelers approaching the city note its smell, a sooty odor. Streets at night are lit with oil lamps, a technology thousands of years old. Buildings are constructed poorly and with shoddy materials—crumbling bricks and knotty timber—and then patched up; it is not unusual for them to collapse. Within buildings, burning coal provides the main source of heat, belching thick clouds of irritating, choking black smoke into the city's air. There is no indoor sanitation and people commonly empty their chamber pots out of their windows and leave garbage on the streets to rot. Open sewers run through the middle of many streets and gutters carry away human waste, while offal from butchers' stalls and horse manure by the ton fill streets daily. London delivers water from the Thames to some residents through hollowed-out tree trunks running underneath the streets. The river, the main thoroughfare for commercial shipping, receives the city's discharge. To avoid drinking the water, residents turn to gin; eight thousand places in the city sell the unregulated intoxicant. Many of the area's wealthy residents avoid these conditions by living outside of the city, commuting by regular coach services into the commercial center and exclusive shopping districts, and navigating the streets in sedan chairs carried by porters.

From this premodern starting point, it took some 150 to 200 years—seven or eight generations of people—for modern cities to fully take shape. Many accounts describe the rise of the modern city as being driven by the Industrial Revolution's technological innovations, starting with the steam engine powered by burning coal; they made mass production, electricity, cars, skyscrapers, and other new things possible. But this urban transformation was not just driven by technological advances.

Modern Ideas

Modern cities were built on a mix of ideas that began to take hold in the nineteenth century. These ideas worshipped the use of markets and capital to create massive wealth and meet social needs. They celebrated the role of ever-increasing material consumption in producing personal and societal benefits. They revered the control of the planet's natural systems through science and engineering. And they admired acts of will that sought to shape the future.

These ideas had an underlying theme: the power of human beings to shape their individual and collective well-being. As philosopher Richard Kearney explains in *The Wake of Imagination*, the idea took hold, especially in Western society, that human beings have the power "to create a world of original value and truth," rather than being subordinate and accountable to a higher power. Emerging scientific knowledge about the material world provided people with the means to manipulate physical reality for their purposes, especially the creation of economic abundance. Construction of the Eiffel Tower in Paris for the 1889 World's Fair exemplified this worldview, as critic Robert Hughes notes: its unique architecture contained "the promise of unlimited power over the world and its wealth."

The developing field of economics, points out social thinker Jeremy Rifkin, celebrated the idea of self-regulating markets driven by man's innate competitive self-interest, saw property acquisition as an inherent biological drive, and proclaimed that nature had value only when people transformed it into productive assets. Founders of economics modeled their thinking on the field of physics and its

URBAN EVOLUTION STORYLINE

Histories of cities embrace a fairly common version of the transformation of urban space and development. They sketch a general sequence, at least for Western cities, which comes alive graphically in *A City through Time*, an illustrated children's book that traces the 2,500-year evolution of a single imaginary settlement from "ancient colony to vast metropolis."

The story starts with "The Greek Colony" in 550 BCE—a small set of buildings several stories high, with a marketplace for merchants and traders, and a temple on a hill, alongside a river, olive groves, and wheat fields.

Seven centuries later, the now-Roman city is larger and surrounded by a wall with watchtowers. Buildings are taller. A bridge crosses the river, with a road connecting the city to other parts of the empire. Merchant ships are moored nearby, and the city's space has more uses: restaurants, bakeries, public baths, and a butcher.

Proceed to the "Medieval City," with a castle and cathedral, greater population density, and horses and oxen pulling freight and people.

Then it's on to the "Industrial Port of 1880." Now the city contains two million residents and many more buildings, trains, and mills in the industrial quarter, which emit smoke. A steam-driven carriage moves down the street; a coal barge floats on the river.

Finally, we arrive at the city of "Steel and Glass": a modern city of cars, buses, high-rise buildings with apartments and offices, streetlights, television antennas, a financial district, retail stores, and a subway. "Everyone seems to be in a hurry," reads the caption.

An illustrated children's book: Philip Steele and Matilda Gollon, *A City through Time: From Ancient Colony to Vast Metropolis*, illustrated by Steve Noon (London: Dorling Kindersley, 2013).

mathematical certainties, Rifkin explains, and they concluded that, "just as the laws of gravity govern the universe, an invisible hand rules over the affairs of the marketplace."

The idea of engineering all of nature became pervasive. The nineteenth century "was the century of the engineer," notes historian John Barry in *Rising Tide*, a history of efforts to control the Mississippi River. The idea prevailed, he explains, "that physical laws as solid and rigid as iron and steel governed nature, possibly even man's nature, and that man had only to discover these laws to truly rule the world." In 1900, as industrialization was still gathering steam, American historian Henry Adams experienced its remarkable sway. As he toured the Gallery of Machines at the Great Exposition in Paris, examining engines, machines, and electricity-generating dynamos, Adams wrote that he "began to feel the forty-foot dynamos as a moral force, much as the early Christians felt the Cross. The planet itself seemed less impressive, in its old-fashioned, deliberate, annual or daily revolution, than this huge wheel, revolving within arm's length at some vertiginous speed. . . . One began to pray to it."

The idea arose that consumption by individuals and nations was a "civilizing force" and that increased consumer demand could drive economic growth, says historian Frank Trentmann in *Empire of Things*, his panoramic account of the past seven centuries of consumption.

These and other big ideas molded thinking about practically everything of concern to people: economic well-being, social order, nature, disease prevention, religion, and more. They inspired numerous innovations in the design and function of urban spaces and systems in existing, expanding, and new cities. Three fixtures of modern urban living—department stores, sewers, and automobiles—provide examples of how new ideas underpinned innovations that altered cities' spaces and, in turn, transformed their economies, metabolisms, nature, and civic cultures.

DEPARTMENT STORES EXHIBITED EMERGING IDEAS ABOUT MASS CONSUMPTION AND SOCIOECONOMIC STATUS

The emergence of department stores in Paris, London, New York City, Berlin, Shanghai, and other cities brought fixed prices, customer service, and the world's goods to urban retailing. "What the department store did was to bring together various innovations under one enormous glass roof supported by a massive iron frame," explains Trentmann. "The biggest stores imposed themselves on the urban landscape like civic buildings and royal palaces. . . . The key to success was flow—flow of people and of goods. Cheap prices demanded large, rapid turnover, and this fundamentally changed the atmosphere inside the store as well as its relationship to the urban environment outside. In comparison to early modern shops, the department store was an extrovert. Instead of creating an exclusive, semi-private space for elite customers, it reached out into the city to grab the masses and pull them in."

Other forms of urban retailing—small shops, local co-ops, markets, and street vendors—competed with department stores. "Cities were battle zones between rival visions of spatial order," Trentmann documents. "More than anyone, it was street sellers who were in the firing line, and their fate shows us both how urban authorities tried to regulate the flow of goods and people, and how difficult that proved to be." As ideas about public health took hold, street hawkers were considered to be carriers of disease and disorder: "Across the world, cities turned to market halls to bring them under central control." The halls made it easier to license retailers, control quality and prices, and regulate the behaviors of sellers and buyers.

SEWERS CHANNELED NEW IDEAS ABOUT WASTE, HEALTH, AND ENGINEERING

As US cities grew in the 1800s, they began to establish public water systems. As supply increased, notes historian Ted Steinberg, households began to connect water closets, precursors to modern toilets, to the water systems: "There was only one problem: the cesspools and privy vaults [that the water closets drained into] could not handle all the waste." In some cities, residents secured permission to hook their drains up to existing sewers. But these had not been designed to "transport glutinous torrents of human waste. As sewers backed up and cesspools oozed, cities across the nation began to drown in their own filth." City officials, engineers, and sanitary experts "rallied around the idea of more underground plumbing," Steinberg says.

The idea of cleanliness shifted from a focus on appearance and clothing to a concern about the body's health, as germ theorists and epidemiologists promoted regular washing to improve public health. "Eventually thousands of miles of sewer pipe were laid, as human waste went flushing into rivers, lakes, and harbors," Steinberg notes. But sewers only went in at the request of property owners who paid for them: "Only those who could afford better public health received it." Discharging untreated sewage into waterways damaged the environment—causing algae blooms, oxygen-poor water, fishery declines, garbage-strewn beaches—and polluted the water supplies of users downstream.

AUTOMOBILES DROVE MODERN IDEAS ABOUT EFFICIENCY, MOBILITY, INDUSTRIALIZATION, AND SOCIAL STATUS

Cities old and new succumbed to the automobile in the twentieth century. Making room for cars and trucks was an essential element of being a modern city. The vehicles were faster and could carry more weight than other transportation methods, and they provided users with more freedom and range of movement, which many people found desirable.

Histories make it clear that the mass motorization of cities resulted from multiple forces and intentions and interwoven developments. Scientific knowledge provided new technologies for energy use, new materials and engineering techniques, and new management methods to boost industrial efficiency. Enormous sums of private capital provided investments to deploy mass-manufacturing methods and promote consumption, generating profits, jobs, wealth, and economic growth. In 1939, automaker General Motors sponsored the highly popular Futurama pavilion at the New York World's Fair, its model of the "city of 1960" featuring a network of highways cutting through the city to connect numerous scattered residential and commercial towers.

Government policies from local to national levels, often swayed by moneyed interests, provided public investments, such as those in the US interstate highway system ($128 billion for forty-seven thousand miles), and regulations and incentives that paved the way for technologies and capital. The rising professions of urban and transportation planning and highway engineering brought their expertise and authority to bear on the redesign of space in cities. A culture that endorsed economic growth and consumption and idolized science and new technology, as well as the "freedom of the road," reinforced the notion that enabling more people with more cars was a sign of society's progress.

As new ideas and the system-changing innovations they spawned took hold and accumulated in cities, they transformed the underlying order of the premodern London and other cities and put into place the blueprint for new cities like San Francisco, Melbourne, and Vancouver.

DÉJÀ VU

The nineteenth-century innovations that shaped the modern city faced a gauntlet of challenges that today's urban innovators would recognize.

Organizers of new urban gas and water services had to cope with daunting technical, financial, political, and economic difficulties, historian Frank Trentmann reports: "One was to decide who should provide the service. Massive investments were required." Private firms stepped in when they secured monopolies and price guarantees. But "these arrangements were a source of endless conflict about fair prices, quality, and supply."

Late in the century, cities in the US, Britain, Sweden, and France municipalized the services to ensure a reliable supply of water and to earn profits from providing gas, which allowed them to fund other city projects. The new systems had endless problems with reliability of service and providing sufficient supply for expanding cities. It was not clear how to measure and meter consumption or how to price the services—through taxes or through user fees, through flat or varying rates? Other decisions had to be made: What rights did consumers have? Which technologies should be used?

Trentmann reports: Frank Trentmann, *Empire of Things: How We Became a World of Consumers, from the Fifteenth Century to the Twenty-First* (New York: Harper Perennial, 2016), 182–83.

All In

Over time, the ideas that formed the modern city turned into a global juggernaut. As we became an urban-dwelling species, we made cities worldwide in the same basic modern image with the same modern systems.

The similarity of modern cities is pervasive, observes Wade Graham, a Los Angeles–based writer on urbanism: "These days, local variation is hard to spot. In the modern era (since about 1850 in Western Europe and America and now everywhere), cities look more alike than they do different, from Singapore to Ulan Bator to Boston to Moscow to Buenos Aires. Aside from those parts of them built before the modern era—the odd churches, squares, and low-rise historic districts—there is a remarkable, global urban monotony: here are tower blocks, there freeways, there shopping malls, over there pseudo-historic suburbs, here a formally ordered civic center, beyond that, mile after mile of car-dependent sprawl."

In some parts of the world, the modern model was imposed by colonial force. Journalist Daniel Brook recounts in *A History of Future Cities* how Western powers "began dotting the globe with Western-style neighborhoods to make their far-flung businessmen feel at home and impress the locals with their technologically sophisticated civilization." In Shanghai, for instance, "the British, French, and Americans carved up open land to build their colonies, each based on the cities of their home country. The British built a bustling port with a pagoda-free skyline and set aside grassy areas for sports fields. The French built gracious tree-lined boulevards sporting elegant cafes while the Americans slapped together a hodgepodge settlement like something out of their Wild West, all laid out along a central spine they dubbed Broadway."

Generally, though, modern cities arose because the new ideas we've described became a widespread way of thinking that urban leaders—elected and appointed government officials, entrepreneurs and business owners, architects, engineers, and other professionals, consumers, and civic activists—found extremely appealing and used to make decisions. These decisions changed city space and, in turn, reshaped cities' economic, social, and environmental fundamentals.

In the last century, for instance, automobile dependence became standard urban practice. American cities led the way because the nation was the first with mass car ownership, and its young, growing cities could be readily adapted to the automobile's needs. Some European cities resisted the trend, as urban planner and historian Peter Hall details in *Cities of Tomorrow*, by controlling suburban growth, investing in public transit systems, and launching large-scale urban renewal and housing projects. But, Hall adds, they only delayed the change: "All that happened was that the automobile revolution came to Europe 40 years later. In the process, it began profoundly to affect both traditional lifestyles and traditional urban structures." Car ownership and driving, and accompanying single-family-home construction, soared; suburbs sprawled; vast networks of urban highways surfaced; and traffic engineers dominated city planning.

The pattern spread worldwide: a 2016 ranking of the cities with the worst traffic congestion placed Mexico City, Bangkok, Istanbul, Rio de Janeiro, and Moscow in the top slots—all worse than Los Angeles, the most congested city in the US. In China, where half of the world's new cars are sold these days, "from Guangzhou to Beijing, Shanghai to Chengdu, there is a common and serious problem: the density of traffic," observes Chinese-city watcher Wade Shepard. "The rapidly rising number of personal cars on the roads . . . are clogging the country's highways and jamming its streets." Not long ago, he adds, 60 percent of the residents of Beijing commuted to work by bicycle, but bike use has dropped to 16 percent.

The modern-city phenomenon has encircled the planet, observes global strategist Parag Khanna: "The lives of any two people in cities across Europe and Asia are increasingly more similar than the lives of fellow citizens living in rural areas." Cities became the places where new and enormous private wealth and public revenues could be generated through real estate development and services for large populations. And they became indispensable hubs in emerging global economic and social networks—connected centers of commercial power, technological development, and cultural invention.

But as modern ideas and innovations reached global scale, they also produced the global warming that now disrupts urban life. This process started with the emergence of factories for mass production in London and other British cities in the early 1800s, an economic innovation that spread into cities in Europe, North America, and Japan before becoming a worldwide phenomenon. Modern cities became the places where the embryonic fossil-fuel economy could organize and obtain the mass labor and consumer markets that factories needed, while not being held responsible for the environmental damage it caused. The interests of capital investors sparked the burning of enormous quantities of coal to power manufacturing machines, explains Andreas Malm in *Fossil Capital: The Rise of Steam Power and the Roots of Global Warming*. Capitalists in Britain favored coal over water, the prevailing energy source, because coal was mobile, while water's power was limited to where and when it could be harnessed. By using coal, investors could concentrate industrial production at the most profitable sites and the most convenient hours. "It becomes imperative to reside in the most favourable place," Malm says, "where the largest markets can be courted, the latest machines purchased, the maximum surplus-value squeezed out of labour." In other words, capital focused on cities. Coal and then also oil replaced firewood as cheaper, abundant, and more transportable energy sources. This "logic of capitalism" entwined with urbanization and spread a fossil-fuel economy worldwide.

Transformational Ideas

Today, cities that are aggressively following a climate-innovation pathway are abandoning the very ideas that made them modern and got them this far. They are turning to a set of new ideas—four transformational ideas that are embedded within the hundreds of climate innovations emerging in lab cities and spreading from city to city. These are not just ideas that cities should in theory be using; they are in play in the cities responding most ambitiously to the imperatives of climate change. In the next chapters, we closely examine each of these four ideas, showing how they came alive and are beginning to inhabit innovation lab cities and their systems. They underpin these cities' efforts to radically alter their business-as-usual trajectories by finding ways to decarbonize and strengthen resilience. We will also show that these ideas are gaining traction in markets, in professions, and with consumers and national and state levels of government, an essential development for supporting and accelerating change by cities.

We frame these transformative ideas as new roles and capacities of cities for the climate-change era.

CITIES CAN EMPLOY THEIR UNIQUE ADVANTAGES TO TURN THE EMERGING RENEWABLE-ENERGY ECONOMY INTO URBAN WEALTH AND JOBS

Modern economic ideas have treated cities mostly as an afterthought: companies, markets, and nations were the drivers of economic growth, and cities were supposed to facilitate companies' efforts by holding down local costs and providing the infrastructure needed for commerce. More recent thinking, however, recognizes that the city is a primary driver of economic innovation and growth. Cities "are assuming an even greater importance in today's knowledge-driven innovation economy, in which place-based ecosystems are critical to economic growth," explains urban studies professor Richard Florida. "Cities are the key economic and social organizing units of the Creative Age."

The primary reason that cities pursue carbon-free energy systems is to address the problem of excessive GHG emissions, but the many innovations they use—offshore wind turbines, on-site solar installations, and more—provide more than clean energy at competitive prices. They also provide local and regional economies with transformational economic opportunities. Cities are developing local clusters of "clean-economy" businesses that sell products and services worldwide. They are localizing and decentralizing the production, storage, distribution, and management of renewable-energy supply, in a shift that creates jobs. And they are becoming increasingly appealing to young, talented entrepreneurs and employees attracted to carbon-free urban lifestyles.

CITIES CAN MORE EFFICIENTLY USE ENERGY, MATERIALS, NATURAL RESOURCES, AND SPACE TO GENERATE A NEW KIND OF URBAN ABUNDANCE

In the modern-city era, economic ideas about abundance drove vast increases in material consumption and shaped worldwide supply about rising standards of living and social progress. Pursuit of this type of abundance brought on improved living conditions for many, but in the process, it sacrificed environmental, human health, and other noneconomic values, promoted short-term growth at the expense of long-term sustainability, and yielded pervasive economic disparities that hobble social well-being and individual development.

Now cities pursue greater efficiency in their core systems, especially energy for buildings and transport, and seek to eliminate all waste, which reduces GHG emissions and increases climate resilience. In the process, they are redefining abundance to embody long-term sustainability of resources, a comprehensive set of noneconomic values, and a wider base of participants sharing in the bounty. "It's a world of sharing and abundance," declares world-renowned architect and product designer William McDonough. "We imagine our cities reducing the things we don't want, increasing the things we do want, and letting our children lead us into this future."

CITIES CAN RESTORE AND TAP THE POWER OF NATURAL SYSTEMS TO ENHANCE AND PROTECT URBAN LIFE

The huge expansion of built urban space in the eighteenth and nineteenth centuries embodied the idea that a city's physical, economic, and social needs were to be met by dominating natural systems near and far—sweeping away, reengineering, or overriding them. "Man's dominion," boosted by philosophies that promoted human agency, was facilitated by emerging engineering and scientific prowess. As a result, observes biologist Edward O. Wilson, an early conceptualizer of biodiversity, "humanity has destroyed a large part of the natural world and withdrawn from the remainder. We have also expelled it needlessly from our daily lives."

Cities that once turned their backs on nature are now turning back to nature to provide environmental, social, health, and economic benefits, as well as reduced GHG emissions and greater resilience to climate impacts. Their renaturing innovations—use of living infrastructure, stewardship of ecosystems and biodiversity, and provision of "biophilic" immersion in nature—invert the modern idea-hierarchy by restoring nature, instead of the city, as the dominant context for urban development.

CITIES CAN CULTIVATE THE CAPACITY OF INHABITANTS
AND CORE SYSTEMS TO ADAPT SUCCESSFULLY
TO THE FUTURE'S NEW REQUIREMENTS

As modern societies developed, they embraced the idea that people could create the future they desired by planning for it, instead of waiting to see what nature's cycles, divinity, or fate imposed upon them. Planning practices emerged as a way of actively constructing the future—to discern the possibilities, assess potential benefits and risks, and decide what to achieve. In cities, planning took on the role of articulating the public interest in determining a collective future.

Now however, given the global unfolding of climate change and destabilizing social and economic forces, the future seems less knowable and controllable, more uncertain and riskier. "The ideal of progress and a blind faith in social control no longer guide our collective futures," observes professor of environmental planning David Connell. The uncertainties of climate change, notes professor of urban planning Yosef Jabareen, "challenge the concepts, proce-dures, and scope of conventional approaches to planning."

Urban planning has begun to emphasize preparing for and adapting to unpredictable change and minimizing risks. Cities are investing in the capacity of residents and civic leaders to understand, deliberate about, and collectively determine responses to complex, changing problems. They are designing the physical infrastructure and service capacities of urban systems so they can be readily adapted as climatic conditions change and technological advances emerge.

During the modern-city era, new methods of thinking about eco-nomic growth, efficiency, abundance, nature, and shaping the future became cornerstones of globally used ways of understanding the world and valuing parts of it. These modes of thinking became mental habits, and habits are hard to change. But they are changing, thanks to innovations built on the four ideas we've identified.

New ideas and their innovations usually disrupt a city, but over time, they can settle into place. Bogotá Mayor Enrique Peñalosa, once a Green Party candidate for president of Colombia, saw a rad-ical idea take hold in his city: "When I was mayor 18 years ago, we created a network of more than 250 kilometers of bikeways. Then, there were no bikeways in New York or in Paris or in Madrid. At that time, I was almost impeached. Now, there are dozens of young people's organizations for cyclists. It's a new consciousness."

Oslo Mayor Raymond Johansen, asked about his city's dramatic decision to ban driving in its central district, points to the normalizing power of time: "I think 10 years from now, people will take this as natural, like not smoking in a restaurant."

Gradually, transformational ideas are becoming a new standard for cities—not just a toolbox of innovations but a radically different way of thinking about, a model for, city development and urban achievement around the world. And businesses, professionals, consumers, community activists, and government policymakers are applying these ideas in ways that help expand and accelerate urban transformation.

The successor to the modern city is busy being born.

CARBON-FREE ADVANTAGE

—

Cities Can Employ Their Unique Advantages to Turn the Emerging Renewable Energy Economy into Urban Wealth and Jobs

Opportunity is the mother of invention.

—JANE JACOBS

Thousands of residents of Copenhagen purchased stock in the city's offshore and onshore wind turbines, providing investment capital that is helping the city reach its goal of becoming carbon neutral by 2025.

Residents of Shanghai bought about sixty-one thousand electric vehicles (EVs) in 2017, attracted by large city financial subsidies— part of a market-growth scenario in which the megacity could have more than 1.5 million electric-vehicle users by 2030.

The one hundred thousand residents of Boulder are taxing them- selves a total of $16.5 million between 2018 and 2020—in addition to $10.4 million they've already spent—to support a fight to free the city from an electric utility that won't increase its renewable energy as quickly as the city needs to reach its ambitious decarbonization goal.

Residents of Cape Town installed forty-six thousand solar water heaters with help from city government, reducing the amount of coal-based electricity they obtain from the national energy-supply monopoly and saving money. The city also went to court in 2016 to force the South African government to let it purchase renewable energy from independent producers instead of having to depend on the monopoly.

These four examples could appear in newsfeeds about cities striking a blow for decarbonizing the world's energy systems: Hundreds of thousands of residents in different cities on different continents all "vote" with their money for renewable energy. Four cities adopt innovative policies and make investments to bolster renewables and even take on big electricity utilities and national governments. But these cities are not just replacing fossil fuels with renewable energy. They are also finding that the switch to renewables creates new ways for them to use a city's advantages in creating economic wealth.

Copenhagen, Shanghai, and other innovation lab cities are forming new geographical concentrations, or clusters, of businesses for "clean energy," "smart technology," and other climate-related products and services by turning themselves into incubators for the development of commercial products and services for expanding global markets. Renewable energy has already reached more than $1.4 trillion in global sales a year, with $200 billion in the US alone. Copenhagen's first offshore wind farm, the forty-megawatt Middelgrunden site, was built by a Danish utility, Ørsted Energy, which has captured about 25 percent of the growing global market for offshore wind power. With China's government investing in its EV sector as a strategic emerging industry, Shanghai has negotiated with Tesla to produce electric cars in its free-trade zone. The city was where, in December 2017, Ford Motor Company announced its commitment to produce more EVs for the Chinese market, and its executive chairman said that "China will lead the world in EV development."

Cape Town and other cities are producing electricity from local wind and solar installations, funded by public and private investment, instead of importing dirty power from utilities. By localizing energy production, they keep tens of millions of dollars in the city economy, supporting businesses and job creation and reducing residents' energy bills. In Cape Town, the typical solar water heater can cut a household's electricity use by about 25 percent. In South Africa in 2017, the price of electricity from new solar and wind projects was lower than what the government monopoly charged to supply cities.

By distributing electricity production and storage among many sites in the city—small and large wind and solar farms, as well as on rooftops—instead of centralizing it in mammoth generating plants, cities are making power generation less susceptible to failure in a storm or other climate disaster and less vulnerable to cyberattacks. In Shanghai and other cities, the growing number of electric vehicles is regarded as a potential new source of renewable energy for the electricity grid that can be tapped while the cars are not in use.

By positioning themselves as leaders in the renewable-energy economy, Boulder, Copenhagen, and other lab cities are enhancing their branding as green and sustainable places where the future is bright—characteristics that appeal to the talented, highly educated, tech-savvy young entrepreneurs and workers who drive business innovation worldwide.

In these ways, cities are changing the role they were given during the reign of the fossil-fuel global economy.

The City in the Economy

Around 1800, Berlin was "an economic backwater languishing on the edge of western Europe," describes Alexandra Richie in a history of the city. But within decades, she continues, the city "had become the mightiest industrial capital on the continent." A new industrial landscape of thousands of firms, founded by "a new breed of Berlin entrepreneur," grew up in Berlin, producing machinery, pharmaceuticals, alcohol, precision instruments, clothing, and more for global markets. In the 1850s, the biggest private company in Berlin, its main factory as large as a small city, supplied the world with entire railway lines, from tracks to locomotives. A new financial district, Behrenstrasse, grew to meet industry's enormous need for capital. By 1914, Berlin contained three million more people than a century earlier.

Berlin's story typifies the urban economic expansion and transformation initiated by the Industrial Revolution, when new fossil-fueled machinery supercharged capitalist markets, which had been emerging slowly for several hundred years. "The factory became the nucleus of the new urban organism," says historian Lewis Mumford. "Every other detail of life was subordinate to it." Throughout the nineteenth and twentieth centuries, cities old and new became growing production centers for large-scale industry, with far-flung supply chains and consumers. People flocked into cities from rural areas and across national borders; about half of the residents of all European cities in 1850 had been born outside the places where they lived. Cities developed ever-heavier concentrations of factories and workers, and succeeding generations of factory workers became habituated to the conditions of industrial work. Factories amassed in cities, and railroads severed cities' traditional arteries for movement. Horrendous housing conditions arose, as did heavy pollution of air and water, and public health deteriorated, eventually triggering waves of urban reform and government regulation that continue to this day.

Cities played a secondary role in the world's intensified pursuit of economic wealth by providing entrepreneurs, investors, and corporations with sizable labor markets with diverse skills, numerous consumers with increasing incomes, and public infrastructure for power and transportation. By concentrating production in growing cities, businesses could implement the essentials for success in the new fossil-fuel economy: financial efficiency and control. They forged economies of scale that boosted market dynamics; reduced costs allowed cheaper prices that encouraged more consumption, which permitted further lowering of costs. Companies also instituted the centralized governance and management structures needed to guide increasingly complex business operations and vast capital flows. This city-based corporate approach emerged in the fossil-fuel sector, says Jeremy Rifkin in *The Third Industrial Revolution*, because it required "top-down command and control systems and massive concentrations of capital to move [fuels] from underground to the end users. . . . The centralized energy infrastructure, in turn, sets the conditions for the rest of the economy, encouraging similar business models across every sector."

The advent of skyscrapers in cities demonstrates the modern economy's need for centralized control. The new towers allowed "hundreds, if not thousands, of people and businesses to be in the same place at the same time," notes an account of the more recent spread of tall buildings in Asia. "By promoting density, skyscrapers confer a competitive advantage and allow a city to become a beacon of commerce."

Cities mattered mostly as settings in which businesses, capital, and markets drove economic growth, supported by national government policies. "The economic importance of place," explains urban studies professor Richard Florida in *The Rise of the Creative Class*, was "tied to the efficiency with which companies can make things and do business there." It was thought, he says, that cities grow "either because they are located on or near transportation routes or because they have endowments of natural resources that encourage firms to locate there." An implication, Florida adds, was that city governments should do everything they could to reduce local taxes and other costs that businesses paid. Cities existed to enable the economic efficiency that businesses and markets wanted.

Ideas about the subordinate economic role of cities have changed, and efforts to decarbonize cities have given impetus to new thinking. In 1984, Jane Jacobs, in *Cities and the Wealth of Nations*, upended orthodoxy by arguing that wealth creation depends on *cities*, not *nations*, and national economies depend on cities. The key to economic growth, Jacobs said, is innovation of goods and services, and this is precisely what happens in productive cities. Other analysts focused subsequently on "human capital" in cities, the concentrations of skilled and talented people that generate innovations with economic value. "Cities are not just containers for smart people," says Florida, "They are the enabling infrastructure where connections take place, networks are built, and innovative combinations are consummated." The urban concentrations generate new ideas and increase productivity: "The clustering force makes each of us more productive, which in turn makes the places we inhabit more productive, generating great increases in output and wealth."

This is especially true in the twenty-first century's high-tech economy, notes economics journalist Eduardo Porter: "Opportunity in the information era has clustered in dense urban enclaves where high-tech businesses can tap into rich pools of skilled and creative people." Cities with capacities for economic innovation use that advantage to get richer and richer. "Before anywhere else can catch up," says economic geographer Michael Storper, "San Francisco has already leapt ahead again with new stuff they've invented."

As the idea that cities are society's main producers of economic innovation bubbled up, the industrial-age market economy experienced two fundamental disruptions—a shift to renewable energy supply and the widespread use of "smart" information technologies.

These changes create huge economic opportunities for innovative cities. Jeremy Rifkin says they amount to a third Industrial Revolution, and he has advised Rotterdam, Rome, The Hague, and other cities and regions, as well as the European Union, to plan for an economic sea change. "The great economic transformations in history occur when new communications technology converges with new energy systems," he explains. "The new forms of communication become the medium for organizing and managing the more complex civilization made possible by the new sources of energy." In the nineteenth century's first Industrial Revolution, Rifkin says, coal-fired steam engines drove industrialization and turned printing, coupled with mass literacy, into the world's primary communications tool for managing the economy's complex operations. In the twentieth century, "electrical communication [telephones, radios, televisions] converged with the oil-powered internal combustion engine, giving rise to the Second Industrial Revolution," which mass-produced the automobile and revved up the global oil industry.

In Rifkin's framing of a third Industrial Revolution, internet-based communications are converging with renewable energy, and this, he says, "will fundamentally change every aspect of the way we work and live." The economy will be characterized by "boutique, high-tech, professional workforces programming and monitoring intelligent technology systems," and education levels required by the renewable-energy sector will increase due to growing digitalization and complexity of its systems.

This convergence creates the prospect of cities using their advantages—innovation and market power—to shape the next global economy, not just accommodate the market forces that are being unleashed.

Urban Renewables

In the early 1990s, when a dozen or so pioneering cities, including Copenhagen, Minneapolis, Portland, and Toronto, focused on developing plans to decarbonize themselves, their options for producing and using renewable energy were quite limited. Global energy consumption included a negligible amount of renewables; in 1995, more coal, oil, and gas were used in a single average *month* than all the wind, geothermal, solar, biomass, and waste power used in the entire *year*. Almost no electric vehicles were available on the automobile market; Toyota's Prius hybrid was not introduced until 1999. The usefulness of storage batteries for electricity was limited by technical and economic factors. Cities were left mostly with ways to reduce energy consumption: increasing the use of mass transit, bicycles, and carpooling and making buildings more energy efficient.

Gradually, though, production of renewable energy has grown. Thanks to lowering costs, worldwide installation of renewable capacity—half of it solar—set a record in 2016 by attracting $242 billion in investment. Renewables provided only 10 percent of all energy but were 24 percent of global electricity. Even at these modest and insufficient levels, the renewable-energy sector provided nearly ten million jobs internationally, with eight hundred thousand in the US and four million in China. A 2016 US government report found more Americans employed in the clean-energy sector than in fossil fuels. The world's expenditure on energy reached $6 trillion in 2010, with a third of the spending on electricity. Global energy consumption is projected to continue growing substantially, as is the renewables' share of the sector. In the next few decades, trillions of dollars could be spent on developing and building renewable production.

Innovation lab cities are intent on boosting the renewable portion of their energy supply. Vancouver's city council voted unanimously in 2015 to shift the city to 100 percent renewable energy sources, and among other actions, the city is developing district heating systems based on renewables. Stockholm is phasing out its last coal-burning plant, replacing it with a biomass generator that can heat three hundred thousand homes and provide up to 8 percent of the city's electricity. Copenhagen plans to produce more wind energy than its residents consume and to sell the surplus into the nation's electricity grid. Rio de Janeiro could use rooftop solar installations to produce nearly twice the energy the city needs, says Luciana Nery, the city's former deputy chief resilience officer. Boulder, Cape Town, and Minneapolis are among cities that have fought with investor-owned and national-government utilities to gain more renewable energy.

Dozens of other cities have pledged to shift to all renewables. When President Donald Trump suggested that withdrawing the US from the Paris climate agreement protected the interests of

Pittsburgh, a city of 305,000 in a coal-mining region, the city's mayor rebutted the notion. "Once famous for its steel mills [Pittsburgh] has emerged as a trailblazer in environmental innovation," declared Bill Peduto. "Pittsburgh will be 100 percent powered by renewable energy by 2035."

But there's more to renewables than changing the sources of energy to reduce GHG emissions. New ideas about expanding the use and altering the design of energy systems are emerging, with implications for cities. The "electrification of everything" envisions that nearly every urban need for energy will be met by electricity produced entirely from renewable sources. This vision greatly expands demand for electricity and builds on the beachhead that electric mobility has established, especially in leading-edge cities—with electric cars, trucks, buses, and trains coming into the mainstream. Full electrification of transportation, according to one analysis, could increase global electricity demand by 56 percent. Electricity-transport products already earn billions of dollars worldwide, and their expansion depends on continued development of and investment in electric-charging infrastructure, storage batteries, and other innovations. By 2020, there will be more than twelve million EV charging stations worldwide, up from one million units just six years earlier, according to market forecasts. Further propelling a shift to electric mobility and to the once-unimaginable "death of the internal combustion engine," Norway, France, Germany, and the United Kingdom have announced efforts to phase out fossil-fuel vehicles. China, already the world's largest maker and buyer of EVs, is heading toward a similar policy.

These trends position cities as the economic hubs of an expanding global market for the production and use of electricity and electric products and services. Oslo is perhaps the city furthest along toward creating an all-electric, all-renewables transportation system. The city's metro, trams, and buses run mostly on hydroelectricity from the national grid. In September 2017, 60 percent of new cars registered in Oslo were fully electric or plug-in hybrids. The city contains twenty-two thousand electric cars, about 7.5 percent of the total private and public fleet, and expects to nearly double that number by 2020, when there will be more than two thousand charging stations. London, Portland, San Francisco, and Stockholm have declared their intentions to become EV market leaders, while Shanghai, designated an EV-demonstration city by the national government, registers far more new EVs annually than any city in the world. Another potential growth market for electric products is the heating of space and water in residential buildings in the US, which consumes large volumes of natural gas and fuel oil. Boulder, New York City, and Washington, DC, have studied how cities, in collaboration with manufacturers, can get building owners to switch to highly efficient electric heat pumps that draw heat out of the surrounding air.

Even as innovation lab cities support new uses of electricity, the structure of energy production and distribution is changing, with economic implications for cities. When electricity gained traction more than a century ago, utility companies took advantage of economies of scale and created a centralized system of power generation, distribution, and management. Large-scale generation occurred at a small number of facilities a long distance from customers. Now, though, a renewable electricity system with numerous smaller and more geographically dispersed sites for power production—primarily rooftop solar panels and wind turbines—is emerging. Some buildings are producing more renewable energy than they need and selling it into the electricity grid. Electric vehicles can also sell their unneeded energy into the grid. Although it's not likely that cities will produce all the power they need, they have an important role to play in transforming the electricity grid to 100 percent renewable energy.

The grid itself is being made "intelligent" through the use of information technology and the internet, which enables distributed producers and consumers to sell and buy electricity based on real-time pricing and other considerations.

Eventually, says Rifkin, "hundreds of millions of human beings will be generating their own green energy in their homes, offices, and factories and sharing it with each other across intelligent distributed electricity networks—an intergrid—just like people now create their own information and share it on the Internet." Within cities, microgrids are connecting distributed producers into electricity networks that can meet the needs of entire neighborhoods and hospital and university campuses. In this next-generation information-energy grid, utilities that no longer provide all of the energy may become managers of a system of digitally connected buildings, vehicles, and everything else using electricity.

What began several decades ago as a new question—what could cities do to decarbonize—has turned into a way for cities to make a significant mark on the world's transitioning economy.

City Clusters

When Mette Søs Lassesen attended meetings that the city of Copenhagen held with local government officials in several US cities a few years ago, the Americans couldn't figure out why she was there. The sessions were intended to explore the potential for city-to-city collaborations between the Danish and US cities. But Lassesen, a native of Copenhagen, didn't work for the city. She works for a Danish engineering firm, Ramboll, which is headquartered in Copenhagen and has been aligning its business around the theme of "livable cities," including energy, mobility, water, buildings, and environmental systems. Lassesen's job is to help Ramboll's livable-cities business find traction in the US market. She joined the meetings with American cities to conduct business for her company—and that's exactly what Copenhagen's officials wanted her to do.

"New York and Washington, DC, were a little mystified by this approach," Lassesen reflects. "They're not used to having the private sector introduced in this way into these city-to-city discussions." But this is Copenhagen's way: "When the city engages in these collaborations, they don't do it just because it's fun and interesting. It's because they can bring Danish businesses into the loop."

Copenhagen routinely establishes and mines its connections to other cities to create opportunities for its local businesses. This economic-development strategy starts back at home. When the city decided in 2011 to become carbon neutral by 2025, says Lassesen, "it realized that the last piece of how to get there was unknown. It was assumed that there would have to be innovation along the way." The city decided to help grow businesses that produced innovative products and services for addressing climate change. Turning itself into an incubator for these companies became a key part of Copenhagen's strategy for its future as a global city, according to Lord Mayor Frank Jensen, an economist and former minister in the national government: "We can see that investments in new green solutions go hand in hand with job creation. Investing in the right solutions is also good for the economy." The city's role as a "customer for green solutions" creates opportunities for local clean technology and other green businesses, Jensen says. Many of the firms sell their green products and services to other cities: "They use the brand of Copenhagen as a leading green center as a selling point when they go to other cities." Delegations of green businesses travel to cities in the US and elsewhere to pitch their products and services.

Several other innovation lab cities—Boulder, London, and Vancouver—also position themselves as markets for and incubators of businesses that develop clean-energy solutions for sale elsewhere. Vancouver has become home to one of every five clean-technology companies in Canada, says Mayor Gregor Robertson. "This," he explains, "is about assembling a center of excellence in how green a city can be, in the same way that Silicon Valley concentrated talent and technology, and all of that technology gets exported around the world." Vancouver is working with Seattle—just 140 miles and an international border crossing away—to develop a technology-business corridor. In the last decade, the two cities have attracted more than $10 billion in venture-capital investments in technology start-up companies. Vancouver also provides clean-tech and smart-city companies with free access to test sites for their innovative products.

London developed plans for a clean-technology cluster that would link a top technical university with companies operating in a redeveloped district called Old Oak and Park Royal. "Imagine the scene," promoters gushed: "A eureka moment in a lab in Imperial College is moved to an Imperial White City Incubator. It is rapidly tested and developed to the point where it earns first round finance. It moves from the incubator to a business growth hub in Old Oak, where it draws upon a range of services and is inspired by other related entrepreneurial businesses. Prototypes can be made in the same zone to prove market demand exists. This is the potential of a cluster." In 2017, Mayor Sadiq Khan announced the development of a clean-tech incubator to support one hundred business start-ups.

Shanghai participates in the development of its nation's Global Innovation Centers program, established in 2015 by the national government with the involvement of city mayors. The initiative establishes pilot cities for development of high-tech business hubs of local companies in energy, automobiles, health, and other emerging sectors. Shanghai has strong positioning in electric vehicles, renewable-energy technologies, and redesign of electricity grids for distributed production, says Guo Jianli, trained in automotive engineering and environmental policy, now the vice director of the Resource Conservation and Environmental Protection Division of the Shanghai Development and Reform Commission. "But it takes time and the right companies to be an innovation hub."

Boulder, with a large endowment of scientific laboratories and three thousand climate researchers, sees the energy transition as an economic opportunity. "For those in our community drawn to Boulder's entrepreneurial spirit," states the city's 2017 climate action plan, "creating new approaches to renewable energy generation, storage and management—and being able to test those approaches here in Boulder—are leading to unprecedented business and local job opportunities."

For Ramboll's Lassesen, participating in the Copenhagen delegation's meetings with US cities, along with other companies from the city, offers a significant opportunity. "When Copenhagen goes into New York, it says, 'these are the companies we have worked with. Why don't you talk to them as well,'" she explains. "You can't get a better recommendation for starting off with a new client."

Copenhagen's path to becoming a major exporter of renewable-energy products and services began in the 1970s, when a cartel of oil-producing Arab nations cut off oil shipments to the US and other nations, sparking worldwide shortages and a steep rise in prices. "Denmark learned the hard way that fossil fuels were expensive and we should not rely on them," says Lassesen. "That's when the national government started looking at renewables." In 1979, the first wind turbine was installed in Denmark, and today more than 40 percent of the nation's electricity supply comes from wind power, much of it produced offshore.

The city and the nation have often moved in concert to develop green-energy technology companies. In 2009, the Copenhagen

Cleantech Cluster formed with twelve partners—energy companies, research institutions, government and nonprofit organizations—and since then has supported more than 126 start-up companies and created more than one thousand jobs. It was the largest cluster project in Europe. The entity became part of a national cluster with more than 170 public and private members. In 2015, Danish companies' wind-power exports earned nearly $9 billion in revenue, making up more than 5 percent of the nation's exports. Denmark's command of the wind sector keeps growing: In 2017, China announced it would use Danish companies to build a wind farm and would partner with Denmark on the development of a test and demonstration center for offshore wind power. In October 2017, the US government signed a deal with the Danish government to expand cooperation on offshore wind power, another boost for Danish companies.

Copenhagen continues to expand its international connections and the economic sectors it is mining. "The city wants to be a place where companies can come and it's easy for them to try things out," says Lassesen. "We're competing with other cities—in Scandinavia and Europe—to be a 'first mover' when it comes to achieving carbon neutrality. We're showing that it can be done and how it can be done."

The city designated its Nordhavn district, the largest urban development project in Scandinavia, as an EnergyLab site to help businesses develop and show ways that electricity, heating, and energy-efficient buildings and electric transport can be integrated into an "intelligent system." The city also declared itself a "living laboratory" for smart technologies for cities; more than 250 companies are involved and global technology companies—Cisco and Hitachi—have located development capacities in the city.

Moving into the US market, Copenhagen joined with Aarhus, Denmark's second-largest city, more than twenty Danish companies, the national government, industry associations, and universities to locate the Danish Cleantech Hub in New York City. The hub's purpose is "to create visibility of Danish cleantech expertise and increase the speed with which solutions are shared." At one Hub event, Copenhagen's mayor was a keynote speaker. At another, Denmark's prime minister gave the closing speech.

LOW-CARBON INNOVATION DISTRICTS

*A*ustin, Stockholm, and Toronto have infused innovation development into new low-carbon districts they are building. These are not "innovation districts" that many cities have created to assemble clusters of entrepreneurs, start-up companies, and business accelerators. They are neighborhoods where tens of thousands of people live, work, and play, just like in any large city, *and* where others—researchers, developers, and builders, for instance—pioneer real-world products and services for decarbonizing cities.

Austin is building out Mueller, a seven-hundred-acre "mixed-use urban village" for thirteen thousand residents and thirteen thousand workers, atop an abandoned airport site three miles from the city center. Located in the district is the Pecan Street Lab, a three-story university research-and-development facility that monitors rooftop solar panels, electric vehicles, and residential microgrids in roughly three hundred homes in Mueller. When this is combined with its other sites in the US, Pecan Street has the world's largest energy and water research database, which is used to improve the performance of solar installations and microgrids, develop mobile apps to manage residential energy demand, and produce strategies for managing "smart-grid" electricity loads.

Stockholm's Royal Seaport District will contain twelve thousand residences with twenty-five thousand dwellers, some thirty-five thousand workplaces, and 6.5 million square feet of commercial space. The district set up an innovation center that has conducted more than twenty research projects and experiments with partners to improve performance. To help with the design of smart grids, it recruited a family of four (two working adults and two teenagers) to live for six months in an apartment equipped with various smart appliances and control systems—energy measurement, motion, and temperature sensors as well as dimmers, regulators, and "away" buttons to decrease consumption.

In October 2017, Toronto, a city of 2.8 million people, unveiled its partnership with Sidewalk Labs, a subsidiary of Alphabet, which

---

Mueller description: "About Us," Mueller, accessed February 6, 2018, http://www.muelleraustinonline.com/about.php.

also houses Google, to develop an eight-hundred-acre waterfront area into a high-tech neighborhood. The Quayside project starts with a twelve-acre neighborhood that sponsors say will combine "the best in urban design with the latest in digital technology" and may include prefabricated buildings with mixed uses, indoor and outdoor sensors and cameras, autonomous vehicles, deliveries and garbage collection by robots, and microgrids for electricity. Project developers intend to invest in and incubate companies that develop tools for use in Toronto and other cities, making the city into "the global hub for urban innovation."

Quayside project: "Press Backgrounder," Sidewalk Toronto, October 17, 2017, https://sidewalktoronto.ca/wp-content/uploads/2017/10/Sidewalk-Toronto-Backgrounder.pdf.
Prefabricated buildings . . . for electricity: Ian Austen, "City of the Future? Humans, Not Technology, Are the Challenge in Toronto," *New York Times*, December 29, 2017, https://www.nytimes.com/2017/12/29/world/canada/google-toronto-city-future.html?.
Project developers . . . urban innovation: "Welcome to Sidewalk Toronto," Sidewalk Toronto, accessed January 18, 2018, https://www.sidewalktoronto.ca.

Local Production

As CEO of the nonprofit Advanced Energy Economy (AEE), Graham Richard worked with hundreds of clean-energy companies, tech start-ups, and global corporations throughout the US to develop a national association for the fast-growing sector. AEE pushed tirelessly for state and national policies favorable to renewable-energy production and issued reports detailing the sector's impressive job-creation numbers. But it's not just businesses that can benefit from these developments. Cities, too, have big opportunities in the emerging "clean economy," says Richard, who served two terms as mayor of a city of 250,000 residents—Fort Wayne, Indiana. The spread of *decentralized* production of renewable energy coupled with smart technologies is gaining momentum, he says: "This model will be implemented community by community. That means creating *local* jobs instead of building large power plants way outside of cities. Production will be popping up in populated areas, because that's where the producers and buyers are."

Efforts to localize energy production are a new entry in an urban dynamic that Jane Jacobs identified as key to city-based economic development: import replacement. "Cities grow and become economically versatile by replacing goods they once imported with goods they make themselves," she explained, and this process "often entails adaptations in design, materials or methods of production, and these require innovating and improvising." In nearly any city, replacing fossil fuels with renewable energy puts a potentially large amount of money into play. For instance, in Washington, DC, a city of 680,000, the residents, businesses, and local government spend $1.8 billion a year on oil, natural gas, and coal imported from Russia, Saudi Arabia, Venezuela, Canada, Mexico, and six US states. Boulder's 2017 climate plan pitches energy-import replacement: "Rather than sending over $300 million each year out of our community to pay for fossil fuels we simply burn up, we can reinvest those dollars in energy systems that could last a lifetime or more."

This model of localized energy contains three linked elements that innovation lab and other cities are beginning to exploit. It installs "distributed energy resources," such as rooftop solar panels, for the production and storage of renewable energy. It uses smart information technologies—network-management software and the "Internet of Things," which is made up of sensors embedded in just about anything and connected to the internet—to link and manage distributed systems. This forms microgrids that can be connected to or separated from the main electricity grid. And it develops an electricity grid made up of networked, distributed resources, such as microgrids, which are the building blocks of a reinvented grid. Where this model has advanced most, energy regulators and policymakers in state and national governments have paved the way by adopting rules that remove barriers and offering financial incentives for investment in small-scale renewable production.

In Australia, of the 1.5 million households that generate their own solar energy, about 275,000 received government-subsidized payments for selling the electricity they generated to the power grid. Some received twice as much as it cost them to produce the electricity. In California, more than 250,000 private solar-energy customers are connected to the grid operated by the state's leading utility, Pacific Gas and Electricity, which also has more than eighty-five thousand electric vehicles registered in its service territory. The utility expects a "dramatic increase" in distributed energy resources by 2025. In New York State, it's estimated that plans for a new "hybrid grid" that uses distributed renewable production and microgrids could generate as much as $8.7 billion in annual revenue for the energy-storage industry alone. Top-level utility executives in Europe, says Richard, predict that twenty years from now, electricity systems there will be mostly organized around distributed renewable production "because that's what their customers want." In Germany, 6 percent of households produced their own renewable energy in 2014, and many more households intended to do the same, drawn by government financial incentives. In the United Kingdom, reports professor of urban and regional political economy Andrew Cumbers, "the emergence of decentralized forms of energy, often linked to new district heat and power schemes, is offering the possibility for cities to meet climate change obligations" and boost energy affordability. Distributed production models may also provide local communities with a greater voice in decisions about energy supply and distribution, since they are no longer just passive customers of the utility system.

For cities, C40 Cities reports in "Deadline 2020," distributed production of renewable energy can result in huge reductions in emissions and can be scaled up rapidly by using microgrids. These innovations also contribute to climate resilience, C40 notes: "Local energy production can be less exposed to supply chain risks as fuel is located on-site" as long as it has been designed, constructed, and operated for future climate conditions. In 2016, Rio de Janeiro published an energy toolkit for buildings that promoted several advantages of local microgeneration, even though the national electricity grid the city taps into is mostly renewable hydropower. It noted that periods of below-average rainfall reduced the reliability of hydropower. The resilience of microgrids is a main reason analysts project that in the US between 2017 and 2022, installed microgrid capacity for renewable production will double.

This networked-electricity future is in early stages of development in cities—part vision, part plan, part pilots. The number of solar installations on residential buildings in New York City rose to 5,300 in 2016, up from under two hundred in 2011. A study for Paris projects that by 2050, almost 20 percent of rooftops in the city will have solar panels. In Hamburg, the publicly owned electric utility has invested in six wind farms within the city's boundaries. Rotterdam's vision for development includes the use of "an Internet of Things infrastructure in and around every building to monitor and manage energy efficiency" and a building stock of "smart, digital nodes interconnected in vast digital networks." In Berlin, the development of smart passive-energy buildings is also demonstrating the extent to which a building can become a power plant—and what a network of buildings can do. "Connected devices in the past have been poorly designed gadgets for nerdy early adopters but smart-home devices are on the verge of becoming mainstream," says Björn Grindberg of Climate-KIC, a public-private organization dedicated to a zero-carbon future. "The spreading of smart meters and smart energy management systems can accelerate the German energy transformation," says Andreas Kraemer, founder and director emeritus of the Berlin think tank Ecologic Institute. Oslo's FutureBuilt program, which develops pilot projects for large GHG reductions, has supported prominent passive-energy buildings—a school, a museum, and a multiuse structure—that use smart technology to manage energy use.

A scenario developed for Shanghai projected that by 2030, electric vehicles could consume as much as 11 percent of the city's electricity. Given driving and EV charging habits, this level of demand could substantially increase the evening peak load on the grid, "thus putting pressure on the safety and stability of the power grid." By coordinating when during the day EVs charge their batteries, the study said, the city could reduce peak demand for electricity and generate several benefits: the utility would avoid the cost of procuring power or investing in new generating capacity to meet peak demand and could pass savings on to customers while paying EV owners to participate. The large number of EVs in the city could also serve as a source of clean power for the electric grid while they are not being used, which is about 95 percent of the time. This also could earn money for EV owners, save the utility money, and allow the utility to obtain clean (stored) power instead of generating more power from GHG-emitting sources, says Barbara Finamore, Asia director for the Natural Resources Defense Council's China program, which cosponsored the 2016 report.

New climate disasters are producing an opening for distributed, networked electricity systems, notes Richard. For instance, thousands of houses in wildfire-ravaged areas north of San Francisco are being built with resilient microgrid systems instead of just being connected to the main electricity grid. In Puerto Rico, after Hurricane Maria leveled the electricity grid for three million residents, energy regulators in January 2018 opened the door to widespread deployment of microgrids using renewable energy—a potentially faster and cheaper way of restoring service.

The new energy and digital technologies are making it much easier for new businesses to enter the highly controlled electricity sector. Some companies in Germany now offer to convert communities to a microgrid system independent of utility grids. "You don't need big utilities anymore," says the head of a German investment firm that put about $12 million into one of these businesses.

City Green Branding

In 2014, Vancouver competed head-to-head against five comparable global cities—San Francisco, Shanghai, Singapore, Sydney, and Hong Kong—in a study to assess the strength of each city as a brand. A city's brand is a measurable asset composed of its reputation and image. Brand Finance Canada, a brand-assessment business, interviewed more than 1,100 business leaders, students, and tourists worldwide, as well as residents of certain cities. Its managing director, Edgar Baum, announced the results: Vancouver had the strongest brand of the selected cities—scoring seventy-seven out of one hundred points, with no other city scoring more than sixty-nine points. The city's strong suit was obvious. "The City of Vancouver brand," Baum reported, "is associated with the environment, 'green' living, and environmental leadership that was discernibly ahead of that of the five other city brands studied." The city trumpets the results on its website: "We are uniquely associated with being clean, green and environmentally sustainable." This branding, says Mayor Robertson, provides Vancouver with an important economic advantage: "Being a green city is a big competitive edge for attracting talent, and with the talent comes private investment."

Vancouver is not alone in paying attention to its image. The "Sustainable Sydney 2030" campaign promotes the two-hundred-thousand-resident city's ambitious goals for becoming "as green, global, and connected as possible" and being "a leader with outstanding environmental performance and new 'green' industries driving economic growth." Copenhagen presents itself as a livable, edgy, and responsible city with an emphasis on addressing climate change. The city "is internationally renowned for its innovative approach to the climate and the environment," states the city's "Co-Create Copenhagen" publication, in English, with full-page color photos of people enjoying life out of doors. "Copenhagen is one of the world's most ecological and climate-friendly cities." In Boulder's climate plan, the mayor and city manager remind residents of their city's identity as a trailblazer: "This is a critical time for our environment and our community—but it is also an exciting time. Once again, our community is positioned to be a leader."

City governments increasingly make "explicit efforts to employ the strategic marketing tactics of companies to 'brand' their city as a Global City," reports Kristin Ljungkvist in *The Global City 2.0*, as they compete for "attention, influence, markets, investments, businesses, visitors, talents and events." Ultimately, though, cities' quests for innovative economic capacity focus on talent. "Global cities are magnets for people—particularly those who are ambitious and highly skilled," observes Richard Florida. "Some three in four residents of fourteen large global cities—London, Paris, Tokyo, Sydney, Shanghai, Beijing, and others—report that they 'chose' their city . . . and didn't just end up there by accident." Trends like this can have a measurable urban impact: between 1990 and 2015, the number of young adults and more-educated and higher-income residents increased in nearly every US city's downtown and central neighborhoods, according to a University of Virginia report.

Although cities have promoted their greenness for centuries— building and touting their parks and forests—urban green branding now includes climate actions and energy efficiency.

A city's look and feel matters to companies competing for talented employees. In 2017, Ford Motor Company's leadership committed $60 million to upgrade downtown areas around its world headquarters in Dearborn, a city of about one hundred thousand people outside of Detroit. The company has been in the city for nearly a century and has some forty thousand employees there. But like other US-based automobile companies, it is becoming more of a digital technology company focused on electrification, autonomous vehicles, and mobility and has to recruit talented, tech-savvy workers. "Younger generations of workers really want to work closer to where they live," says Donna Inch, head of Ford's real estate office. "And to be able to live where they want to work, they really need vibrant downtown areas." Ford's ten-year plan focuses on creating a walkable, aesthetically pleasing environment in Dearborn.

When Amazon ignited a 2017 bidding war among North American cities to become the location of its second corporate headquarters, the company emphasized that, in addition to seeking a "friendly business environment," "optimal fiber connectivity," and financial inducements, it was looking for a city with "the potential to attract and retain strong technical talent." It anticipated hiring as many as fifty thousand highly educated employees who would earn an average annual income of $100,000. The company preferred a place with a diverse population and excellent institutions of higher education, its Request for Proposals stated: "We want to invest in a community where our employees will enjoy living, recreational opportunities, educational opportunities, and an overall high quality of life." Amazon touted its own green brand, noting that at its headquarters in Seattle, the "buildings' interiors feature salvaged and locally sourced woods, energy-efficient lighting, composting and recycling alternatives as well as public plazas and pockets of green space. . . . We also invest in large solar and wind operations and were the largest corporate purchaser of renewable energy in the U.S. in 2016."

Even as cities position themselves to be the innovation drivers of an emerging global clean economy, breathing life into a new urban economics, they recognize that replacing fossil-fuel sources is insufficient to address the global warming crisis. Given political, technological, and financial constraints and uncertainties, a world of 100 percent renewable energy won't be achieved quickly enough to avoid exceeding the global "carbon budget" for the atmosphere. "People in China think cutting emissions means substituting [old] sources of energy with new ones," notes Zhu Dajiang, director of Shanghai Tongji University's Institute of Governance for Sustainable Development. "That's a major misunderstanding."

Cities also prioritize the reduction of their appetite for energy, which could cut the amount of new renewable energy that needs to be produced. But consumption of energy is deeply embedded in the systems and lifestyles of modern cities and the production of prosperity.

08 EFFICIENT ABUNDANCE

—

Cities Can More Efficiently Use Energy, Materials, Natural Resources, and Space to Generate a New Kind of Urban Abundance

Cities must be regarded as more than engines of wealth; they must be viewed as systems that should be shaped to improve human well-being.

—CHARLES MONTGOMERY

New York City has more buildings than most cities in the world have people: one million of them. Known for its skyscrapers, the city shelters 8.5 million residents and hosts roughly six hundred thousand inbound commuters on weekdays. The buildings in which they live, work, and play consume energy for heating and cooling space, heating and moving water, lighting, ventilation, cooking, and running electric appliances, machines, and devices. The energy comes mostly from fossil-fuel sources: 60 percent from natural gas and fuel oils, much of the rest from a state electricity grid that generates three-quarters of its power from carbon-emitting sources. Buildings produce about 70 percent of New York City's GHG emissions.

It was natural, then, that in September 2014, attention focused on the city's building stock when Mayor Bill de Blasio committed to reduce the city's GHG emissions by 80 percent by 2050. The plan that the de Blasio administration released, "One City: Built to Last," called for a 30 percent reduction by 2025 in GHG emissions from energy used in buildings—on the way to a 60 percent cut by 2050 from the 2005 level. Efficiency improvement is the city's biggest opportunity to achieve GHG reductions while it also pursues its limited options for increasing the use of renewable energy.

New buildings sprout up in New York and other cities all the time. Between 2004 and 2015, construction added 8 percent to the total floor space in the city. Many advances in design and equipment make it possible to hold down *new* buildings' energy use substantially, often to nearly zero, and some buildings even produce enough energy to run themselves and send the excess into the electricity grid. But, the city projected, 90 percent of the buildings standing in 2015 would still exist in 2050. The great majority of those buildings were not designed, constructed, and equipped with energy efficiency in mind. Fossil-fuel energy was relatively inexpensive in the twentieth century; how much was used (or its impact on the environment) was not a paramount concern for architects, engineers, building owners and managers, or even many tenants paying the bills. "We've been living on an enriched diet of fossil fuels, because it was so cheap," observes John Lee, deputy director for green buildings and energy efficiency at the Mayor's Office of Long-Term Planning and Sustainability. "Especially in the economic boom in the 1960s and 1970s, we built buildings in a way that didn't care about energy. And they last 50 to 100 years, or more."

The design of buildings has been based on principles set up in the early 1900s, when modern architecture and the International Style were born, explains architect Ed Mazria. At the time, architects and planners were responding to several developments: industrialization had created overcrowded slums and heavy air pollution in cities; advances in reinforced concrete building technology and central heating, cooling, and ventilation systems allowed for the construction of high-rise buildings with glass "skins" and larger interior spaces; and the arrival of the automobile led cities to favor large blocks of tall buildings and redesign wide street grids for more efficient movement of people and goods. The International Style, Mazria says, "divorced the building from place and location, and overpowered the climate and external environment by using abundant inexpensive energy to condition and light interior space." The same glass building could be located almost anywhere in the world.

Now, though, buildings have to be turned into much more efficient structures, retrofitted for a different world than the one for which they were designed and built. "Our buildings will need to become high-performance structures," Mayor de Blasio's report announced. "Walls and windows must be insulated, building equipment must become more efficient and intelligent. . . . Residents would need to conscientiously conserve energy and water, and building operators will need to become skilled in the latest energy efficiency technologies." Experts estimated that existing technologies and strategies could reduce energy use in typical buildings by 40 to 60 percent. The challenge is to get these "deep" efficiency upgrades to happen in nearly every building in the city even though few building owners, managers, and occupants have compelling financial reasons to act. "We haven't priced the energy input into buildings to the point where efficiency to cut costs matters enough," explains Lee, noting this is true even though New York's energy costs are among the nation's highest. "The potential return on investment for efficiency has to compete against other, more profitable investments."

Most innovation lab cities face a similar challenge with reducing emissions by buildings, although not at New York's vast scale, and they have dedicated substantial resources and effort to figuring out how to boost building efficiency. In the absence of strong financial drivers for private investment, cities use government and utility programs to incentivize or subsidize weatherization and other energy-reduction projects on buildings. But they recognize that the pace of this "retrofitting" is much slower than what's needed to achieve their goals for building efficiency—and doing a great deal more of it would require a huge amount of taxpayer or ratepayer money.

The energy consumed by buildings is just one target among many for ramping up urban efficiency to reduce fossil-fuel energy use and increase cities' resilience to climate disruptions. Climate innovators also push to cut energy use in transportation and processing solid waste. Gradually, they have expanded their sights to cover nearly everything that a city consumes: food, water, materials, natural resources, and even the time people spend traveling. They want to reduce overall levels of consumption and waste that have been baked deeply into the physical, economic, social, and political structures of modern urban life.

This, it turns out, requires a change in modern thinking about abundance: what it is and how it can be produced.

The Rise of Abundance

A big gain in efficiency ignited the Industrial Revolution. James Watt, an instrument maker in Glasgow, redesigned a rudimentary steam engine that had been used for nearly sixty years to pump water out of mines. In the 1780s, Watt reduced the engine's waste of heat, which increased the mechanical power it produced by burning coal to generate steam. The boost and other adjustments made it commercially feasible to use steam engines in mills for paper, flour, cotton, and iron; in distilleries, canals, and waterworks; and to power trains and ships.

So began the global rise in consumption of fossil fuels that continues to the present, setting a record in 2015, even as the amount of renewable energy in the world also reached a new height. But the past two centuries are more than a story of ever-peaking energy consumption. Before the 1800s, material consumption worldwide had been increasing for several centuries, summarizes Frank Trentmann in *Empire of Things*. By 1800, he says, values and practices "favored greater consumption and kept the momentum going." Industrialization in Europe spurred consumption, as did globalizing markets and expanding colonial empires. This rising tide, reports another history of consumption, swept away earlier agrarian-society behaviors in which "clothing and household possessions were extremely limited [and] individual material goods were used, with repairs if needed, for decades."

Ideas about consumption began to change. "The new prominence of consumption was part of a mental shift in industrial societies," Trentmann explains. Economists had previously agreed there were natural limits to economic growth, but economic expansion brought on by industrialization broke through the presumed ceiling. "Growth unsettled assumptions about the social order, the nature of wealth, its origin, use and distribution," says Trentmann. The concept of a standard of living, with an emphasis on material and financial well-being, took hold as a measure of society's performance and a priority for government policy. Economists contended that consumption helped civilize nations and generate abundance.

Potential drivers of consumption, such as keeping the cost of supplying goods low and continuously stimulating consumers' desires, became enshrined in modern business practices and public policies. "When the Industrial Revolution manifested itself, people wanted simply to keep supply as high as demand," observe William McDonough and Michael Braungart in *The Upcycle: Beyond Sustainability—Designing for Abundance*. Increasing supply meant consuming more natural resources to make things. "Nature never said no," recaps McDonough. "Everything was there for the taking." The process of turning resources into products expanded throughout the twentieth century. In 1987, the Brundtland Report noted that global industrial production had grown more than fiftyfold, with most of the increase since 1950.

Along the way, *economic* thinking about social well-being gained dominance. "The mass of humanity," observes Richard Heinberg, senior fellow of the Post Carbon Institute, "came to be motivated by … the belief in material progress—the notion that life itself is getting better, is meant to get better, with every passing year, with every new generation. As time goes on, technology improves, scientific knowledge accumulates, and we get richer." To promote material progress, Heinberg adds, economists touted the idea that "the optimal benefit to humanity is to be obtained through perpetual economic growth."

Beginning in the nineteenth century, economic thinking also captured the concept of efficiency—the amount of useful work performed by a machine or a process compared to the total energy expended. Efficiency was worth pursuing if it cut financial costs, which could improve the bottom line of producers and reduce prices paid by consumers. Focusing on economic benefits minimized or ruled out other concerns, such as environmental and health impacts and social and racial equity. In the 1940s, when nations adopted a new measuring tool, the gross domestic product (GDP), it was a way, explains journalist Elizabeth Dickinson, to "capture all economic production by individuals, companies, and the government in a single measure, which should rise in good times and fall in bad."

Consuming Cities

Mass consumption reshaped cities. To meet growing demand from residents and businesses, cities had to build new systems for delivering services and goods. Urban use of water, gas, and electricity soared. "Streets, neighbourhoods and their inhabitants were networked, connected through pipes, gas lines, the omnibus and the tram," Trentmann documents. "In the second half of the nineteenth century, any modern city worth the name aspired to be networked." By 1867, Paris was lit by twenty thousand gas lamps. The use of water closets in houses and apartments spread in Boston, New York City, London, and other cities. In the 1890s, London became the first city to provide a "constant supply" of water rather than intermittent service.

Cities enabled the movement of growing flows of people and goods. Between 1890 and 1905, for example, US cities began to deploy electric streetcars, constructing thirty thousand miles of electric street railway. By 1923, the industry's national ridership had reached 15.7 billion passengers. Cities also accommodated enormous expansions of housing, industrial production, and shopping—which forced them to rethink land use, urban form, and the regulation of real estate, retailing, and other markets. "Cities served as the hothouses of consumer society" in the seventeenth and eighteenth centuries, notes European historian Deborah Cohen. "By the late nineteenth century, cities had not just lavish department stores, with spectacular window displays . . . but the infrastructure for the inconspicuous consumption that came to define a civilized life—running water on demand, gas lighting, indoor plumbing, and electricity."

With consumption patterns driving city development and use, New York City in 1916 introduced America's first citywide zoning code—designed, according to a report at the time, to "check the invasion of retail districts by factories and residence districts by factories and businesses" and "prevent an increase of the congestion of streets and of subway and streetcar traffic in sections where the business population is already too great for the sidewalks and transit facilities." Cities adopted zoning to keep land uses and densities separated—a regulatory model with substantial impacts. Separating residential areas from shopping areas made it "difficult to go from one to the other without a car," note urban planners Jonathan Barnett and Larry Beasley. Zoning codes with many residential areas based on differing lot sizes, they add, perpetuated social distinctions, spread out urbanization unnecessarily, and "contributed to making new housing unaffordable for ordinary families."

Rising material consumption generated mounting quantities of waste—and management of waste had an economic basis. Before the 1800s, cities used a blend of methods for dealing with waste. Reuse and recycling depended on pickers and collectors taking and selling materials—coal ash, rags, bones, human waste, and horse manure—that served as inputs for industrial and agricultural processes locally and even in other countries. Paris in 1884 had around forty thousand rag pickers. London used dust as fertilizer and for the bricks used to rebuild Moscow after the 1812 fire. In the 1920s and 1930s, Shanghai's licensed collectors of "night soil," human manure, wheeled their carts to the city's docks where hundreds of farmers in boats waited for the "liquid cargo." Shanghai's night soil was "considered superior and especially fertile," explains historian Hanchao Lu, "thanks to the rich diets of the people."

For items with no apparent market value, city dwellers routinely dumped their household waste into streets, ditches, and waterways. The growth of uncollected waste and fears about its impact on public health pushed cities into action. Odors arising from open sewage trenches in Melbourne in the nineteenth century led to the city being dubbed "Smellbourne," with doctors urging the city to install a modern sewage system. When medical researchers linked human waste to the spread of cholera and other diseases, cities initiated a wave of engineering to design and build "sanitary" sewers that carried dangerous human discard away for treatment and disposal. Eventually the send-it-away approach—disposing into waterways, the ground, or the air—was applied to all manner of waste. "What started as a crusade for public health and civic renewal ended up in the hands of engineers who focused on finding the best and cheapest technologies for getting rid of waste by either burying or burning it," Trentmann notes. British cities began to burn waste systematically in the 1870s. In 1883, all Parisians were ordered to put household refuse into waste bins for collection in the morning. Two decades later, Shanghai required households to place all refuse into iron bins for pickup; later the city introduced concrete house-refuse containers with locks to keep out the rag pickers. In 1885, New York City built the first garbage incinerator in the US. By the early 1900s, incinerators and landfills for disposal had spread through urban America.

By the beginning of the twenty-first century, the world's cities generated ten times more solid waste than a century earlier—more than three million tons every day. Around 1900, residents of Stockholm threw away an average of sixty-six pounds of waste a year. By 2017, per capita annual disposal in the city had reached more than one thousand pounds. New York City alone produces ten million tons of solid waste annually, according to a 2013 report—two-thirds of it from everyday activities, the rest debris from construction and demolition of buildings.

Through a gradual process of change, modern cities came to serve as epicenters of a global consumer society in which buying, selling, and disposing of goods and services are predominantly social and economic activities.

The New Abundance

The growth of material abundance has been a double-edged sword. One edge is the production of undeniable benefits for humanity. "In 1665, half a billion humans sweated to sustain the species near subsistence with their crude implements," notes philosopher Leif Wenar. "Now our global economy is so productive that 16 times that number—some 8 billion humans—will soon be alive, and most will never have known such poverty." It's an affirming judgment often made. In 2017, writes *New York Times* columnist Nicholas Kristof, "a smaller share of the world's people were hungry, impoverished or illiterate than at any time before."

Abundance's other edge produces downsides, especially in cities. But global warming due to fossil-fuel burning is not the only danger that consumption has brought to our door. The processes of taking wood, coal, and other natural resources laid waste to vast ecosystems and continue to do so. Since the 1970s, according to the Global Footprint Network's calculator, humanity has been consuming resources at a faster rate than the planet can resupply them—a chronic "ecological overshoot" of consumption. "It now takes the Earth one year and six months to regenerate what we use in a year," the network reports. In 2005, Calgary, a city of 1.2 million, used the network's calculator to assess its footprint. "If everyone on earth had the same Ecological Footprint as the average Calgary resident," the analysis concluded, "we would need five Earths to maintain that level of resource consumption." The barely constrained taking of natural resources is simply not sustainable. It's possible, McDonough and Braungart note, that "humans will run short on easily accessible, clean biological and technical materials from which to build and create a beneficial civilization."

At the same time, the processes of making, using, and disposing of goods releases pollution and hazardous and toxic wastes that further damage the environment. Government regulation has had some mitigating effect, but every day seems to bring headlines of growing or newly detected problems: mounting plastic waste in the oceans, for instance. Researchers recently identified the four-thousand-mile-long Yangtze River, flowing near Shanghai and other Chinese cities, as probably the planet's top waterway carrier of plastic pollution.

Of course, consumption-driven abundance and its economic and environmental effects vary greatly among and within modern nations. "Industrial countries and the world's richest people consume and pollute far more than other nations and groups," notes ecological economist Robert Costanza. In 2011, points out urban designer Peter Calthorpe, the average person on earth accounted for 4.9 tons of carbon emissions, but the bottom quarter of the world's population by income emitted only 0.3 tons per capita; they "do not own cars or air conditioners, live in large homes, or eat steaks." Uneven levels of consumption and GHG-emissions production are also evident within cities.

These and other severe environmental, social, and economic problems with the consumption-abundance model have inspired a new set of ideas that radically redefine what abundance is and how it is produced.

ABUNDANCE MUST BE SUSTAINABLE, NOT JUST SHORT TERM

Abundance is not abundance if achieving it depletes and pollutes the environment—the natural systems and resources on which we depend for future abundance. The rate of consumption of natural systems should not outpace the systems' capacity to renew themselves, as the Brundtland Report specified: "A new era of economic growth . . . must be based on policies that sustain and expand the environmental resource base."

The design of products should avoid unnecessary resource inputs and minimize, if not eliminate, waste. "As modern engineers and designers commonly create a product now," explain McDonough and Braungart, "the item is designed only for its first use, not its potential next uses after it breaks, or grows threadbare, or goes out of fashion, or crumbles." Products become waste that has to be put somewhere else. But there is no "away" to which waste can be sent without environmental repercussions for someone. Instead, McDonough and Braungart argue, all products can and should be designed for complete recycling and reuse: "If human beings were to devise products, tools, furniture, homes, factories, and cities more intelligently from the start, they wouldn't even need to think in terms of waste, or contamination, or scarcity. Good design would allow for abundance, endless reuse, and pleasure."

ABUNDANCE MUST BE HOLISTIC, NOT JUST ECONOMIC

Abundance is more than material and economic well-being: it includes human health, social well-being, happiness, environmental conditions, and the way people use their time. "'Bounty' doesn't mean simply more cheap consumer goods and empty calories," say Erik Brynjolfsson and Andrew McAfee in *The Second Machine Age*, noting other types of abundance that matter: "It also means simultaneously more choice, greater variety, and higher quality in many areas of our lives."

To increase abundance requires more than ever-increasing consumption of goods and services. "Consumerism replaced satisfying experiences of making, growing, repairing, and sharing with the momentary buzz of buying a new manufactured product," says Heinberg. People want "more," he continues, but more can be redefined "in terms of relationships, community solidarity, and shared experiences rather than the mere acquisition of stuff."

The theme of nonmaterial abundance resonates with millennials worldwide. "This generation has an abiding interest in looking out for the welfare of the group, not just their own satisfaction," notes Morley Winograd, coauthor of three books about millennials. "As the results of overconsumption and unsustainable growth become more apparent to young adult millennials, their consumption patterns shift to focus on how the goods they buy are produced, the ethics of the companies they do business with, and extracting the maximum value for the least amount of cost. Often this leads them to spend more heavily on experiences and less on 'stuff.'"

Critiques of the abundance-is-economic-value school of thought abound. The gross domestic product is "notorious for overweighting market transactions, understating resource depletion, omitting pollution damage, and failing to measure real changes in well-being," Costanza says. A more holistic version of abundance would recognize values that have been sidelined but are critical for cities, says Richard Florida: "Back in the industrial age, pounding out more steel, more cars, and more consumer durables seemed good proxies for growth. Wasted energy and pollution were accepted as unfortunate but unavoidable byproducts. That no longer holds today in an era where knowledge, innovation, creativity, and human potential drive the economy."

ABUNDANCE MUST BE WIDELY SHARED, NOT NARROWLY POSSESSED

The failure to broaden the base of beneficiaries of abundance, the Brundtland Report contended, is unfair to the poor and weakens the prospect of sustained economic growth. More widespread abundance would minimize problematic disparities in society, especially those driven by economic and social discrimination against particular categories of people and places. In the US and in other nations, more and more cities have taken up this argument for increased economic and social equity in the use of resources.

Seattle has been a global leader in publicly acknowledging disparities due to racial discrimination. On Earth Day in 2016, then-mayor Edward Murray released Seattle's Equity and Environment Agenda, acknowledging that the city's progress in reducing pollution and energy consumption and its investments in public transit had not addressed evident inequities. Residents in low-income neighborhoods "often deal with higher levels of pollution," Murray said. "They often face greater risk of severe health problems, and have limited access to healthy foods and open space. Yet, they benefit the least from our environmental progress. This is particularly true for communities of color."

Urban disparities come to light especially when cities consider their vulnerability to climate changes. In most cities, the populations and neighborhoods most vulnerable to climate impacts also face other significant economic, social, and health inequities. "Conventional approaches to adaptation and mitigation view vulnerability as a characteristic or condition of groups of people and not as a circumstance or consequence of the ways social groups have been historically and systematically marginalized and excluded from opportunity," explains an overview on climate resilience by the collaborators in the Movement Generation project. Boston's resilience plan notes that expected climate impacts "will disproportionately affect communities of color, and overlapping socially vulnerable communities such as older adults, children, people with limited English proficiency, people with low to no income, and people with disabilities."

Cities also are increasingly concerned about how their climate actions affect affordability—the cost of housing, energy, and transportation for people with low incomes, for instance—and might cause displacement of low-income people. Portland's climate plan stresses that energy-efficiency upgrades should not result in increased cost burden to low-income populations and communities of color that are already under financial stress. Austin, one of America's fastest-growing cities, unveiled a plan in 2017 to allow developers to build larger housing projects as long as they ensure a portion of the units will be affordable to renters or they build affordable units elsewhere in the city.

In innovation lab cities, these new ways of thinking lead to three approaches to generating abundance in climate-smart ways. The cities reduce consumption of energy, water, and other resources, conserving in ways that save money as well as materials. They reduce waste disposal by developing "circular" pathways to recycle and reuse products and materials. And they redesign urban compactness—the proximity of people to necessities—to reduce the use of automobile transportation that consumes energy, city space, and people's time and money.

Reducing Consumption

Different motivations may fuel people's efforts to reduce their consumption. Some individuals and businesses value having a small environmental footprint or rejecting wastefulness. For them, this is personal, a way of being—call it *green*, *responsible*, or *sustainable*—and they will often go out of their way, experiencing inconvenience or additional cost, to enact it. When New York City analyzed the "greenness" of its residents, it found that about 40 percent were "young urbanites" or "aspiring greens" who felt "high concern for the environment" and empowered to act.

Some people want to do what others are doing; they are motivated to be with or join others—and many green behavior-change campaigns tap into this social desire by communicating to target audiences what their peers are doing or saying.

A powerful motivator is the financial savings that can be obtained by reducing consumption. Efficiency gains in the US save electricity customers $90 billion a year, according to the American Council for an Energy-Efficient Economy. Some savings may be "free" thanks to behavior changes—using less heat or water, turning lights and appliances off when they're not needed. But most energy savings require investments in equipment that reduces consumption: insulation for buildings, more-efficient appliances for homes, or less-wasteful machines for industrial processes.

In many innovation lab cities, the combination of these motivations has spurred development of new or retrofitted green buildings with high levels of energy efficiency. In 2017, seven of the top ten US cities for energy efficiency were innovation lab cities, according to a scorecard released by the American Council for an Energy-Efficient Economy. But the payoff for energy efficiency in buildings has not yet motivated anything like the widespread and immense gains in reduced energy consumption that innovation lab cities need to meet their GHG-reduction targets. The average building energy retrofit in the US typically involves "shallow" improvements that only reduce energy use about 15 percent.

INNOVATION LABS: BOOSTING BUILDING ENERGY EFFICIENCY

- Washington, DC, a city of nearly seven hundred thousand residents, has more than 1,400 commercial and residential projects certified by LEED (Leadership in Energy and Environmental Design; the green-building rating system) and in September 2017 was named the world's first LEED Platinum city. It is also the leading US city for Energy Star–certified buildings, a voluntary federal government program; owners of 790 Energy-Star buildings in the city have saved an estimated $167 million in energy bills.

- In Austin, San Francisco, Seattle, Toronto, and eleven other North American cities, downtown commercial-building owners, organized as "2030 Districts," have committed to cut energy and water use 50 percent by 2030 in 1,300 buildings.

- Berlin won an award from C40 Cities for its energy-efficiency program that retrofitted 1,400 large government and commercial buildings, saving more than $10 million in annual energy costs after paying for the upgrades.

- Boulder focused on cutting energy consumption of its city-owned buildings and reduced emissions by more than 40 percent, saving almost $700,000 a year.

Washington, DC, . . . LEED-Platinum city: Ayda Ayoubi, "Washington, D.C. Named the World's First LEED Platinum City," *Architect*, September 7, 2017, http://www.architectmagazine.com/technology/washington-dc-named-the-worlds-first-leed-platinum-city_0.

Energy Star–certified buildings: Kim Slowey, "DC Is the World's First LEED Platinum City," *Construction Dive*, September 6, 2017, https://www.construction dive.com/news/dc-is-the-worlds-first-leed-platinum-city/504315/.

2030 Districts: "About the Network," 2030 Districts, accessed February 6, 2018, http://www.2030districts.org/about-network.

Berlin won an award from C40 Cities: C40 Cities, "Case Study: Energy Saving Partnerships," accessed November 21, 2017, https://c40-production-images .s3.amazonaws.com/case_studies/images/1_berlin_energy.original .pdf?1389915616.

Boulder focused on cutting energy consumption: City of Boulder, "Boulder's Climate Commitment: Rising to the Climate Challenge, Powering a Vibrant Future," May 2017, https://bouldercolorado.gov/climate/climate-commitment.

New York's John Lee estimates that a minority of building owners in the city voluntarily invest in efficiency. "It happens at the margin of the market," he says, mostly by owners who intend to hold onto the building for several decades—long enough to benefit financially after making the necessary investment. "Retrofitting is expensive and the payback period is long," Lee notes. At the same time, because the cost of energy is a relatively small portion of a building's overall cost, most owners won't see big financial gains from acting, Lee adds: "If I can command $100 per square foot in rent and my energy expenditure is $3 per square foot for that space, and I can cut it to $2, it only adds up—maybe to millions of dollars—if you're a big owner who commands enough space."

In US cities, says Vincent Martinez, COO for Architecture 2030, commercial buildings are sold every eight years on average, and residential buildings sell every nine to twelve years. "This timeframe pushes longer-term investments in energy efficiency, such as replacement of the building's whole energy system or improvements to the building's exterior, off the table," he explains, because building owners won't capture the financial return on these big investments with longer payback periods.

These daunting financial barriers set the stage for cities to use another type of motivation for reducing consumption. Even as they increase incentives for efficiency—tax rebates, loan programs, and eased development regulations—some cities are turning to mandates. "The market is far from perfect, so policymakers have to go beyond the normal market influencers like information and prices," explains Lee.

In September 2017, for instance, New York Mayor de Blasio proposed that the city require twenty-three thousand existing commercial buildings—apartment houses, office buildings, and warehouses—to cut their carbon emissions by 2030 or face significant financial penalties. The mandate would cover buildings with more than twenty-five thousand square feet of floor space, setting caps on their energy consumption. If buildings exceed the cap, then owners would be fined. New York would be the first US city to use this approach to get buildings to make GHG reductions.

About two months earlier, Vancouver adopted a plan that requires all new buildings in the city to produce no GHG emissions at all, the toughest building code in North America. The Zero Emissions

Building Plan phases in the zero standard by 2030, starting mostly in 2020. "This is a Plan to fundamentally shift building practice in Vancouver in just under 10 years," says Sean Pander, the city green-building manager, estimating that by 2050 about 40 percent of all floor space in Vancouver will be in buildings built after 2020.

Embedded in these two cities' aggressive approaches to boosting energy efficiency in buildings are key elements of the approach that innovation lab and other cities increasingly use:

- After a period of encouraging voluntary change by building owners and renters, cities require reductions in levels of consumption. Increasingly, they are tying the necessary changes to key points during which major renovations occur, including after a building purchase or refinancing, a change in occupancy or zoning, or a building upgrade for flood or earthquake protection. An analysis prepared by Architecture 2030 found that if buildings sold in New York in 2013 had been required to meet higher efficiency standards, more than twenty-six thousand buildings would have been upgraded.
- The cities target certain segments of the building market for change, focusing on where there is the highest potential to reduce GHG emissions. In New York, for instance, the city's largest buildings (more than fifty thousand square feet in area) make up 2 percent of the building stock but account for 45 percent of citywide energy use.
- The cities phase in new requirements over a period of years to give businesses and consumers in the market time to adjust, and they provide financial and technical assistance to help them implement the changes.

Local real estate market conditions can affect just how far cities will go with introducing mandates. Most lab cities' markets have strong demand for housing and office space, which tends to allay building owners' concerns about small cost increases due to efficiency. In Vancouver, Doug Smith, director of the city's sustainability group, says that meeting the zero standard for new buildings will add 2 to 5 percent to the cost of construction: "In Vancouver's market this has a negligible impact on housing prices as the prices are based on what the market can bear and are not directly linked to the price of construction, which only accounts for one quarter of the cost of a single-family home. High-performance buildings actually improve affordability, health, and equity, since the reduction in utility costs is typically larger than any potential increase in mortgage costs. Combine this with having healthier, more resilient buildings for owners and renters and there is no reason not to pursue these standards." In cities with weak housing markets, however, there may be more pressure from owners and occupants to avoid policies that increase buildings' costs and prices, whatever the long-term benefits and financial gains might be.

Even as lab cities focus on electricity use in buildings, they also seek to cut GHG emissions by reducing consumption of other types of energy—gasoline, natural gas, and fuel oil—and of water, food, and other goods. They use an array of behavior-change campaigns, financial subsidies, public investments, pricing signals, and regulatory mandates. Some also look to sharing-economy models as a way of reducing consumption.

But these efforts also face obstacles. Water utilities, for instance, built their business models on encouraging more consumption and have difficulty shifting to a model that promotes reduced use of water. Using carbon-emissions trading markets or congestion fees to cut consumption will have little impact if the prices are too low, but high prices can generate political opposition. Analysts of sharing-economy models see conflicting impacts on efficiency. Some members of car-sharing programs sell their cars or avoid purchasing a car. But there's evidence that ride programs like Uber actually increase vehicle traffic on streets and take away passengers from mass transit. Similarly, space sharing through, say, Airbnb, increases the use of existing space but also increases the consumption of energy in the space.

Lab cities' aggressive efforts to curb energy use have important limits. Most target energy and emissions used operationally within their borders—to heat and cool buildings and move vehicles, for instance. This is the internationally recognized way of measuring and inventorying emissions by cities. But it doesn't include emissions generated outside of the city to produce or deliver what is used and consumed within cities, such as food. San Francisco, Vancouver, London, Portland, Seattle, and other cities have pioneered the development and use of consumption-based inventories that include the full life cycle of emissions of products consumed in the city wherever they were released. This approach, San Francisco notes, is especially relevant for affluent places "where the high level of income enjoyed by many households leads to increased consumption of goods and services, as well as more spending on leisure activities such as vacation travel." Typically, a consumption-based analysis reveals that a city has a much higher level of GHG emissions than previously recognized.

As innovation lab cities push harder for consumption reduction, they are also innovating at other stages of the consumption cycle—before use, when goods are being designed and produced, and after use, when they are being disposed of.

INSIDE SHANGHAI'S CARBON-EFFICIENCY MARKET

The price of a ton of carbon emissions in 2017 reached a high of about $6 (36 yuan) in this city's unique trading exchange, which regulates more than three hundred local enterprises, including the world's busiest port and the enormous Pudong airport. Shanghai's four-year-old "cap-and-trade" market is one of just a few city carbon markets in the world, set up as a pilot for the national market that China has started to roll out.

The city designed the Shanghai Environment and Energy Exchange (SEEE) from scratch, looking at the experiences of the European Union and California markets. It had to figure out how to operate the market—which is housed inside an unremarkable building on Shanghai's North Zhongshan Road, alongside one of the city's elevated highways. In a quiet office, as many as sixty employees work at computers or leave to visit with companies in the market. On one wall, a gigantic computerized board displays trading prices.

Since opening in late 2013, the market has expanded coverage to companies in twenty-six sectors. More than 50 percent of Shanghai's carbon emissions are included in the market, explains Guo Jianli, vice director of the Resource Conservation and Environmental Protection Division of the Shanghai Development and Reform Commission. Through July 2017, Exchange officials report, some 26.8 million tons of local carbon-emissions allowances have been traded at a total cost of more than $70 million. After a three-year start-up period, the market required companies to obtain emissions allowances annually. The enterprises report on the previous year's emissions, which are verified by a third party.

A critical element of the market's design was a decision not to create a price floor or ceiling for the market, says Zang Ao Quan, supervisor of the Exchange's Trading Department. At one point, the trading price went down to seventy-five cents per ton. Compared to other carbon markets in the world, the overall Shanghai price has been relatively low—which can diminish the financial motivation of companies in the market to reduce their GHG emissions. The overall cap on emissions in the market is set by national policy, which aims to peak carbon emissions nationally in 2030. Shanghai's goal is to peak emissions before then, by 2025. Its market operates in parallel with the national carbon market that launched in 2017 but only covers a few industrial sectors so far.

Circular Motion

In 2013, Oslo's bus company made an announcement that puzzled city residents: "Now buses are fuelled by your banana peels." The explanation lay in a climate innovation: a year earlier, households in the city had been required to put their food waste into special green plastic bags for collection. The city wanted to use the organic material to produce biogas to power its buses—a way to reduce GHG emissions from decaying waste and burning fossil fuel in the vehicles. But it's also part of a greater effort the city and other innovation labs are pioneering to eliminate waste completely—to conserve valuable resources and reduce environmental impacts.

For similar reasons, San Francisco implemented a program for composting food scraps, collecting from residents and businesses and turning the material, along with yard trimmings, into compost used by local farmers on their soil. This initiative, too, was part of a bigger plan for the city that in 2002 set a 2020 goal of "zero waste," defined as "nothing going to landfill or incineration." By 2012, about 80 percent of the city's waste met that standard, the highest "diversion rate" of any North American city. About half of what still goes to landfill, the city says, can be recycled or composted, which would boost the city's rate to 90 percent.

Reusing food waste—turning it into fuel or fertilizer—is one way that cities are experimenting with "circularity," replacing the modern city's linear take-make-dispose model with an approach that changes what and how things are taken, made, and used so that nothing needs to be disposed of. "We transform a big problem, waste, into a massive opportunity," explains William McDonough. Circular systems build on cities' traditional recycling and reuse systems, of course, but go further "upstream" to the development and use of products. They look at how products can be initially designed for durability, reuse, and repair. Circularity "is designed to mimic the material and energy flows in mature ecosystems where resources are continuously appropriated, used, redistributed, and recycled for future use," notes Jeremy Rifkin. It also defines waste as more than just what cities' waste-management systems handle. "The things we make are consistently underutilized," notes a 2017 report for the Ellen MacArthur Foundation. In Europe, for instance, the average car is parked 92 percent of the time, and the average office space is used only 35–50 percent of the time.

Circular systems generate abundance by reducing the unneeded consumption and cost of materials and energy for producing goods and decreasing the cost of waste collection and management. A recent European Commission study projects that the circular economy for manufacturing in Europe alone could save $630 billion a year. As fewer new materials are needed for production, circularity also reduces society's environmental footprint. The value of materials that can be reused numerous times increases, and some recycled materials, such as biogas, can be used as renewable energy. In the case of composting food waste, fertilizer can have a regenerative impact on soils. The system can also stimulate development of more locally based production and repair of goods, functioning as a local "closed loop."

Oslo and other cities are pioneering circularity with four types of experiments, explains Håkon Jentoft, senior executive officer of Oslo's waste-management agency and chair of the European Union Partnership for Circular Economy.

INNOVATION LABS: EXPANDING CIRCULARITY

- In 2016, Austin, Boulder, Copenhagen, London, New York, Rio de Janeiro, Toronto, and Vancouver, as well as four other cities, formed a Circular Cities Network to learn together how to design and implement circularity in urban systems.

- Cape Town joined a regional effort, Western Cape Industrial Symbiosis Program, which connects businesses that may profit from recycling and reusing each other's unused or residual materials. The city's online Integrated Waste Exchange links individuals, schools, and businesses that wish to exchange their waste or excess materials.

- In 2017, Google announced it would create "circularity labs" in New York and San Francisco, with a focus on innovations for the building industry. "The idea is to demonstrate what the circular economy model looks like in the setting of the built environment," says Kate Brandt, who leads sustainability across Google's worldwide operations. The labs will look at "designs for disassembly, material innovation, technical and digital solutions, all of which is very relevant to the circular cities discussion."

- Paris reuses excess heat from household wastewater and computer servers to heat community swimming pools.

Circular Cities Network: "The Ellen Macarthur Foundation Launches Circular City Network," Ellen MacArthur Foundation, October 6, 2016, accessed February 6, 2018, https://www.ellenmacarthurfoundation.org/programmes/government/circular-cities-network.
Western Cape Industrial Symbiosis: "Welcome to WISP," Western Cape Industrial Symbiosis Program, accessed November 1, 2017, http://greencape.co.za/wisp/.
Cape Town Integrated Waste Exchange: City of Cape Town, "Integrated Waste Exchange: About," accessed November 2, 2017, http://www.capetown.gov.za/Family%20and%20home/Residential-utility-/Residential-solid-waste-services/Integrated-waste-exchange-(IWEX).
Brandt quote: Joel Makeover, "Google's Search for Business Value in Circular Cities," *GreenBiz*, September 20, 2017, https://www.greenbiz.com/article/googles-search-business-value-circular-cities.
Paris swimming pools: Aurelien Breeden, "If the Pool Is Warm in Paris, Thank the Washing Machine," *New York Times*, December 12, 2016, https://www.nytimes.com/2016/12/12/world/what-in-the-world/if-the-pool-is-warm-in-paris-thank-the-washing-machine.html.

CITIES START DIALOGUES WITH INDUSTRIES
WITHIN THEIR CITIES

"To have better resource management, you have to talk to industry about how things are produced and encourage them to change the way we are producing the goods we consume," Jentoft says. "We use our knowledge of waste management to say, 'See what problems your products are creating for us.' What can you do about that?" To start this sort of exchange, Jentoft adds, a city "must know what the company is doing and how they are thinking and planning." These efforts are crucial because development of circular markets depends on actions by businesses to design their products and take "producer responsibility" for the entire life cycle of products.

CITIES USE THEIR PURCHASING POWER, PROCUREMENT, TO
DEMAND PRODUCTS WITH A MORE CIRCULAR APPROACH

"Cities are big consumers; there's a lot of power in their procurement," Jentoft says. Oslo is one of the biggest procurers in Norway, "from buildings to daily life things, for schools and homes." Previously, the city focused on green procurement, which applies environmental criteria, including carbon emissions, to products: "Now we want to introduce the circular idea into procurement, looking at the life cycle of the product, adding the production and waste phases of the product to our criteria."

CITIES SEEK TO INFLUENCE THE WAYS
THEIR CITIZENS CONSUME

"This is about offering guidelines and recommendations about how my fellow citizens are consuming, and gaining their acceptance," Jentoft says. "This is difficult. There are such strong forces every day trying to get us to consume more."

CITIES THINK ABOUT HOW TO USE MATERIAL RESOURCES
IN BETTER WAYS

"Instead of looking at what they will be discarding tomorrow from the waste coming in every day," says Jentoft, "they look for what could be the resources of tomorrow that are in the waste flow. We know what people are throwing away, what products are ending up as waste, and if they could be reused or not."

Oslo's circular system for food waste has been gaining traction. More than 150 city buses run on biogas from food waste and wastewater, while biofertilizer is sent to farms. Since 2012, when Oslo residents started to separate food waste and plastic at home, the rate of material recovery has increased. But by 2016, it had only reached about 40 percent—and the city's biogas plant, the largest in Norway, had unused capacity. Even so, this system was a good starting point for Oslo's innovative efforts, because the city could generate both supply from its residents and demand by converting its bus fleet and waste-hauling trucks to use biogas. The city had to invest in the technology and facilities that could separate the green bags from households' other waste. "You have to make investments to create a circular market," Jentoft points out. Getting farmers to use the biofertilizer the city produces hasn't been easy, he adds: "It's a huge step for them to move from industrial fertilizer to our product when they don't know the quality and the reaction that their crops will have."

Compact Living

Density of population and buildings defines cities in general, but for urban climate innovation labs, it can be a crucial advantage. A city's density of habitation, especially its quantity of high-occupancy buildings, generally makes the city more efficient in using energy. When journalist David Owen writes that "New York"—with its miles of concrete, air pollution, and traffic congestion—"is the greenest community in the United States," the idea may seem preposterous. But not when density and public transit are part of the equation. As Owen explains, "New Yorkers, individually, drive, pollute, consume, and throw away much less than do the average residents of the surrounding suburbs, exurbs, small towns, and farms, because the tightly circumscribed space in which they live creates efficiencies and reduces the possibilities for reckless consumption."

Urban *compactness* offers an efficiency advantage that builds on density, one that many cities had before they were designed for the automobile and that innovation lab cities are busy reclaiming. Compactness refers to the proximity of stores, jobs, and amenities to where people live—a development pattern that shortens routine travel distances and changes how people travel. "Mixed use is a rarity in sprawled cities where homes, workplaces, schools, hospitals, and shops are segregated from each other," notes Michael Renner, senior researcher at the Worldwatch Institute. The more compactly these necessities are located, the less often and less distance people must drive to get what they need. Instead, they may choose more often to walk or bike to nearby destinations, which reduces energy consumption for mobility.

Compactness can also decrease traffic congestion, which wastes human time and reduces economic productivity. Research shows that congestion-related problems cost US drivers nearly $300 billion in 2016 in lost time and economic productivity. In Seattle, for example, the average commuter wasted an estimated sixty-three hours a year stuck in traffic in 2014. Urban compactness can also reduce the cost of living, since a car-free lifestyle (no purchase, insurance, or garaging) becomes more feasible and attractive. And it may enable the repurposing of public space dedicated to cars—roads, streets, and parking spaces.

"Mixed-use, walkable, economically integrated, and transit-rich places define good urbanism in any city," says Peter Calthorpe, a founding member of the Congress for the New Urbanism and a global advocate for transit-oriented development (TOD). China's newer cities, says Calthorpe, have high density, but they also sprawl: "Single-use residential blocks of largely identical units are clustered in superblocks surrounded by major arterial roads. Vast distances separate everyday destinations and create environments hostile to pedestrians. Sidewalks rarely are lined with useful services, and crossing the street is death-defying. Job centers are distant and commutes are long, especially for low-income people." This urban design reflects a desire "to move cars efficiently; people are an afterthought," Calthorpe concludes.

In 2015, however, China's national government adopted a version of TOD standards for cities' growth. "All future urban development must feature dense road networks, small blocks, and other sustainable urban design principles," notes Energy Foundation China. "The new guidelines prioritize walking, biking, and public transit. . . . This is a radical departure from the country's last 30 years of urban development." A year later, a street-design guide for Shanghai focused on reclaiming streets from automobiles by

INNOVATION LABS:
INCREASING COMPACTNESS

- A scenario for future growth of Mexico City, a sprawling, heavily congested city, assumed that most new development to accommodate 2.7 million more housing units by 2050 would be mixed-use, walkable, and located around bus and train-line stations—a transit-oriented development approach that builds up a set of compact centers with residential and commercial density around access to mass transit, which connects the centers to each other. Compared to a business-as-usual scenario for development, the TOD scenario projected dramatic changes for the city: reduced use of land, infrastructure costs, water consumption, carbon emissions, household costs, congestion, and air pollution, along with reduced auto miles driven and average travel time per day.

- Cape Town's five-year transportation plan, adopted in 2017, embraces TOD—"prioritising the right development in the right locations, along major road and rail corridors in Cape Town," an approach that "will reduce travel times and costs, as well as deliver important environmental benefits." So important is TOD to generating "spatial transformation" and sustainability of Cape Town, that the city expanded its Transport Authority to include all urban development.

- Four other innovation labs—Melbourne, Paris, Portland, and Vancouver—featured in a "green-growth" study by the Organisation for Economic Co-operation and Development, which detailed a cluster of innovations involved in urban compactness: targeting infill development for greenfield and brownfield areas, setting minimum density requirements for new development, promoting mixed use of land and TOD in built-up areas, and encouraging the greening of built-up areas.

Scenario for future growth of Mexico City: Peter Calthorpe, "Urbanism and Global Sprawl," in Worldwatch Institute, *Can a City Be Sustainable?* (Washington, DC: Island Press, 2016), 103–5.
Cape Town TOD quote: City of Cape Town, "Integrated Transport Plan," July 2017, http://resource.capetown.gov.za/documentcentre/Documents/City%20 strategies%2C%20plans%20and%20frameworks/HYS_Draft%20Comprehensive %20Integrated%20Transport%20Plan%202017%20-%202022.pdf, i.
OECD study: Organisation for Economic Co-operation and Development, "Compact City Policies: A Comparative Assessment," 2012, https://www.oecd .org/cfe/regional-policy/50524895.pdf. Study also included Toyama in Japan.

"paying attention to how people meet and live" and "promoting the joint development of neighbourhoods and streets."

In Portland, a growing city with 640,000 residents, a push for compactness began four decades ago—before climate-change awareness—when a coalition of farmers and environmentalists got the state to adopt an urban-growth boundary around Portland and other cities in the region to prevent sprawl. "It was assumed that how we grow and accomplish this regional objective was inextricably tied to our transportation planning," says Joe Zehnder, Portland's chief planner. "It's the bedrock of our compact planning." To reduce dependence on automobiles, the city embraced mass transit: "There's a very strong transit culture in the city, and support for continuing to build out that system." But having mass transit isn't enough, Zehnder says. "We need to design transit to support compact development, so the benefit of being a household in one of the city's centers is that you're less dependent on the car."

As Portland expanded its transit system, it also promoted the idea of the "20-minute neighborhood," places where residents can meet their daily nonwork needs by walking or cycling. Portland's Climate Action Plan calls for neighborhoods in which 90 percent of residents can walk or bicycle to meet these needs. The city's long-range, comprehensive plan envisions "complete neighborhoods" with "multistory buildings, well scaled streets and businesses and shops and restaurants that meet the everyday needs of residents."

Urban abundance generated through efficiency, not consumption; circularity, not take-make-dispose; and compactness, not spread: this is more than an ideal or a far-off vision. It's an emerging reality in leading-edge cities, the beginning of new ways of managing urban consumption in the climate-change era. It aims to change habits of consumption and disposal, the design of products and services, and the underlying economics of using materials and producing goods. It raises the development of a new abundance, a new quality of life, above the accumulation of material wealth.

But if consuming and wasting far fewer natural resources is a critical part of the urban future, so is the even-larger relationship that cities have with natural systems. What cities use nature for is the subject of another transformational idea.

09 NATURE'S BENEFITS

—

Cities Can Restore and Tap the Power of Natural Systems to Enhance and Protect Urban Life

If you look after the country, the country will look after you.

—ABORIGINAL SAYING

Every tree's life matters in Melbourne.

To encourage developers to design projects with minimum removal of trees, every publicly owned tree in the city has a financial value—$100,000 or more for a big, mature elm—that must be paid if construction plans are not altered to avoid its removal. To prevent damage to trees during development, projects must set aside money to insure against potential injury. Each of Melbourne's seventy-seven thousand trees in public space has its own symbol on the city's digital urban-forest map. A click on the orange dot near the corner of Elizabeth and Collins Streets, a downtown intersection, reveals a London planetree, ID#1024658. It is in decline, a pop-up box discloses, with less than half of its leaf canopy and maybe ten more years to live. Another click provides an email template; you can write to this tree, expressing admiration, asking it a question. Every tree in the city also has advocates in a ten-person city-government unit of foresters, ecologists, and an arboriculturalist and among residents of the city's precincts and conservation and horticultural organizations.

Until 2009, Melbourne, a coastal city of fourteen square miles and 140,000 residents in a much larger, sprawling metropolitan region, cared for its trees much as other cities did—mostly as amenities that enhanced city life. Settlers in the nineteenth century had set aside land for public parks and gardens and planted trees, favoring species that recalled Britain's trees, that could have value as timber supply or were considered to have health-giving properties. In the twentieth century, though, a history of the city's forest explains, "Melbourne was keen to be seen as a modern and Australian city" and planted trees that formed avenues, shapes, and colors "popular in global urban landscaping trends." For today's residents, the trees are a key characteristic of Melbourne's identity as Australia's "garden city."

Then came the worst drought in Melbourne's recorded history—a twelve-year dry spell that lasted into 2009. Annual rainfall declined more than 25 percent on average between 2002 and 2009, and water-level capacity plunged to about 25 percent of normal. Heat waves killed hundreds of people. Low availability of water killed trees and shortened the life expectancy of others. Residents adapted, cutting water use 50 percent and buying rainwater-holding tanks, while the city invested in a pipeline to deliver water over mountains. To save water, city officials removed trees lining streets and drastically reduced irrigation of public greenery—until community concerns about the declining state of urban trees prompted a change.

"The drought made us rethink about water and trees," says Ian Shears, the city's urban-sustainability manager. Melbourne's many older trees—those lining boulevards and in parks are more than one hundred years old—were especially vulnerable to the harsh conditions, as were irrigated trees. Climate scientists predicted that average annual temperatures would keep rising, with twice as many days of extreme heat (above 95° Fahrenheit), less annual rainfall, and more extreme storms. All of this would increase stress on trees and damage caused by pests, diseases, and soil erosion. By 2030, it was estimated, 39 percent of the city's trees would be ending their useful lives. "There was the realization," says Shears, "that an asset was being lost that people thought was always going to be there."

At the time, Shears, armed with a graduate degree in horticulture and a city job as a steward of the urban landscape, saw a strategic opportunity. "The loss of a lot of green and the potential loss of the big trees really drew people up short," he says. "I used that as a stepping stone to say, look, we have to do something, so what is it we should do?" He and his colleagues started talking about an idea unused in the city: "urban forestry," a practice developed in the 1960s in Canada, which recognizes that urban trees and other vegetation are part of a city's essential infrastructure and provide environmental, social, and economic benefits, not just recreational and amenity value. Thinking about the trees this way, says Shears, "changes people's paradigm about what a city can and should be. We live within a *green* infrastructure and it's just as important as transport, telecommunications, etcetera."

The new framing focused the community's conversation on the city's broader relationship with nature, starting with its trees. "The way we've established our city has been in spite of nature rather than with it," Shears observes. "What we needed to do was recognize that if we work *with* nature, and if nature is at the heart of our urban design, then we'll be able to have a much higher livability within the city."

Melbourne's award-winning plan to strengthen its urban forest, unveiled in 2012, identified a wide range of potential benefits. The forest provides shade that cools the city and reduces flows of storm water and nutrients—nitrogen, phosphorous, and heavy metals—into waterways. It reduces air pollution and greenhouse gas emissions. It provides wildlife with habitats and enhances biodiversity of an area. It helps a community build local identity, brings people together, encourages outdoor activity, and improves mental well-being. It reduces energy costs, increases property values, avoids infrastructure damage, decreases health costs, stores and sequesters carbon emissions, and plays a role in marketing the city as an attractive setting.

The forestry plan, Shears says, "has something for everybody in it. What's been fantastic—the community wants it. Every time we go out and have a conversation with people, they exhibit a palpable desire for more green in their lives. Look, there are a lot of pressures in living in Melbourne. Climate change is with us. Extreme heat days are going up. There's rapid population growth—they're saying that by 2050 Melbourne's going to double in population. People are feeling the effects of urbanism hitting them very heavily. Whether consciously or subconsciously, there's a desire to get in touch with nature."

The Way Forward

Obtaining nature's benefits, for Melbourne, involves more than just planting trees. The city has to undo its development patterns—the design and use of space—and change them for a future of even more development, when many more residents, workers, and visitors will be present. Development has left most of Melbourne without substantial tree canopy and shade. It covered the land with impervious hard surfaces—paved roads, streets, sidewalks, parking lots, and building roofs—that keep water out of the soil, channeling it into an extensive built drainage system that empties into the city's river and bay. The combination of hard surfaces and low vegetation cover, as well as the use of vehicles and air conditioners, contributes to the urban "heat-island" effect that makes the city warmer—by 7 to 12° Fahrenheit—than nearby suburban and rural areas, especially at night. Even the way the city has irrigated its parks and gardens for many years proves to be a problem. Surface irrigation encouraged trees to develop superficial root systems that did little to support soil moisture and left trees vulnerable when irrigation ceased. The city needs "water-sensitive" urban design—permeable paving, rain gardens, green roofs and walls, and other green infrastructure—to promote healthy growth of vegetation.

What unfolded in Melbourne during the years after the drought followed much the same winding pathway you'd see in other leading-edge cities engaged in renaturing: rounds of technical analysis and planning; extensive community-engagement processes; goal and target setting by elected officials and top government managers; design and implementation of new policies, demonstration pilots, and bigger projects; and the gradual embedding of new thinking into the city's regulatory, budgetary, and other deep operating structures. Melbourne developed extensive plans for urban forestry, open space, biodiversity, climate adaptation, regional resilience, and management of water, the "blue" that is essential for keeping a city's "green" healthy and growing. These provided the city's big-picture destination—a set of broad goals—and a roadmap at the citywide scale. They became the basis for development of precinct-level and water catchment–area plans that set the context and criteria for prioritizing potential projects.

To drive change at an ambitious but feasible pace, the city adopted a set of citywide targets for increasing its tree canopy, diversifying the urban forest's tree species, expanding green space in the city, increasing permeable surfaces, increasing understory plants— small trees, shrubs, vines, and grasses—on city land, and boosting municipal water sourced from non-drinking water sources such as reused rainwater and storm water and recycled wastewater.

Since 2012, the city has spent about $8 million a year on its urban-forestry strategy and planted about three thousand trees a year—on the way to adding as many as fifty thousand trees. It adopted a Tree Retention and Protection Policy that put a dollar value on every tree. "If a new building is going up in the city and they need to take out two trees to do it," Shears explains, "we will go through all lengths possible to keep the trees. If we can't, then the developer pays the value of those trees and for regreening the site." In 2016, the city collected about $700,000 for trees that had to be removed—funds it invested in its greening strategy. Developers also have to provide financial guarantees for trees that could be injured or killed during a site-development process. By mid-2017, developers had put up a total of nearly $5 million in bonds to cover 267 trees at risk. Putting a price on trees often causes developers to change their plans for sites, Shears says, as they try to avoid the potential costs.

In 2013, the city launched its digital map of the city's trees and an email channel to connect to any tree (map at www.melbourneurban forestvisual.com). "Everybody loves trees, but if you express a love for a tree, you're seen as a bearded tree hugger who wants to protect forests from logging," says Shears. "We decided we needed a way to enable bankers in suits to show their desire for trees. The emails to trees become this twenty-first-century technological way to hug a tree." Thousands of emails have been received.

In May 2017, the city unveiled an Urban Forest Fund, with about $1 million in initial capital, to promote the greening of privately owned property, which contains twenty thousand trees. "Our existing strategies have ticked most of the boxes of the public realm," Shears explains, "but the next really big step is to start to influence

When touring Melbourne with Ian Shears, it seems there's a city-greening project around every corner. The city focuses heavily on converting roads into green space. "About 80 percent of our public jurisdiction is in roadways. That's the space to play in," Shears explains. "We're repurposing the city."

University Square is a residential area where the city, in financial partnership with Melbourne University, is expanding a small park by 40 percent by tearing up 160 parking spaces and closing off the ends of two streets: "We're also working on putting green roofs on the university's apartment buildings that border the park."

On Errol Street in North Melbourne, where the city turned 5,300 square feet of roads into a 1.2-acre park, "we had a small island with three double-lane roads around it and a primary school nearby. So we went from what was a bit dangerous for pedestrians and cyclists down to a one-way road system." The repurposed park cost about $1.5 million, but purchasing this much land for a similar-size park would have cost nearly ten times that amount.

About Royal Children's Hospital, he says, "We did a lot of work with them when it was being designed. When doctors first meet kids coming in, it's traditionally a difficult time for them to connect with the kids, to find a comfortable conversation space." The new hospital site included a natural play area where these conversations happen: "You go out there on sunny days and you see kids on hospital trolleys with their drips, out in the landscape." A new large playground next door has plantings designed to bloom during each of the Aboriginal culture's seven seasons.

Shears points down one of Melbourne's celebrated laneways, alleys lined with hole-in-the-wall cafes, restaurants, and bars: "We mapped all the laneways: the physical space needed for rubbish trucks, the sunlight they get, and which ones have capacity to green. We worked out that the whole city had 170 hectares [420 acres] of wall space available for greening, then put the map online and said, 'Who wants to join with us to green the private realm?' We had 800 nominations come back in two weeks and chose four of them. This is one of them. See the planters from which plants will grow up the outer wall? We've got a tree that will go in near where that blue rubbish bin is."

Shears drives past a median in a street: "The pine trees are in poor condition. I'm busting to get hold of it and rejuvenate it, to rebuild the median. It's ripe for storm water harvesting and capture."

what happens in the private realm—land and rooftops—and how that can come together with the public strategy." The fund offers to match private investments in green roofs, walls, and facades and other greening projects.

In 2018, the city approved regulations for privately owned green roofs, walls, and facades, culminating a twelve-year effort to set new rules in place.

Melbourne's many greening efforts have had two major effects, Shears says. "We're in a really new place. We've raised awareness, created knowledge, and created the desire of people to participate." This, in turn, has helped get city officials on board with massive greening: "We've been able to demonstrate to our elected officials that this is what the community's demanding."

Living in the Garden

To obtain an extensive array of nature's benefits, Melbourne and other cities—Portland, Oslo, San Francisco, Singapore, to name a few—have advanced comprehensive, multifaceted, citywide approaches.

These communities are embracing a far-reaching shift in their mental models about the city's relationship to nature. In modern times, the city has been thought of as the dominant context in the natural environment; its physical, economic, and social needs were to be met by shaping the landscape near and far. To do this, cities cleared and built upon the land, sweeping away natural habitats and species. They engineered control over waterways, consumed vast amounts of natural resources, and dumped enormous amounts of waste. Their inhabitants lost direct connection with the natural world and its processes. Urban areas did contain parks, garden areas, and tree-lined streets, but these mostly were limited "postage-stamp" parcels in the larger urban scheme of things.

In the 1800s, Melbourne, Vancouver, San Francisco, and other new cities exploded into existence. Historical geographer Gray Brechin describes the transformative effect of San Francisco's growth on a windswept peninsula without freshwater or firewood: "Forests were leveled on all Pacific shores, rivers and lakes vanished, and the bay from which the city took its name was filled, poisoned, and plundered, while wildlife and natives within the vortex were speedily exterminated." Older cities—London, Boston, New York, Berlin, Tokyo, Shanghai, and others—expanded horizontally and vertically. By 1987, the Brundtland Report on sustainable development was warning that an "urban challenge"—the unhealthy and degrading environments of cities in a rapidly urbanizing world—stood in the way of managing environmental resources to ensure sustainable human progress and human survival.

Many factors explain the modern transformation: population growth, the desire for improved material well-being, development of unfettered markets for goods and property, and society's increased technological prowess harnessed to cheap, portable supplies of fossil-fuel energy. But ideas mattered too. Religions upheld the dominion of people over nature. Especially in Western society, the notion took hold of the primacy of human agency. Cities, says Richard Register, urban ecologist and designer, generated a kind of human creativity unknown in the collective, careful, slow-moving villages that preceded them. It was "specialized, narrow, blind to its long-range effects, and powerful in its new integration of ideas, tools, and products." It quickened the pace of change, "bringing the novelty of conspicuous change into the short span of a single lifetime and giving people the experience of witnessing personal creativity right before their eyes." The village's cyclical sense of time "was transformed into a vector later thought of as Progress. In the brief cycle of one life, the personality could now see oneself as participating in the process of change in society and nature, experiencing a tiny shred of earthly immortality and god-like creativity, causing something to actually happen and be part of a permanent change."

The rise of self-importance has been pervasive, observes landscape ecologist Eric Sanderson, author of best-selling *Mannahatta*, about mapping the natural ecology of Manhattan Island before Western settlement: "It is a conceit of New York City—the concrete city, the steel metropolis, Batman's Gotham—to think it is a place outside of nature, a place where humanity has completely triumphed over the forces of the natural world, where a person can do and be anything without limit or consequence."

Another key modern idea that transformed urban areas was embedded in the scientific way of analyzing the world in parts rather than as a whole. The natural world was seen as a set of distinct resources—land, water, minerals, animals, plants, and so on. In cities, land was treated "as a commodity to be divided among different uses rather than as a living, complex, integrated ecosystem," explain urban planners Jonathan Barnett and Larry Beasley. As a result, "there is often a serious mismatch between what is permitted—or required—and the actual ability of the landscape to survive such changes."

As urban denaturing proliferated in the nineteenth and twentieth centuries, conservation and environmental movements arose to protect and preserve natural spaces—outside of cities. "You enjoyed nature by leaving the city and going to visit someplace: Yosemite, Yellowstone," reflects Timothy Beatley, a professor of sustainable communities and prominent advocate of green urbanism. Today, nearly 15 percent of all land on the planet is under some type of protected status. Other efforts added public parks within the city to provide residents with relief from urban stresses and improve public health. Some urban designers promoted the development of "garden cities," smaller communities that contained green space and were surrounded by green belts. However, as Beatley notes, "most visions of a modernist city seemed not to include nature."

The emerging idea inverts the modern-city hierarchy, restoring nature, instead of the city, as the dominant context. "We're discovering," Beatley says, "that a modern city should understand itself as a city in nature." Melbourne, whose residents have cherished the forest within their city, now talks instead about being a city within a forest. Singapore, a dense city-nation of more than five million people, once envisioned itself as a city with gardens but now sees itself as a city within a garden. The city remains the shaper of its built environment, but it shapes with an altered perspective.

The idea of renaturing cities is being applied at multiple urban scales. In the 1990s, promotion of green buildings—structures designed and constructed to be environmentally friendly and energy- and water-efficient—began to influence the development of individual building sites in cities. At the time, these were viewed curiously by North American cities, but that has changed. In the US, *National Geographic* reports, spending on green construction hit about $125 billion in 2014, more than twelve times the level in 2005, and by 2018, green construction could "account for one-third of the entire construction sector."

The whole city came to be understood as an "urban ecology," the complex dynamics and interplay of multiple natural ecosystems, with many animal and plant species, built systems, and flows and exchanges of materials and energy. The scientific concept of an ecosystem, a living natural system, was formulated in the 1930s, while the concept of urban ecology, the study of distinct city-based ecosystems, emerged in the 1970s. Now the urban ecosystem has become a crucial scale of analysis and city planning, as reflected in Melbourne's approach.

Cities also apply renaturing to the scale of the neighborhood, district, and precinct. Melbourne's overall urban-forest plan, for instance, includes tree canopy–building plans for each of the city's ten precincts that the city codesigned with community members. The district scale is significant because ecosystems and environmental conditions, as well as vulnerability to flooding and heat, vary throughout an urban area.

Part of urban renaturing is a restorative exercise, a way to reinstate balance and sustainability to the city's relationship with nature. Another part introduces new designs to a city's space. "It is a bit 'back to the future,' but it's also a creative new future," says Beatley. "There are elements of the old, but there are entirely new things: the incorporation of nature into the vertical realm [walls and facades of buildings], for instance. Even the notion of 'hybrid nature' as seen in Singapore's 'super trees': large, human-designed and built metal objects that house living plants."

The green future of a city like Melbourne, says Ian Shears, "goes well beyond the European thinking that's led to these major avenues, big broad streets, and stunning trees. It's not the imposition of the European mind-set on Melbourne's ecology, it's the development and understanding of a uniquely Melbourne ecology." That doesn't just mean going back to a previous ecology; climate change makes that unfeasible and scientific knowledge about forests offers new options. "When we think about which trees will be good trees for Melbourne into the future," Shears says, "it doesn't matter whether it comes from Melbourne or Mozambique. What matters is, it needs to survive in a changing environment and it needs to give us the best environmental services it can."

State of Practice

When cities renature themselves, they pursue three distinct, inter-related applications of the idea. They expand the use of green infrastructure. They protect and enhance ecosystems and biodiversity. And they provide people with ways to immerse in nature. Each of these methods involves innovative practices used at multiple urban scales, and each applies to new developments on "virgin" or cleared sites and to retrofitting of densely built parts of the city.

EXPANDING THE USE OF GREEN INFRASTRUCTURE

Cities use various green-infrastructure methods—rain gardens, rainwater harvesting, bioswales, permeable pavement, tree canopies, green space, green roofs and walls, constructed wetlands, and more—to address excess storm water, excess heat, rising sea levels, and other practical problems. This is not a new practice; for centuries, architects, builders, landscapers, and city planners have tapped nature's capabilities to absorb and channel water and to cool the air. But in just the past few decades, green infrastructure has gained significant momentum in local government planning and policy worldwide as a favored way to respond to climate change and to increase cities' sustainability and appeal. The impetus stems from three factors.

Performance
Experimentation and research are increasing the performance predictability and reliability of green infrastructure. The US Environmental Protection Agency's website alone contains links to more than fifty performance studies and databases and numerous other

scientific and regulatory agency research, modeling tools for designing and costing, guidebooks for operations and maintenance, and design manuals.

Cost Effectiveness
Cities find that using green infrastructure instead of or in combination with "gray, hard" infrastructure can provide cost savings— reducing initial construction costs and holding down operational and maintenance costs due to less need for labor and heavy equipment. This is especially true when it is used for storm-water management.

Cobenefits
Green infrastructure can deliver other important value for a city, such as improved water and air quality, upgraded habitat, and increased recreational space. Cities can quantify these benefits, measuring reduction in air pollutants and chronic diseases, for example, and they can assess the financial value of the benefits so that a return on investment in green infrastructure can be assessed.

As cities recognize the increased reliability, cost effectiveness, and cobenefits of green infrastructure, they have expanded the practice from one-off projects to city-scale approaches.

When Copenhagen faced a substantial increase in the frequency and intensity of rainfall, it decided not to expand its sewer system, an expensive "hard" approach to managing excess precipitation. Instead, the city selected a neighborhood, St. Kjeld, as a test site for green infrastructure designed to manage heavy rainfalls, aiming to turn 20 percent of the district's paved surface into green areas and to retain and manage 30 percent of rainwater rather than have it end up in sewers. The approach prevented damage and traffic disruption during heavy downpours. Then the city committed to invest as much as $4 billion over fifteen years for three hundred projects that take the green-infrastructure approach citywide.

When Rotterdam developed its citywide climate-adaptation plan, it selected a neighborhood, the Zoho, in which to pilot the combined use of many green-infrastructure innovations designed to work together to capture, store, and use rainwater or slowly release it into the ground, rather than channeling it to overloaded sewers. The innovations together function as a district-wide "sponge" for water. "These measures are particularly effective in areas with high consumer pressure and little available space, such as the compact city centre and the neighbouring urban districts," notes the city's adaptation plan. The Zoho is a bustling nineteenth-century district with modern buildings and streets. Green infrastructure—soil, plants, trees, and gardens on roofs, in streets, along the facades of buildings—is taking over. Pavement on underused streets and roads has been replaced with permeable pavement that allows rain to filter through into the ground. Rain barrels collect water for reuse in buildings. The district's greenery works in combination with gray infrastructure. At the district's heart sits the Benthemplein Water Square, the world's first water square—a large public space for mingling, events, and recreation that also serves as a giant rainwater collector.

A CITY OF WATER ENGINEERS

*R*otterdam has built an economic development strategy around water management for climate adaptation. "Month in, month out, delegations from as far away as Jakarta, Ho Chi Minh City, New York and New Orleans make the rounds in the port city of Rotterdam," reports the *New York Times*. "They often end up hiring Dutch firms, which dominate the global market in high-tech engineering and water management."

Water engineers based in Rotterdam helped design low-lying Jakarta's strategies for coping with sea-level rise. "Our government believes that Rotterdam has the most expert water management in the world," says Aisa Tobing, Jakarta city planner and director of international cooperation. "I have visited Rotterdam several times," she adds, noting that her city sends students to Rotterdam to study water management, supported by Dutch scholarships.

New York Times quote: Michael Kimmelman, "The Dutch Have Solutions to Rising Seas. The World Is Watching," *New York Times*, June 15, 2017, https://www.nytimes.com/interactive/2017/06/15/world/europe/climate-change-rotterdam.html.

INNOVATION LABS:
CULTIVATING GREEN INFRASTRUCTURE

- Washington, DC, decided that instead of building a gigantic holding tunnel to provide extra drainage capacity during heavy rainfalls, it would invest $90 million in large-scale green infrastructure to reduce the amount of storm water that had to be handled by tunnels.

- Paris's overall greening program includes planting twenty thousand trees and creating 10.7 million square feet of green roofs and walls and eighty-one acres of urban agriculture by 2020.

- Mexico City installed more than 226,000 square feet of green roofs, mostly on government buildings, schools, and hospitals and offered private residential buildings a 10 percent property tax break for putting in their own green roofs. "Dramatic advances have been made" in addressing "initial fears—leakage and humidity issues to the property have been completely subdued," says Tanya Müller García, the city's secretary of the environment. With the city having modeled the practice, she adds, "greenroofing is seen as a component of sustainable design."

- Berlin, with 3.4 million residents living in 343 square miles, has pursued a city-greening strategy since the 1990s—developing nearly three hundred miles of green walks for pedestrians and bicyclists and keeping 44 percent of the city's area in forests, preserves, lakes, and other green and blue spaces. In 2015, it adopted a citywide strategy that included plans for green and open spaces for climate adaptation, building a habitat network for biodiversity, and

---

Washington, DC, green infrastructure: "Green Infrastructure Plan," DC Water, accessed October 7, 2017, https://www.dcwater.com/green -infrastructure.
Paris greening program: "The Paris Greening Program," C40 Cities, accessed November 8, 2017, http://www.c40.org/awards/2015-awards/profiles/66.
García quote: Brendan O'Driscoll, "The Green Roofs of Mexico City," Innovate Development, January 15, 2016, http://innovatedevelopment.org/2016/01/15/ green-roofs; and Tanya Müller García, "Areas Verdes de la Ciudad de Mexico and Azoteas Naturadas," video presentation for Green Roofs and Walls of the World: Virtual Summit 2013, 11:21, accessed August 10, 2017, https://www .youtube.com/watch?v=ZTL7A7b65vM.

advancing historical and contemporary landscape architecture, urban agriculture; and nature experiences in the city.

————

Berlin greening strategy: Holle Thierfelder and Nadja Kabisch, "Viewpoint Berlin: Strategic Urban Development in Berlin—Challenges for Future Urban Green Space Development," *Environmental Science & Policy* 62 (2016): 120–22, https://www.researchgate.net/publication/282423349_Viewpoint_Berlin _Strategic_urban_development_in_Berlin_-_Challenges_for_future_urban _green_space_development.

PROTECTING AND ENHANCING ECOSYSTEMS AND BIODIVERSITY

A number of leading-edge cities have launched efforts to protect and restore the ecosystems and biodiversity of their urban regions. They want to ensure and enhance the delivery of essential services provided by nature outside, as well as inside, their boundaries.

Melbourne's attention to its urban forest evolved into broader concerns about nature and the city. In various planning processes, it looked at the regional ecosystems of which the city was a part and on which it depended and their animal and plant biodiversity. "By considering our city as a wider ecosystem, there is the opportunity to actively foster connections amongst people, plants, animals, and the landscape," declares the city's "Nature in the City" report. Especially important is the Yarra River, 150 miles long, starting in pristine mountain forests, running through the city, and ending in the sea—covering a catchment area of nearly 1,600 square miles, more than one hundred times larger than the city. The river is the city's lifeblood, one report declared; it provides water supply; supports agriculture, industry, and recreational activities; transports people and goods; and enables urban development. The river, like the city's trees, is an essential part of Melbourne's identity and well-being.

In San Francisco, the five feet of sea-level rise projected to occur by 2100 could inundate highways, airports, and some of the estimated $75 billion of property on the city's shoreline. In response, the city and eight urban counties ringing the San Francisco Bay decided in 2016 to invest $500 million to restore and expand the Bay's wetlands, a vast tidal-marsh ecosystem that for a century-and-a-half had been severely altered by people. "As the population grew," writes environmental journalist Jane Kay, "newcomers from around the world brought a diversity of lifestyles, filled the tidal marshes, dumped mine tailings, and brought exotic species by railroad and ship. Later came dams, sewage, oil refineries, and plastic pollution." The two-hundred-thousand-acre estuary shrank to about forty thousand acres in 1999. But now the Bay is expected to serve as a natural buffer against storm surges and rising high tides, absorbing water and energy; assessments have called for the addition of sixty thousand acres of marshland. This type of restoration is a newly valued environmental service for many of the world's cities built where rivers meet the ocean.

In 2015, Vancouver released its "Greenest City 2020 Action Plan," with urban-greening goals of leading the world in green building design and construction, planting 150,000 new trees, ensuring every resident lives within a five-minute walk of green space, and increasing the number of urban farming businesses, farmers' markets, and community gardens. But the city also recognized that its water supply, food system, and air quality depended in large part on what happens outside the city's borders. Its drinking water, for instance, comes from reservoirs fed by a 202-square-mile watershed that captures rainwater and snowpack melt. Production of food in the region relies on having agricultural lands. And the city's relatively clean air—under threat from population growth that could increase transportation exhaust and from climate warming that could increase forest fires and smoke—can only be maintained through action at regional and provincial levels.

The growing urban attention to ecosystems extends to maintaining and increasing an urban region's biodiversity, which is key to maintaining ecosystem health. "When we allow one species to die," explains Edward O. Wilson, "we erase the web of relationships it maintained in life, with consequences that scientists seldom understand . . . we break many threads, and change the ecosystem in ways still impossible to predict." Singapore developed a City Biodiversity Index to measure its biodiversity and assess progress in maintaining and increasing the number of species. The city published a user's manual in English and Chinese that eighty cities worldwide have used.

Climate changes have been leading more and more cities to recognize the need to protect and enhance a wide range of ecosystem services. Governments in Western Europe and the US have adopted an ecosystem-services framework for planning processes. "Ecosystem services have recently emerged as a policy priority" for cities, reports the United Kingdom's Future of Cities project, adding that cities vulnerable to flooding, heat waves, or drought will have reasons to tap more into ecosystems' benefits. A number of environmental and conservation nonprofit organizations, such as The Nature Conservancy (TNC), are helping cities to restore ecosystems. "Restoring source watersheds [of cities] . . . may be a cost-effective approach for cities to reduce drinking water treatment costs while enhancing supply resiliency and protecting biodiversity among other co-benefits," explains a TNC report.

Cities generally use a combination of regulation and investments to manage ecosystems, but to date, there isn't consistency in this emerging urban practice, and cities lack useful data about ecosystems and species. Cities almost always work in partnership with other government entities that also have control over relevant ecosystems. They advocate for tougher regulation and enforcement to prevent pollution and incentives to preserve agricultural lands from development. They also increase their efforts to reduce consumption of water and other natural resources, which can ease pressure on ecosystems. Some cities are instituting new resource-management models, such as integrated water management, which coordinates the traditionally separate functions of providing drinking water, managing storm water, and treating wastewater, as a way of approaching ecosystems as a whole. The plan to protect the Yarra River emphasizes the need for a new management model that covers the length of the river, recognizes community expectations, has an "integrated, overarching strategic plan," and provides clear accountability.

Melbourne turned to Aboriginal people for help in thinking about its ecosystem-management strategies. Its "Caring for Country" initiative recognizes that "local knowledge passed down through generations of Aboriginal people can provide great insight into the way land is managed, even in today's urban context." Researchers in Melbourne note that the Aboriginal perspective on nature is quite different from the modern Western view: Caring for Country "is a practice of resource use whereby human modification and employment of nature nourishes Country rather than degrading it. . . . Embracing Caring for Country into mainstream sustainability work provides avenues to transform Western views of and relationships with nature."

Within cities' many actions, an emerging practice is the financial valuation of ecosystem services, which helps make the case to policymakers for investments in restoration and enhancement. This valuation typically combines different types of value—financial/economic, social/cultural, short- and long-term, environmental, public health, and insurance value—which makes for notably difficult calculations, because each type of value uses a different analytic framework. For now, valuations tend to be more a way of raising awareness of the ecosystem's services than of providing a rigorous and reliable return-on-investment model for decision making. In some cases, cities have compared the cost of investing in ecosystem-service maintenance and enhancement with the cost of alternative proposals. New York City, which relies on a two-thousand-square-mile upstate watershed to deliver clean, unfiltered water to the city, famously invested $1.5 billion to buy seventy thousand acres in the watershed, protect reservoirs from pollution, and subsidize environmentally friendly economic development. The alternative was to spend $6 billion for a large water-filtration plant. The eye-catching savings prompted more than one hundred other cities to consider watershed conservation—an investment in an ecosystem service—instead of building filtration plants.

PROVIDING PEOPLE WITH WAYS TO IMMERSE IN NATURE

A growing number of cities around the world, including Melbourne and six other climate innovation lab cities—Austin, Oslo, Portland, Rio de Janeiro, San Francisco, Washington, DC—are going beyond green infrastructure and ecosystem and biodiversity restoration to harvest nature's benefits. They are among the twenty-four city-members of the Biophilic Cities Network—communities working in ten countries to bring more contact with nature into city dwellers' daily lives.

The term *biophilia* was defined three decades ago by biologist Wilson as "the innately emotional affiliation of human beings to other living organisms." Tim Beatley, who started the Biophilic Cities Network in 2013, describes the basis for "biophilic urbanism": "Human beings need contact with nature and the natural environment. They need it to be healthy, happy, and productive and to lead meaningful lives. Nature is not optional, but an absolutely essential quality of modern urban life." Beatley's 2016 *Handbook of Biophilic City Planning and Design* cites a range of studies that show exposure to nature provides emotional, mental, and physical benefits, reducing stress, boosting the immune system, aiding in recuperation from surgery, and increasing happiness. The biophilic approach in cities, Beatley says, responds to "long-term chronic stress, the unhealthiness of indoor living, reconnecting us to family and community. It addresses many pathologies of modern life: emptiness and lack of meaning. There's a hunger for this."

Cities committed to a biophilic approach focus on increasing the amount and quality of nature that is present in the city—and on improving access to it. They publicly commit to setting biophilic goals, taking initiatives and other actions—including green infrastructure and biodiversity projects—and using indicators to assess progress. Projects range in physical scale, from sites and buildings to citywide efforts, and in function, from design of physical space to education and outdoor activities.

San Francisco, for example, has supported the creation of more than one hundred street parks and parklets—small parcels of land repurposed as green community space. The city estimates that 98 percent of its residents live within a half mile of a park. The city and region's public transit authority bought light-rail passenger cars with larger than standard windows to provide riders with better views of the Bay and other sights. Oslo has developed a 226-mile citywide trail system, along rivers and through forests, one of the most extensive city systems in the world. It has designated quiet areas in the city where outdoor, recreational, and cultural experiences are shielded from urban noise.

"The important thing," says Beatley, "is to move cities closer to that immersive experience. And that means looking to many other ways to layer nature into cities. . . . It doesn't necessarily have to sit in a large contiguous block of forest but could be the sum of many things."

GREENEST OF THEM ALL

"*You arrive at the airport* and the first thing you see in the lobby is a dramatic 300-meter-long wall covered with plants, with a butterfly garden and hatchery nearby. Then you drive down roads with closed tree canopy overhead. Walking structures that cross the roads are planted with flowerbeds. The underpasses are planted, unlike what you'd see in any other city. Khoo Tech Puat Hospital is the most biophilic hospital I've ever been in: green roofs, a treed interior courtyard with a waterfall. They recognize the healing power of nature."

Tim Beatley is taking us, by phone, on a short tour of Singapore, a financially wealthy Southeast Asian city that incorporates sixty-three islands.

No city in the world is as green, biodiverse, and biophilic as it could be, Beatley says, but "Singapore comes the closest; it is almost in its own category. The city feels, sounds, and smells different." What started as a major tree-planting initiative fifty years ago has turned into a multifaceted, citywide renaturing effort. Singapore's remarkable tree canopy covers about 50 percent of the city. "The city has embraced the idea of biophilic urbanism like no other city yet," Beatley says. City plans envision an integrated, nature-immersive city, while policies and regulations incentivize and push the idea into development projects. "Developers have internalized these ideas and the market supports them." In 2012, Beatley went to Singapore to make a video about the city's approach. He's returned there several times since then.

In 2011, Singapore started to install tree-canopied corridors to link parks and natural areas. Now more than ninety miles of connectors serve pedestrians. Green roofs are connected to each other. To provide habitats for all kinds of animals, the city's forest is designed in layers—ground shrubs, smaller trees, and the overarching tree canopy. More and more buildings feature living

Singapore's remarkable tree . . . of the city: Grace Chua, "How Singapore Makes Biodiversity an Important Part of Urban Life," *Citiscope*, January 23, 2015, http://citiscope.org/story/2015/how-singapore-makes-biodiversity-important-part-urban-life.
Beatley video about Singapore: See Linda Blagg, "Singapore: Biophilic City," YouTube video, 44:06, May 7, 2012, https://www.youtube.com/watch?v=XMWOu9xIM_k.

walls, vertical hanging gardens. The city turned a straight con-crete drainage channel into a two-mile-long river that captures storm water and winds through refurbished, 153-acre Bishan Ang Mo-Kio Park.

Singapore "is beginning to see a kind of holistic urban nature fabric emerge," Beatley says. "The Singapore model has been embraced and held up, not just as a set of projects, but as a whole vision for a city."

When cities live and work with nature, instead of against her, they may lose the comforting sense of control that built solutions seem to offer. Depending on green infrastructure to suck up a certain amount of water or cool the air a certain number of degrees or on wetlands to protect property from a certain level of ocean surge may seem riskier than installing concrete sewers and barriers. But as the practice of renaturing urban space advances, its performance is becoming more reliable and predictable and, as we've seen, it offers important additional benefits that cities need.

In the climate-change era, however, the relationship that cities have with nature is not limited to figuring out how to obtain the full range of nature's benefits. Cities are finding that nature, in the form of climate change and its risks, is altering how they can shape the future.

10 ADAPTIVE FUTURES

—

Cities Can Cultivate the Capacity of Inhabitants and Core Systems to Adapt Successfully to the Future's New Requirements

In a time of drastic change it is the learners *who inherit the future.*

—ERIC HOFFER

Boston and Shanghai live a half-planet apart, 7,285 miles by air, a trip that would emit about a ton of carbon per passenger. Boston's climate has cold winters averaging fifty-two inches of snow a year and warm summers. Shanghai rarely has any snowfall and features humid summers much hotter than Boston's. Despite their differences in location and climate, the New England city and the Chinese megacity share a new and persistent concern about climate change.

Boston got lucky in October of 2012, when Hurricane Sandy swept through the city after striking New York City two hundred miles to the south. The city experienced high winds and coastal flooding and shut down its subway as a precaution, but the storm arrived five hours after high tide. The timing spared Boston from the oceanic surge that devastated New York. But amid the city's relief, alarm bells sounded. How often had Boston, a city with more than 650,000 residents and annual economic output of $160 billion, dodged climate disasters before? Research found dozens of near misses—hurricanes that with a little shift in direction could have socked the city. This was much more risk of climate calamity than anyone had realized. And when the city looked at projections of future climate changes, the risks appeared even bigger. A 2013 study announced that with a sea-level rise of just two-and-a-half feet, a Sandy-like storm could inundate 30 percent of the city.

In Shanghai, one of the most developed areas in China, with twenty-five million residents, a potential Sandy-like disaster looms from a combination of factors. A typhoon could produce extreme rainstorms that flood the Huangpu River, which flows through the city. It could also drive a tidal storm surge into the city from the nearby East China Sea, which, due to sea-level rise, could be three to six feet higher than today's tides. The excess water would hit a city that is sinking nearly four inches every decade and whose drainage system was designed to handle a much smaller volume of water. Just a year after Sandy hit New York, two typhoons struck near Shanghai with winds approaching one hundred miles per hour and as much as nine to eleven inches of rain in a day. They killed dozens of people, forced evacuation by hundreds of thousands of others, destroyed houses and crops, flooded streets and riverside parks, and closed trains, ports, and airports. Climate changes have already increased the frequency in Shanghai of downpours of more than five inches in a day. When city officials used data from actual typhoons to simulate a future typhoon, in 2050, the computer modeling predicted there would be more rainfall, a higher storm surge, and extreme flooding—as high as three feet—in much of the city, with a swollen Huangpu breaching its containment walls. "Flooding is Shanghai's biggest risk," explains Tian Zhan, Head of the Shanghai Climate Center's Climate Change Division.

What should Boston and Shanghai do about these potentially disastrous climate risks? What options do they have?

On January 4, 2018, a winter storm in Boston whipped new urgency into answering these questions. A record tide sent waves surging through downtown streets. "Many were stunned by the sight of water inundating large swaths of the city's waterfront," the *Boston Globe* reported. "What we saw yesterday is absolutely more of what we should expect in the future," Bud Ris told reporters, and he should know. For nearly two years, Ris cochaired the

Climate Preparedness Working Group of the Boston Green Ribbon Commission (GRC), leaders of the business, university, and
civic sectors working with the city to develop a long-term response
to climate changes.

Ris had been CEO of the New England Aquarium, located har-
borside in a building that houses thirty thousand animals and is visited by 1.3 million people a year. "Every time I saw a flood map for
the city," he says, "we were in the epicenter." From the aquarium,
he could look inland and uphill to where the city's shoreline was
four hundred years ago. Over the centuries, Boston grew out into
the water, adding buildings and streets on top of more and more fill.
Today the harbor is ringed with residential and commercial facilities
worth billions of dollars and containing tens of thousands of residents and workers—all on low-lying, artificial land. "If you look at
maps of where the flooding problem will be, it is all the filled land,"
Ris says.

Boston has a deep fifty-square-mile harbor in which tides fluctuate by as much as nine feet. "In the past century, the harbor's water
level has risen about 9 inches, but an inch or so a decade is barely
noticeable," says Ris. Looking ahead, though, the much larger and
more rapid potential increase can't be dismissed. A few years ago,
Ris recalls, the aquarium considered having an outdoor exhibit to
illustrate what's coming: "We were going to suspend a boat 6 feet up
in the air. People would ask, 'Why is that boat up there?' We'd say,
'Because that's where it's going to be in 2100.'"

Other cities around the world face similarly apocalyptic climate scenarios, and many have already experienced the devastation
caused by surging tides, extreme rainfall, or prolonged heat waves.
The US opened 2018 having set a record in the previous year for
the cost of damages due to weather events—$306 billion because of
hurricanes, wildfires, hailstorms, tornadoes, drought, and a freeze.
In the days after Boston's January 2018 flooding, climate disasters
filled headlines worldwide: Paris's Seine River flooded for the second time in three years due to heavy rainfall. Cape Town warned
residents that it "very likely" would run out of water due to a two-
year drought that has cut rainfall by two-thirds. Sweltering heat in
Melbourne crippled power distribution, leaving forty-one thousand
homes without electricity, melted road surfaces, and disrupted train

service. San Franciscans were still reeling from wildfires north of the city that destroyed thousands of buildings and scorched nearly four hundred square miles of land, with smoke prompting air-pollution alerts in the city and warnings to keep children inside.

Of course, cities have a long history of protecting themselves from natural disasters. For thousands of years, they have built embankments to protect against river and ocean flooding. Rotterdam, at the intersection of the North Sea and three rivers, has fended off water since its origin 750 years ago. San Francisco and other cities have imposed seismic standards on buildings to protect against earthquakes. But climate change is not just a natural disaster; it is a disaster of nature. It disrupts the relatively stable climatic conditions that shaped the physical and biological realities within which cities developed. "It's not only that the climate is no longer stationary," says Robert Lempert, senior researcher at RAND Corporation who works with city and utility planners. "It will keep changing and the changes will get bigger and bigger."

The climate turbulence that has been forecast presents cities with a new category of risk, challenging them to think differently about the future—what it can be and how it is made.

Sharing the Future

The modern city was designed primarily for the economic growth that the Industrial Revolutions made possible. Few cities, whether newly made or of ancient stock, escaped from this model for urban development. The city's center was organized for business and finance, where once religious or government institutions might have prevailed. Arteries designed for efficient flows of people and goods, the citywide traffic of commerce, and delineated zones with single functions—industry, retail, finance, or housing—eclipsed the organic mosaic of self-contained, mixed-use neighborhoods. As we've seen in the preceding pages, the city was an instrument used to bend the natural environment, which was thought to be a stable, known entity, and the social order to the aim of creating economic wealth.

The idea that people could control the future was a modern one. "The revolutionary idea that defines the boundary between modern times and the past is . . . the notion that the future is more than a whim of the gods and that men and women are not passive before nature," says Peter Bernstein in the bestseller *Against the Gods: The Remarkable Story of Risk*. "The ability to define what may happen in the future and to choose among alternatives lies at the heart of contemporary societies." In cities, this ability became central to planning. "By the start of the twentieth century," explains professor of environmental planning David Connell, "the professional practice of planning embodied society's belief in its ability to control a discernable future."

Taken only on its own terms, the planning of modern cities for a future of economic growth has been a remarkable success. "We pushed ourselves forward like a bulldozer, designing our cities and infrastructure out of our desires and ideas for proximity, mobility, and prosperity," says urban planner and water-system designer Henk Ovink, the Netherlands's special envoy for international water affairs. But this single-minded focus has had severe negative environmental and human impacts, producing "externalities" such as environmental pollution, vast slums, social conflicts, and disparities in economic wealth. As the damage spread and became increasingly intolerable, challenges arose to the goal of unconstrained economic growth. Constraints were placed on which future could be chosen; the potential for economic activity to produce negative impacts had to be anticipated and limited. The goal of sustainability—a balancing of economic, social, and environmental interests—contended for the urban future.

As the idea of sustainable development took the stage, climate change emerged from the wings and altered the future. Nature, it turns out, has an existence of its own, a complex, dynamic balancing act—the climate—that shapes the entire planet's chemical, physical, and biological existence. It is not just a factor to be reckoned with in some future that people chose. It has the power to define what might happen in any future we might want. Even though some cities face worse potential climate impacts than others, nature is filling *all* futures on the planet with climatic risks—potential disorder and shocks unlike any since city building began. "Climate extremes are becoming *really* extreme, and it turns out we are not ready for this," says Ovink. "Look at places in the Middle East and Africa where there is no water and millions of people are on the run."

A new goal is emerging for planning a city's future: resilience—being able to prepare for future climate shocks and stresses, recover from them, and adapt and grow after disruptions. Planners, says Connell, now "emphasize adaptation and mitigation rather than confidence and control." The future is no longer an open slate on which we can write our chosen adventure. We have to get ready for it, survive it, and learn to benefit from it.

The disruption of the future by a newly and dangerously unstable nature presents cities with great risks, persistent uncertainties, and technical, social, and political complexities. Shaping a path forward means figuring out what the city wants its resilient future to be, what options it has for getting there, and how it should go about deciding which future and options to pursue. These are urban-planning problems, but the plans that are emerging in innovation lab and other cities depart in significant ways from twentieth-century norms. They pose resilience as more than a climate problem; instead, it is framed as a "whole-city" set of interconnected environmental, social, and economic problems. They set new standards about who should be involved and in what ways in deciding what the city should do. They introduce a new approach, adaptive management, for the types of actions cities can take in the face of climate uncertainty.

A Nascent Practice

No city is likely to escape the impacts of the planet's changing climate—if not because of direct stresses and shocks, then because of the environmental, economic, social, and political disruptions that will ripple out from other impacted sites, including the expected migration of millions of "climate refugees." And yet, an assessment of the state of climate adaptation and resilience building in the US, released in early 2018, says that "a sense of urgency is lacking, and too many adaptation efforts are stalled at the planning stage." Echoing other studies, it notes that the knowledge, tools, and skills needed for effective adaptation, especially in cities, are still in an early stage of development.

Many cities and experts identify formidable barriers to taking effective action, including scientific uncertainty about climate forecasts and their potential impacts; difficulties of developing complex analyses of potential environmental, economic, and social impacts; fragmentation of government control over resources and decisions among numerous agencies and levels; disconnection between scientists and public policymakers and between knowledge disciplines; differing interests and values of various stakeholders in cities; difficulties communicating and building the public's understanding of complex climate analysis; lack of resources for investing in long-term resilience, given other near-term priorities; and reluctance to take actions that might constrain development in certain areas of the city or increase the cost of development or living. It's especially difficult for cities to decide to "retreat" from existing development or from land for future development that may no longer be feasible for use because of significant climate risks.

Networks of cities in the US and worldwide are emerging to advance the practice of adapting to climate changes. The Urban Sustainability Directors Network (USDN) is developing a "climate resilience accelerator" to support cities and connect them with potential partners in the private, nonprofit, and university sectors. Sixteen of the twenty-five global innovation lab cities we've described are members of 100 Resilient Cities, created in 2013 to help cities become more resilient to physical, social, and economic challenges. But only a few cities in the world are regarded as cutting-edge leaders. For example, Melbourne's green-infrastructure initiatives respond ambitiously to the risks of extreme heat and drought. The adaptation plan for Paris won a C40 Cities award. When C40 Cities held its first adaptation academy, it used Rotterdam, well known for its sophisticated water management, as the host. Many other leading-edge cities—including Amsterdam, Boston, Copenhagen, New York City, San Francisco, and Seattle—are addressing risks mostly due to sea-level rise or extreme precipitation.

Several initiatives unveiled in 2018 aim to create additional urban pioneers around the world. Cape Town and Mexico City were selected in 2018 to help create a global standard for water resilience, in partnership with Arup, the World Bank, 100 Resilient Cities, the Rockefeller Foundation, and three other cities. Meanwhile, Ovink worked with the Asian Infrastructure Investment Bank, a China-led international financial institution, 100 Resilient Cities, and others to gather the world's talent—urban, climate, and water experts, architects, engineers, designers, social scientists, economists, and local coalitions—to collaborate on developing water-oriented resilience approaches for new pilot cities in Southeastern Asia: Chennai, India; Khulna, Bangladesh; and Semarang, Indonesia. The "Water as Leverage for Resilient Cities" initiative, Ovink says, will help cities turn "a landscape of problems into a landscape of solutions."

The most apparent problem in the landscape, of course, is the physical damage that climate changes may cause in cities. But that's just an opening view of the new environment in which cities must develop their futures.

Physical Exposure

Cities building their climate resilience face an initial significant choice: how narrowly or expansively will they define the problem? Climate change obviously poses physical dangers for cities—and these must be assessed and addressed. Decision makers have to navigate through scenarios for future climate projections and analyses of potential damage. They have to determine how much physical risk is acceptable, given that there's no way to eliminate all risk and there will be limits to how much the city can invest in actions to reduce risks.

Boston and Shanghai, like other cities, are taking or considering short-term measures to cope with climate changes. Actions to prevent property damage in just two of Boston's at-risk neighborhoods, including using portable floodwalls and elevating streets, could cost as much as $262 million over several decades. Shanghai has already built levees and dikes along its rivers to hold back the water.

But there's much more for these cities to ponder: How will they protect their sewers, water and energy systems, and subway tunnels? What resilience standards should they impose on new construction already slated for at-risk areas and in the future? How much green infrastructure can they use to soak up excess water and hold down heat? Should they erect massive barriers to prevent storm surges? A sea barrier in Boston Harbor would likely cost more than $10 billion, according to initial estimates. Shanghai is assessing the option of building a storm-surge barrier, either at the mouth of the Huangpu River or two miles inland where the river is narrower, says Tian. A barrier would function in combination with an upgraded drainage system, deep tunnels to handle excess water, and additional green infrastructure throughout the city.

Constructing barriers, tunnels, and sewers and "hardening" physical protections that already exist will be necessary to protect assets from potential water damage, but they lock cities into fixed and costly actions even though what the climate future will bring is somewhat uncertain. That's why cities are also pioneering a new class of actions, including the use of green infrastructure, which may allow them to "coevolve" with an increasingly dynamic climate.

Adaptive Management

As Shanghai contemplates its options, it has recognized that the combination of long-term climate-adaptation strategies it chooses (barriers, tunnels, etc.) will have to be flexible enough to perform under different scenarios of the future climate. The city's plan, Tian says, needs a "robust combination" of strategies and an "implementation pathway" that sequences and adjusts strategies in response to inevitable revisions in the climate scenarios.

This sort of flexibility helps a city cope with the uncertainties of climate change due to our inability to know what the global GHG-emissions levels that drive change will be and the gaps in our incomplete understanding of the planet's climate system. The idea is to make sure that future decision makers are not locked into past decisions that no longer meet the conditions they have to deal with—a development that could jeopardize the city's resilience and cost it money because previous investments were wasted and new investments cost more than if they had been made earlier.

Innovative cities designing more adaptable resilience-building actions are investing in flexible infrastructure.

They use green infrastructure such as the widespread planting of trees and vegetation, as Melbourne, Rotterdam, Singapore, and other cities described in chapter 9 have been doing. The diversity of a city's green infrastructure is also an important factor in building resilience. Melbourne plans to increase the diversity of tree species in its forest as a way of preventing the spread of diseases and other calamities. Cities can restore natural systems by "day-lighting" creeks and rivers that were covered up, turned into sewage channels, or diverted—changes that reduced their contribution to resilience. In the Netherlands, for instance, the "Room for the River" initiative, begun in 2007 and costing more than $2 billion, restores the natural floodplain of rivers so they will serve as storage sponges that protect populated areas from flooding. Cities also build infrastructure that mimics natural systems. The $60-million Living Breakwaters project in New York City will install submerged structures offshore, designed to maximize the ecosystem while protecting against shoreline erosion, reducing the severity of waves, and restoring oyster beds.

Cities also use modular and distributed infrastructure such as energy-producing microgrids and site-based storm-water capture systems, which are less susceptible to widespread failure during a climatic event than large-scale grids. The failure of one module does not severely affect the other modules. In Boston, the Charles River Watershed Association (CRWA) has modeled the use of decentralized wastewater treatment and renewable-energy production in several neighborhoods instead of relying on big centralized facilities—an approach that, CRWA Executive Director Robert Zimmerman says, increases resilience to flooding and drought, restores natural hydrology, reduces environmental damage, and doesn't cost more money than the traditional centralized model.

Innovative cities design convertible infrastructure such as the water plazas that Rotterdam pioneered—hard infrastructure whose purpose can be easily changed to deal with climate events. They also design movable barriers, such as the enormous gates that protect London, Rotterdam, and Venice from ocean surges while allowing shipping traffic to continue most of the time and minimizing environmental damage.

The use of flexible infrastructure may require changes in government standards and regulations for infrastructure that have been designed for stable structures and guaranteed outcomes. These emerging flexible approaches also require an additional component: a commitment to and the resources for monitoring and regularly reviewing the performance of infrastructure—and changes in climate projections—as well as a readiness to adjust actions based on the new information. The city has to make a systematic effort to obtain the new information that could drive adjustment. "You need indicators of when to make a change, triggers to take the next step," explains Paul Kirshen, professor of climate adaptation at the University of Massachusetts–Boston. Melbourne, for example, uses aerial and thermal images to monitor its tree canopy's capacity and performance, partners with a university to monitor "microclimate" conditions at the street level, and installed weather stations to measure temperature differences between shaded and unshaded streets.

As with any model for public policies, there may be concerns about and opposition to flexible approaches. "Explicitly signaling that policies will undergo change may impede enforcement, make decision makers seem indecisive, and make it easier for them to succumb to political pressure from special interests," note RAND's Robert Lempert and Debra Knopman. Stakeholder groups, they add, "may prefer stability rather than repeatedly contesting policy choices, especially when such groups fear they may lose influence in the future." The alternative, however, may be to take no action at all or to make decisions that could prove ineffective and costly.

Social Vulnerability

Even as cities learn to cope with the serious and uncertain physical risks they face due to climate change, some have recognized that the "social vulnerability" of specific groups, communities, of people in the city poses another critical risk.

In Boston, for instance, it was projected that a three-foot rise in sea level would flood twelve thousand buildings, twenty-five subway stations, and four neighborhoods—and this would impact an estimated 104,000 children, 60,000 elderly people, 327,000 people of color, and others with low incomes, disabilities, chronic and acute illnesses, and limited English proficiency. These people are not just in the way of the water; they likely have less resilience, less physical, social, and economic capacity, to bounce back from disasters. They may live in housing that is less able to withstand inundation. They may have chronic health problems, such as asthma, which make them more susceptible to extreme heat. They may have fewer resources— insufficient wealth, technology, education, institutional services, information, and social connections to neighbors and other potential support—to prepare sufficiently for climate changes and recover from climate disasters. They are at a disadvantage, and often this is because of a city's historic patterns of discrimination against low-income, minority, immigrant, ethnic, and religious populations.

Cities that decide to boost the resilience of vulnerable groups usually seek to engage their members in planning processes to decide what to do. This often starts with an acknowledgment that traditional planning has marginalized the voices, knowledge, and interests of these populations. Cities try to establish a dialogue with vulnerable communities, to codevelop understandings of the climate-change problem and potential actions. In a few cities, engagement extends to empowering vulnerable communities to develop and implement actions themselves, by providing funding to participate in planning and the authority to make some decisions. Sooner or later, though, the city has to decide whether or not to prioritize resilience building for vulnerable communities and how to design and implement actions for specific vulnerabilities, such as limiting cost increases of essential services, providing early warning alerts, improving local health services, and increasing access to training, education, and transportation for local jobs resulting from resilience investments. A USDN "racial equity" guide released in 2017 contained examples of these planning processes and actions drawn from Boulder, New York City, San Francisco, Seattle, Washington, DC, and other cities.

In some cities, innovators have recognized they could do more than seeking to reduce social vulnerability to climate-change impacts. They could put tackling the root cause of social vulnerability—discrimination—at the core of their efforts to strengthen the city's resilience.

Bouncing Forward

"Our first crime against nature was a crime against ourselves," says Taj James, cofounder of the Oakland-based nonprofit Movement Strategy Center, which supports movements for justice and equity and is one of many emerging advocates for resilience-through-equity. "Resilience is about the relationships of human beings to each other," he explains. "The organizing principle is about repairing the harm that humanity has done to itself."

James's analysis is readily translated to the task of making a city's future: the way it's been done in the past has deliberately excluded and deeply injured certain populations, and this cannot be the way to a resilient future. "To effectively build resilience," says a publication he coedited, "frontline communities—including low-income communities and communities of color that are most vulnerable to climate impacts—must be at the center of policy and practice. . . . Our vision of climate resilience is not about 'bouncing back.' Instead, it is about bouncing forward to eradicate the inequities and unsustainable resource use at the heart of the climate crisis."

The idea of bouncing forward offers cities an important insight. It recognizes that city making is a collective exercise in economic, social, and political power. One way that power is used is through urban planning, which, says environmental planner Connell, "is the representation of a collective, public interest in the use of the power." When cities plan their long-term climate resilience, will power be available to those who have mostly been excluded from it in the past? In other words, who is the "collective" that decides the city's future? This is not just a technical question, James points out. It's ultimately a matter of a city's values and identity: "We cannot technocratically transition; we have to transition our values and worldview." If we want to "construct an identity in which we are not separate from nature," he concludes, then we have to repair and end the "domination and extraction" that have been inflicted on some populations.

This idea also poses a challenge for city leaders: how will they define resilience? Is it about bouncing back, maintaining a city's basic functions and structures in the face of disruption and change? Or is it about bouncing forward, changing a city's functions and structures—intentionally disrupting economic, social, and political arrangements—so it can build a different resilience than it has had in the past? The Rockefeller Foundation chose the bounce-forward approach when it launched 100 Resilient Cities—to develop "the capacity," as then foundation president Judith Rodin put it, "to create and take advantage of *new* personal, social, and economic opportunities."

The bounce-back-or-forward distinction may be more or less relevant in different cities, depending on their history, degree of inequity, and type of political system for making decisions. City leaders may choose to pursue a mix of both approaches based on the opportunities for change they perceive.

But any city that is planning its way to a resilient future has to reckon with the role that planning now plays in how the future is made. The "postmodern" purpose of planning, says Connell, is to make "the future visible in a socially acceptable way." What will be socially acceptable, given the uncertainties driven by climate change and the social and economic divisions and tensions at the heart of modern cities, is still being formed in most cities. "In cities," reports Ovink, "you see an emerging capacity: coalitions of the willing that link institutions and individuals to work on the challenges and get to transformative solutions."

Not all of what will be socially acceptable and will occur in cities will be determined by planning. A city has a mind of its own, says Spiro Kostof, historian of architecture and author of *The City Assembled*: "Those who see themselves in charge will legislate a built order," but the city "may refuse to go along with what has been prescribed, or find its own mode of obedience that leaves it free to metamorphose."

Beyond Climate Change

It's difficult for cities to assess the climate changes they face, but the changing climate is only the beginning of their resilience challenge. To deal with potential changes, cities have to do what they don't fully know how to do yet: codevelop the future with the climate by designing actions that are acceptable in the complex present and adaptable in the uncertain future. "All nature is at the disposal of humankind and all humankind is at the disposal of nature," explains William McDonough. "We are to work together, for without working together we cannot survive."

Survival—staying in the game—is a necessary goal, of course. Avoiding calamity and potentially mortal shocks will be difficult enough for many cities, but it is not the same as having a sustained capacity for renewal, growth, and dynamic evolution.

By reshaping the future possibilities of cities, climate change has opened up a new space for urban transformation.

PART III

—

The Road Ahead

11 NEW THINKING SPREADS

—

It always seems impossible until it's done.

—NELSON MANDELA

The four ideas for urban transformation that we've described alter cities in fundamental ways. Cities responding to the imperatives of climate change incubate business innovation so they will thrive during the economic transition brought on by global decarbonization. They reduce their consumption of the planet's bounty. They reengage and collaborate with nature to obtain its life-enhancing benefits. They develop new capacities to prepare for a future filled with unprecedented challenges.

While these ideas are alive and well worldwide in innovation lab cities, they are also taking root in many "early adopter" cities, thanks to Rebel Alliance networks and organizations and other efforts that connect cities to each other to share information, lessons learned, and practical advice about climate innovations and other changes that improve urban livability. But cities cannot by themselves accomplish the urban evolution that has begun, not even through increased efforts. Even the most advanced innovation lab cities and early adopters can't get all the way down the road of transformation alone. They simply don't control enough of the factors for success, such as energy-market regulation, transportation-investment policies, corporate investments, and engineering practices. Nor can they always influence those who do command those levers.

Lack of control and influence is not the only barrier to a complete global urban makeover. The vast majority of the world's thousands of cities are not innovation labs or early adopter cities. Their leaders may be unenthusiastic about embracing a new mind-set and approach to city affairs and going through the difficulties and risks of change. They may be politically constrained, limited by a lack of financial resources and technical competencies, or may feel that the city has more pressing priorities. Or they may be reluctant to take climate actions that increase costs to businesses or residents, fearing negative impacts on the city's development and economy or on their own careers. These cities don't change because of self-drive and learning what works, the main motivations that spur innovators and adopters. Some of them may decide to act when the potential economic benefits for the city are compelling because changes would save city government money, reduce the cost of living or doing business, create more jobs, or generate a favorable cost-benefit ratio for public investment. But this willingness limits them to using innovations, such as switching outdoor lighting to LEDs or substituting green infrastructure for gray infrastructure, which can meet these financial criteria with certainty. Most climate innovations do not produce easy and sure financial wins like that. And as innovation lab cities show, just adopting an innovation here and there isn't nearly the same as transforming core city systems. It's only a step in that direction.

The bottom line: many of the world's cities will not transform their systems until they have no other choice. They will change eventually, but instead of inventing the future, they will be ensnared by it.

That's how the current modern city model took hold globally. In some cases, it was imposed by national governments, such as when Western colonial empires designed Asian, African, and Australian cities in their own image or when the US government built the national highway system into and through cities. Sometimes markets acted as a driving force: businesses wanted to make new products, such as cars, and consumers wanted to buy and use them, and eventually cities changed to accommodate the new mobility. Often, architects, engineers, and other professionals adopted new standards for their practices, much as modernist design of buildings and transportation engineering for efficient movement of vehicles became urban norms. In many cities, civic activists organized to support modern development because it offered opportunities for economic gain, deployed impressive new technologies, or inspired a sense of city betterment and human progress.

These various forcing functions for modern urban development didn't just spread city-to-city. They were part of a *gestalt*, a widespread way of thinking that emanated in the society's cultures, in the hearts and minds of people. A culture's values and beliefs guide action; they provide people with decision-making criteria that allow for local discretion. This is how an idea takes hold in the world; it lets people choose what precisely they will do in service of the idea. The key ideas of the modern age—unfettered economic growth, consumption-based abundance, financial efficiency, and the dominion of built environments over nature, for example—caught on because they appealed to many people in many different situations.

Some values and beliefs endure across generations and eons, while others change. Modern-age values—consumerism and economic efficiency, for instance—replaced traditional values of previous centuries. In our time, the rise of widely held "cultural creative" values—love of nature, awareness of planet-wide issues, embrace of cultural diversity, and gender equality—has been documented. This sort of sweeping change may be tied to what William Strauss and Neil Howe in *The Fourth Turning* call "the seasons of history," cycles of generational change that strengthen civil order, then attack it, then give rise to new values, then replace old values with the new ones.

Now this process of gestalt formation is happening with the new ideas that are transforming cities. It's not just innovative and adopter cities that are using ideas that engender urban climate innovations. Businesses—large corporations, small local enterprises, and entrepreneurial start-ups—are creating products and services out of these ideas, and they look for cities to support them in doing this. Professionals—architects, engineers, real estate developers, water- and electricity-utility managers, city planners, financiers, and others—are developing new practices and standards of practice that incorporate these ideas. It was, for instance, a small group of architects, engineers, and environmentalists that developed LEED standards for green buildings that are being used worldwide. Consumers, community activists, and city residents are also demanding that cities embrace innovations in local policies and make investments based on these ideas, as are some state/provincial and national levels of government the world over.

As this self-organizing dynamic advances, it will continue to result in policy mandates issued by higher levels of government, such as building codes that increase requirements for energy efficiency. It will produce more standards that are adopted and widely used by architects, engineers, water-utility managers, and other professionals. It will generate even larger markets for innovative goods and services, such as electric vehicles and on-site water reuse systems, and suppliers and customers will demand more supportive city infrastructure and policies to enable what they care about.

This dynamic accelerates the pace of change in innovation lab cities and early adopter cities by reinforcing the validity and feasibility of the transformational ideas and bringing new resources to support their application. But it will also increasingly impact decisions of other cities—by creating government mandates, professional standards, and business, consumer, and community-based demands that cities cannot ignore. This is how the next urban model will replace the modern city model worldwide.

Boston's Tentacles

When Boston's Green Ribbon Commission (GRC) met in November 2017, its members—more than thirty CEOs and representatives of leading companies, property developers, nonprofits, utilities, financial institutions, and universities in the city—discussed their collective effort to support the city's plans to achieve carbon neutrality and prepare for climate turbulence. They considered how to create a "carbon-free" city and embed climate strategies into the city's long-term comprehensive planning, a crucial step for sustaining momentum and deepening transformational impact.

But many commission members have other formidable goals on their minds. They are spreading climate innovations throughout the world. Some have shaped the carbon-reduction goals and plans of their large companies in multiple cities and nations and are pioneering critical innovations: offshore wind farms, district energy systems, and "zero-net-carbon" buildings that meet their operational needs entirely through renewable energy, for example. Some are bending entire US and global economic sectors—health care, commercial real estate, private capital investment—toward adopting climate-smart approaches and standards of sustainable practice. Some are teaming with Boston to develop new tools and research capacities to help other cities, as well as states and regions, decide which policies to use to reduce GHG emissions. These urban climate rebels in Boston are reaching far beyond the city's borders, using markets, professional standards, and public policies in ways that affect cities everywhere.

Amos Hostetter, a philanthropist and longtime Boston civic leader, was a founding force in launching the commission in 2010—using his convening power to bring together leaders from multiple sectors in the city. Then the Barr Foundation, which he and his wife, Barbara, started, provided funding for the GRC, a total of almost $4 million by 2018. Mindy Lubber, a former federal environmental regulator in the Clinton administration and cochair of the citizen leadership committee that shaped Boston's 2009 Climate Action Plan, had urged Hostetter to start the commission. "She came to me and said, 'You've got to do something like this,'" Hostetter recalls. "Mindy was my rabbi. You can't spend fifteen minutes with her without getting charged up. My role was knowing most of the movers and shakers in the city and getting them to return calls."

Lubber is CEO of Ceres, a Boston-based nonprofit that works with some of the world's largest corporations and public and private investment institutions on climate change and other challenges of moving toward a sustainable economy. Members such as Apple, General Motors, and Bank of America have committed to use 100 percent renewable energy, JPMorgan Chase agreed to stop financing new coal mines, and the California Public Employees' Retirement System bought 25 percent of a 550-megawatt solar farm. Since December 2017, Ceres has been working with 225 investors with $26.3 trillion in assets under management to get the world's largest GHG-emitting corporations to curb their discharges. "We need capital markets to be part of this fight against climate change," Lubber says, "not only because it's a good thing, but because there is no economy without the capital."

Under Lubber, Ceres has become a $16-million-a-year organization with ninety staffers and broad access to business leadership in the US. It has focused on getting companies and investors to identify and assess the financial risks they face due to climate change. "I spend a lot of time in corporate boardrooms, with senior executives, with CEOs of publicly traded companies, with the world's largest institutional investors," Lubber says.

If I say, "We have got to stop this problem because our kids' lives are at stake," that will get me three minutes and thank yous, and everybody will feel good. But it will have no transference to what I want them to do with their investment portfolios. When we started defining climate as a financial, investor, and corporate risk, *then* it became something I could go into a corporate boardroom and speak about. If you're The Gap and the cotton crop dies, or an insurance company and there are two more Hurricane Sandys, or an oil company and your credit rating drops: these things affect their bottom line, and that's what they largely think about. That's the argument we make.

Lubber urged the creation of Boston's Green Ribbon Commission because, she says, it was yet another way to get the private sector to work on climate change, bringing its substantial resources to the city's important effort: "You have to show what addressing climate change looks like as a comprehensive model in a place, and Boston is such a great laboratory for change."

For another GRC member, Bryan Koop, change due to global warming was a personal experience before it became about how his business and sector operate. Koop is executive vice president of the Boston region for Boston Properties, one of the biggest developers of large office buildings in the US, with 164 properties in Boston, New York City, San Francisco, Washington, DC, and Los Angeles. For the first fifteen years of his three-decade career, Koop says, "I was hanging around with just real estate people, and you'd think that the purpose of real estate is to make a profit and get wealthy." When he first encountered the topic of sustainability, he says, "a little bit of green was being discussed in real estate. My inclination was, this is kind of bullshit." But he read more about it, talked with people outside of real estate, and then a friend suggested he watch *An Inconvenient Truth*. "I watched it five times," Koop recalls. "I started to realize that sustainability principles were really in keeping with what I hold dearly. Why wouldn't I want to develop property while doing as little harm as possible to the environment and the community around me?"

Koop became an evangelist in his sector, bucking the status quo, seeking a broad transformation: "The industry will be changed by a few people standing up, and I want to be one of those people." He also started to incorporate energy-efficiency and climate-adaptation innovations into buildings. He took business risks such as developing the first green office building in New England "on spec," meaning it had no rental customers lined up before his company spent $150 million to build the facility. Making the building conform to LEED Gold standards added to its cost, and Koop told his bosses they'd earn the money back with premium pricing. But when the first large potential renter, a technology firm, took a tour of the space, he had a moment of severe doubt. The company CEO cut off his pitch about the building's sustainability features: "All of a sudden the CEO goes, 'Bryan, just stop for a minute. I don't believe in all this stuff. Let's go take a tour and then talk about price.'" During the tour, Koop recalls, "two of the young leaders of this company pulled me aside and whispered to me, 'We're really sorry about that.' I go, 'No, no, no, not a problem.' And they go, 'It *is* a problem and we're going to enlighten him on this.'"

Months later, Koop continues, the company moved into the space, and the CEO addressed a ribbon-cutting ceremony: "He says, 'One of the things I'm most proud of is that this building is LEED Gold certified. I'll be the first to say that I didn't value it.' And he turns to his board of directors and these young leaders and says, 'But I was educated otherwise.'" The triumph Koop felt at that moment, he says, was more than about making a sale: "I went from severe doubt to, oh my god, it worked—and we *changed a company*. If we can change them, we can change others. We can provide leadership to our customers, because it isn't our customers' responsibility to know this stuff. It should be our responsibility."

Other global activists on the GRC include David Torchiana, CEO of Partners Healthcare, the largest employer in the State of Massachusetts, and one of the leaders in Health Care Without Harm, a nonprofit working with thousands of hospitals worldwide to reduce their carbon footprints and press for public policies to reduce GHG emissions; Thomas Brostrom, representing Ørsted Energy, the Danish firm that is the world's leading offshore wind developer, now entering US and Asian renewable-electricity markets; Robert Brown, a chemical engineer and president of Boston University, which is developing a center to provide cities, states, and regions with state-of-the-art modeling capacity to assess the potential impact of policies for reducing GHG emissions; and Jeremy Grantham, chief investment strategist for a $77 billion asset management firm and founder of a research institute on climate change at the London School of Economics.

These activists wear two hats in the Rebel Alliance of climate-change agents—city and world. Many more like them are busy all around the planet, pushing ideas and innovations into markets, professions, public policies, and communities, making it possible for cities to go further and faster toward transformation.

A Changing Context

A world that is more renewable, efficient, green, and adaptive: nearly every day brings news that these ideas and their innovations are advancing—and not just in cities. Some are particularly important for the evolution of cities, supporting both the urban innovation leaders and early adopters but also signaling changing conditions for all cities to consider.

Energy-supply markets are shifting toward renewable-energy production, driven by investor and corporate decisions and technological advances in generation and storage, despite weak or nonexistent carbon-pricing incentives and regulatory mandates. Half the coal plants in the US have closed or are being phased out. Large pools of capital—Norway's sovereign wealth fund, European insurance giant Axa, the World Bank, New York State's pension fund—are turning away from fossil-fuel investments. "Something big is starting to shift," notes Bill McKibben, founder of 350.org. "There are signs that the world's financial community is finally rousing itself in the fight against global warming." In December 2017, the US Congress was on the verge of eliminating tax credits for investment in and production of solar and wind energy and purchase of electric vehicles, until an alliance of companies committed to producing and using renewables stepped in and persuaded legislators to relent.

Distributed production of solar and wind power is moving toward notable size. According to Bain and Company's Global Utilities practice, the proliferation of distributed energy resources (DERs) and the smart software to manage decentralized electricity is creating demand for more investments in redesigned electricity grids "to accommodate and integrate a growing influx of supply from these distributed sources of electricity." Graham Richard, former CEO of Advanced Energy Economy, notes that as the cost of "clean-economy" technologies comes down, especially battery storage costs, more companies are stepping into the distributed renewables market with products and services for consumers, communities, and utilities. In March 2018, the California electricity-grid operator cancelled or modified $2.6 billion in planned transmission projects, in part because an increasing amount of residential rooftop solar-energy generation was reducing forecasted local demand for electricity.

China is fueling a boom in electric vehicles, as other nations announce future bans of fossil-fuel vehicles. China had more EV sales in 2017, some three hundred thousand vehicles, than the rest of the world combined and is recruiting electrical engineering talent from around the world. Norway, which intends to phase out sale of diesel and gasoline cars by 2025, reported that in 2017 more than half of the vehicles sold in the country ran on alternative fuels. By 2018, automotive producers have turned away from the internal combustion engine, as more and more of them announce they intend to electrify their entire product lines in the next two decades. Germany's highest administrative court ruled that cities can ban vehicles from streets to reduce air pollution. Even oil companies have noticed the emerging EV market; in 2017, Royal Dutch Shell purchased one of Europe's largest car-charging companies.

These and other developments support growth of clean-energy and "smart-tech" businesses—potential opportunities for cities to grow economically.

Real estate markets are moving toward greater energy efficiency—despite weak and misaligned financial incentives. That momentum is especially strong in new construction, where the increased cost can be relatively low and "green" new facilities can command premium prices. LEED standards for green buildings have been used worldwide in more than ninety-two thousand projects. In September 2017, in Shanghai, Chinese architects, planners, and building-sector professionals attended the nation's first-ever training session for the design of low- to no-carbon buildings. Chinese architecture and design entities and Architecture 2030 cohosted the event and have developed for worldwide use a new "zero-net-carbon" building code—for highly efficient buildings that produce on-site or procure enough carbon-free energy to meet their annual operating needs.

Health Care Without Harm members—735 health systems in forty countries, representing more than twenty-one thousand hospitals and community health centers—have pledged to adopt "green and healthy" procedures, including increasing energy efficiency and reducing food waste.

In 2015, the European Commission adopted a comprehensive Circular Economy Package designed to stimulate recycling and reuse. "Many cities across Europe have started their journey of transition to a more circular economy," says Amsterdam Deputy Mayor Abdeluheb Choho. "Some have engaged in small projects in specific sectors, whereas others have taken more holistic approaches by developing circular strategies." Meanwhile, some companies are taking more responsibility for the life cycles of their products, efforts that usually come company-by-company, product-by-product. In October 2017, for instance, IKEA U.S. announced that, in keeping with its corporate zero-waste goal, it would recycle all old mattresses, of any brand, that are picked up when it delivers new mattresses. About 80 percent of a mattress can be recycled, according to the company, which noted that roughly eighteen million mattresses are disposed of in the US every year.

Hundreds of European cities have committed to plan for climate change, and many have started the process, most without waiting for a catastrophic event to trigger action. "In recent times," reports the European Environment Agency, "cities that have not suffered such an event had started to take action too. Increasingly, they see climate change adaptation as an opportunity to create a more attractive and vital city."

In December 2016, Mexico City issued a city green bond, raising $50 million from private sources to fund energy efficiency, public transportation, and water-treatment projects. A few months later, Cape Town issued its first green bond for $77.2 million to finance low-carbon public transit and water-treatment projects.

In a prod to US cities, in November 2017, Moody's Investors Service, a leading credit-rating agency, cautioned cities, especially those on seacoasts, that their access to long-term loans for infrastructure and other uses could be damaged by failure to increase their resilience to climate changes. Also in 2017, a Swiss foundation issued a new standard for assessing the climate resilience of physical and digital infrastructure. Projects voluntarily submitted for certification must demonstrate the ability "to withstand identified climate change risks and hazards in plausible scenarios throughout [their] lifecycle."

Along with these developments, work continues in academic and professional communities on a set of analytic and management frameworks and tools relevant to key transformational ideas for cities, including the measurement and monitoring of urban metabolisms, the flows of materials and energy within cities, and the assessment of return on investment in environmental services, the range of economic and noneconomic benefits created by natural systems.

Green Is the New Urban

In one of the more noticeable global trends, urban green infrastructure is no longer a luxury or just an idealistic value or aspirational goal. It is happening now in many different urban contexts and at every urban scale because cities need it for dealing with climate change, and it generates a range of demonstrated, tangible, and desirable financial and cobenefits that the engineering profession has begun to promote. A 2014 publication, "Cities Alive," produced by Arup, a London-headquartered engineering firm with offices in thirty-five countries and a staff of thirteen thousand, uses one hundred fifty pages and numerous examples to extol the emergence of urban greening in terms that green urbanist Tim Beatley might favor: "The approach seeks to create healthier, more socially connected cohesive and biodiverse urban environments and a connected city ecosystem for people and wildlife that also builds in resilience measures against climate change."

Greening is becoming a mainstream professional practice with extensive practical know-how, replicable methods, planning processes, measurable standards, and dependable cost advantages. "Professions must fundamentally rethink 'green,' not as an optional add-on, a desirable enhancement or a dutiful nod towards biodiversity, but as a fundamental part of the solution," says Sue Illman, president of the Landscape Institute, a British professional body for six thousand landscape architects.

URBAN GREENING

The greening of individual buildings, now a worldwide phenomenon, has extended to increasingly large new developments.

In Berlin, regulations known as the Biotope Area Factor establish the proportion of green space needed for densely built districts and are used to ensure that proposed new development projects support the city's greening goals.

Seattle's Green Factor regulation requires new commercial development of four thousand square feet or more to have at least 30 percent of the site use tree planting, green roofs, permeable pavement, rainwater harvesting, drought-tolerant plants, or other green landscape features.

In southern China, the groundbreaking in June 2017 for a 342-acre "forest city" with up to thirty thousand residents—containing forty thousand trees, almost a million plants, and seventy buildings—is taking the know-how for greening to the scale of a self-contained district. The project was commissioned by the urban planning department in nearby Liuzhou, a city of more than one million people, and was designed by a Milan-based architecture firm that had planned tree- and plant-covered towers in European cities and a green hotel and two green skyscrapers in China.

Berlin Biotope Area Factor: Arup, "Cities Alive: Rethinking Green Infrastructure," 2014, download available at http://www.arup.com/publications/research/section/cities-alive-rethinking-green-infrastructure, 116.
Seattle Green Factor: Timothy Beatley, *Biophilic Cities: Integrating Nature into Urban Design and Planning* (Washington, DC: Island Press, 2010), 132.
China "forest city": Allyssia Alleyne, "China Unveils Plans for World's First Pollution-Eating 'Forest City,'" *Architecture*, July 20, 2017, http://www.cnn.com/2017/06/29/architecture/china-liuzhou-forest-city/index.html; and Sarah Benton Feitlinger, "Italian Architect Envisions 'Forest Cities' to Combat China's Air Pollution," *DOGO News*, May 8, 2017, https://www.dogonews.com/2017/5/8/italian-architect-envisions-forest-cities-to-combat-chinas-air-pollution.

European, Chinese, Australian, and US governments have bought into urban greening with regulations, guidance, and support, although to varying degrees. Increasingly, the business case for investing in green infrastructure shows that cities can save money and realize cobenefits such as improved health and increased value of property, although this raises concerns about increased property values leading to displacement of low-income residents. There is growing interest among city dwellers for green, healthy living conditions, not just places in which to live and work. More and more people want green products and services—organic food, renewable energy, for instance—and they extend this desire to the buildings and streets they use. In many cities, community groups representing low-income neighborhoods are demanding environmental justice, which includes the fair spatial distribution of and access to a city's green infrastructure and environmental services.

Decision Time

These market, professional, and other developments aren't a substitute for cities making key decisions now about their future, but they inspire confidence that widespread reinvention is in the cards, even though it is still happening much too slowly. Transforming energy supply, real estate, mobility, and other markets will take much bolder measures. "Even if many of the companies are getting it," says Ceres's Mindy Lubber, "there are many more companies behind them who don't have a sustainability officer, who don't know climate change. In the end you're going to need changes in the law. You cannot have radical change without it."

We agree, but telling people what they have to do and giving them financial reasons to do it are only a part of how to accelerate progress. They also have to be aware of and understand what is in it for them—and for others—beyond money, and this requires painting a credible picture of a desirable future. It means understanding what community members want and helping them to have it. Greening in Singapore, says Tim Beatley, "is being driven by a sense of the positive draw of the vision itself. You can only do so much by hitting people over the head by telling them to stop driving and turn down the thermostat. They're going to be motivated by wanting to live in a particular place because of its positive, uplifting qualities."

Transformation of the commercial real estate business, says Boston developer Bryan Koop, will be sparked by what more and more customers—businesses, schools, and other organizations—want in the future: "They will want to know how they can get the most out of their human talent. They will want space that enhances productivity." That's not a demand for the cheapest possible space or for climate-friendly space; it's a growing market willing to pay for the type of space that the real estate industry doesn't yet provide much of. It is space that can be climate smart.

Koop offers the example of designing space to maximize natural light, which reduces the need for energy-consuming artificial light: "We know that people produce better with natural light. But our industry doesn't believe it. Whenever I bring this up, people say, 'Prove it, Koop.' The other day we gave a pitch to potential renters, which included lots of natural light in the space. For a week they kept calling us about the natural light: could we get them another case study about its benefits? My team said, 'They're becoming a nuisance.' I said, 'No, they're not. They're becoming aware.'"

For now, though, building professionals, real estate markets, and potential driving forces of urban change are themselves in an early stage of a long-term innovation transition. The decision to apply the transformational ideas and innovations of urban climate action remains mostly in the hands of city leaders. The most innovative cities are deciding to develop clusters of cutting-edge climate-oriented businesses, initiate consumption-reduction efforts and foster circular economies, install green infrastructure and promote biodiversity and biophilic immersion, and invest in communities' future-making capacities.

These decisions, the cities realize, are crucial for their own well-being in the coming decades.

12 CONTINUOUS INNOVATION

—

A map of the world that does not include Utopia is not worth even glancing at, for it leaves out the one country at which Humanity is always landing.

—OSCAR WILDE

What will cities be like if—when—the four transformational ideas we've described take hold? The ideas and their innovations have traction in cities worldwide, and in markets, professions, and government policies, but they have a long way to go to gain unstoppable momentum and widespread impact. Others who have peered into the future of the climate-change era provide utopian images of urban life.

"Everyone would live in a small, efficient home of about 46 square meters [495 square feet], eat a vegetarian diet, and get around on non-fossil-fuel-based transportation," offers Jennie Moore, an urban sustainability expert at the British Columbia Institute of Technology, describing what a sustainable Vancouver would look like. She and colleagues have a jokey shorthand for this: "closet-dwelling vegans on bikes."

Eric Sanderson, author of *Mannahatta*, which reconstructs what the hilly island at the heart of New York City was like in 1609, before Europeans arrived, looks ahead four hundred years: "One thing is certain: The city of the future will be different from the city of today." He envisions a city operating on renewable energy, buildings layered with gardens, streetcars running along greenways, suburbs replaced by dense cities and agricultural belts, sustainable fishing in the harbor, streams with headwaters in green rooftops, and beavers in Central Park: "More than ever, we will be a city of walkers and talkers, drawn from cultures all over the globe."

Gino van Begin, secretary-general of ICLEI-Local Governments for Sustainability, paints a street-level picture: many people are riding bicycles, the air is fresh, native trees line the streets, parks host people of different languages, rain gardens absorb storm water, organic waste feeds green space, and dark night skies show constellations of stars. City residents reuse, share, and exchange things in new patterns of consumption without waste. They share electric cars, sell their excess solar power to the grid, and ride biofuel buses to work. Green jobs grow the city's economy.

These imagined (and hopeful) futures evoke new technologies and lifestyles, the applications of the big ideas that are already shifting the model for urban development. They emphasize that in cities intensely engaged in climate innovation, the true prize is city livability and well-being, and climate action is a way to get there.

"For some," van Begin says, "the notion of living in a sustainable city can feel vague and distant, a dream of the future. But others are already living in this city or are advancing quickly towards it." He's right: many of the advancing cities are the innovation labs we've described and other leaders or early adopters.

But no city has put together the entire package of climate-driven innovations. You have to stitch together selected features from certain cities—Copenhagen's bicycle network, Melbourne's tree canopy, Shanghai's electric vehicles, San Francisco's recycling system, Rotterdam's water-management infrastructure, Mexico City's bus rapid transit corridors—to form a made-up whole.

In some lab cities, though, a version of low-carbon and more climate-resilient living is becoming available.

Living in the Royal Seaport

When Christina Salmhofer started working at Stockholm's Royal Seaport in 2011, the 583-acre industrial site along the Baltic Sea had been prepared for new development, but nothing had been built on it yet. Seven years later, the Seaport is in one of the world's growing number of low- or no-carbon and climate-resilient districts, a place where urban climate innovations are being integrated at district scale. More than three thousand apartment units have been built—half are rentals, half for sale—but this is only about a quarter of the way to a build-out of twelve thousand residences with thirty thousand dwellers, some thirty-five thousand workplaces, and 6.5 million square feet of commercial space. Demand for the living space "is very, very large," says Salmhofer, and people are paying market rates.

The Royal Seaport is an experiment in making a future city within an existing city. The city-owned site, once a royal hunting area, is two miles from the city center, contains an active port with ferries and cargo ships, and connects by subway and electric bus with the rest of the city of nearly one million inhabitants. It's a beehive of construction and demolition, torn-up roads, detours and large trucks, and cranes and partly completed buildings. But in neighborhoods that have been completed—streets with wide sidewalks and five-story, balconied apartment buildings with ground-floor shops, as well as green-certified buildings for preschools, all surrounded by green space, plantings, and trees—everyday city life is under way.

"This is a beautiful area, close to a national park," says Salmhofer, director of the seaport district's four-person sustainability team and an experienced environmental manager in the real estate sector. Back in 2009, the city decided the area should become an international model for urban sustainability. It developed a master plan with standards for energy and water use, waste management, and green space, then put opportunities for development up for bid. When completed in 2030, at a projected cost to the city of $2.6 billion for streets, parks, and other infrastructure, the seaport will be a dense, fossil fuel–free, inner-city neighborhood of diverse buildings with four to eleven floors and some high-rise towers. A third of its energy will be produced in the district, including by rooftop solar panels, a district heating system will run on biofuels, and a smart electricity grid will manage building energy consumption.

People will use a network of bicycle and walking lanes, electric-vehicle charging stations, and a bus fleet running on biofuels. The landscape will contain parks, urban gardens, green roofs and walls, a water arena and canal, and even beehives. A vacuum disposal system—color-coded chutes—in buildings and on streets will handle plastic packaging, paper, and general waste; kitchens will have disposal units for collecting food waste that will be used to produce biogas. The entire waterfront site has been designed to handle climate changes—increased rainfall and heat, rising seas—by raising ground levels for buildings and using green infrastructure extensively.

LOW-CARBON DISTRICTS FROM THE FUTURE

Cape Town's Old Mutual Mupine Development is a mixed-use, affordable-housing district being built on a golf course in the city's downtown. With seven hundred housing units planned alongside recreation facilities and space for small businesses, the project is part of a broader effort to reverse decades of racial segregation that forced black people to live outside the city. The project also incorporates green infrastructure, limited on-site parking, connections to the city's rail system, biogas digesters for on-site wastewater treatment, and the positioning of buildings to maximize natural lighting and ventilation.

Paris is redeveloping Clichy-Batignolles, a 125-acre mainly industrial district on the city's northeast edge, with 3,400 housing units, offices, a shopping center, and the twenty-five-acre Martin Luther King Park.

Sydney's Barangaroo waterfront development will accommodate twenty-three thousand office workers and some three thousand residents in a carbon-neutral district.

Most low-carbon districts involve cleared land, but some also arise in fully built areas. Washington, DC's Southwest Ecodistrict involves fifteen blocks, just south of the National Mall, containing federal government and privately owned commercial buildings as well as the usual urban infrastructure. It is being transformed into a walkable, high-density, mixed-use neighborhood with more residential and retail development, solar and geothermal energy, and reduced GHG emissions, water consumption, and waste for landfill.

Old Mutual Mupine Development: See Julian Smith, "Oregon to South Africa: Incubator 2017," EcoDistricts, July 11, 2017, https://ecodistricts.org/oregon -south-africa-incubator-2017/; and "Mupine Sustainable Residential Development," Design Space Africa, December 28, 2017, http://www.designspaceafrica .com/mupine-sustainable-residential-development/.
Clichy-Batignolles: Paris Batignolles Aménagement, "Clichy-Batignolles," accessed November 15, 2017, http://www.paris-batignolles-amenagement.fr/pba/ sites/default/files/publications/exe_depliant-mipim_en_web.pdf.
Barangaroo: Barangaroo Delivery Authority, "Sustainability," accessed January 18, 2018, http://www.barangaroo.com/the-project/progress/sustainability/.
Southwest Ecodistrict: "Southwest Ecodistrict: Washington, D.C., U.S.A., July 2017," Ecodistricts.org, accessed November 7, 2017, http://ecodistricts.org/wp -content/uploads/2017/08/ed-case-study-swecodistrict-FINAL-august-3-2017.pdf.

Steady Work

The development of low-carbon districts is spreading, but real progress toward a fully realized new global model for urban development lies in the decades ahead. Even in lab cities, innovations advance along a ragged edge, some running ahead, others behind.

As climate innovation moves into the global urban mainstream, innovation lab cities must continue to be sources of continuous advancements. This is a crucial and difficult role even for experienced cities. The many real-world challenges of innovation don't disappear, even as a city gets better at making changes happen. The course of innovation never does run smooth. Innovation lab cities keep having to overcome the everyday difficulties of innovating—sustaining political will, developing technical capacities, engaging community members, managing the economic impacts of change, and balancing climate innovation with the city's other priorities. Ambitious cities start many projects, but fully implementing them and impacting systems and the entire city is hard to do and takes time.

Innovation lab cities must continuously improve the innovations they already have under way. They must address key challenges that arise from the successes they've had: how to integrate innovations in districts, systems, and citywide and how to ensure that cities have the authority and resources needed to keep pushing urban transformation. And they must deal with questions that come when advancing the transformational ideas we've identified.

Lab cities have to keep refining already-developed innovations to improve their performance, even as they work on new ones to drive transformation even further.

Copenhagen, for instance, is a world leader in the use of bicycles to get around the city, but it wants to increase this habit even more. "A lot of the solutions for our network for bicycles, which is so important here, are developed in cooperation with bikers," says the city's Jørgen Abildgaard. "We ask them, 'Where are links missing? How can we transform the city so it's easier to bike?'" When the city published an online map of the bicycle network, within ten days, citizens placed ten thousand dots on the map—red ones for a lack of safe infrastructure, black for too narrow a bikeway, and blue for high levels of congestion. City planners use the data to plot new investments.

Cities are still at an early stage of understanding just how well a green-infrastructure project will perform—how much water it will retain, how much it will cool the air. Performance depends on a number of variables, including soil condition and the maturity of the trees and plants. Some research shows that although large trees (at least fifty feet in height) produce much more canopy than small trees, their environmental performance does not become significant until they are thirty feet tall. A 2015 assessment of some of New York City's installed green infrastructure—including green roofs, permeable pavement, street swales, tree pits, and rain gardens—noted success in retaining up to one inch of storm water but found that the underlying soil's condition impacted this performance. Shanghai and fifteen other Chinese cities are experimenting with using green infrastructure to capture and reuse at least 70 percent of rainwater, in a "sponge cities" initiative to address chronic and worsening urban flooding and water shortages.

Lab cities often have to build on previous innovations so they can be used to transform an urban system. For example, as alternative fuels are increasingly used in transportation, it becomes critical to develop widespread fueling infrastructure to supply vehicles. Sydney, Melbourne, and Yokohama used a grant from the Carbon Neutral Cities Alliance (CNCA) to study how cities can support the deployment of refueling stations for hydrogen fuel-cell electric vehicles, which are being mass-produced by some automobile manufacturers. The cities developed a blueprint guide to help cities prepare, review, and approve applications for hydrogen refueling stations in accord with international best practices. Meanwhile, other cities have been researching and experimenting with the use of new technologies for transportation innovation, such as autonomous vehicles and "dockless" bicycles for bike sharing.

Edges of Innovation

As lab cities install and accumulate climate innovations that apply transformational ideas, they encounter "next-generation" puzzles that must be addressed for long-term urban evolution.

They have to figure out how to integrate innovations so they function effectively at the neighborhood/district scale, like Stockholm's

Royal Seaport, and also at the scale of core urban systems and city-wide plans and regulations. How will innovations for reducing GHG emissions in buildings, transportation, waste, and energy supply fit together? How will they fit with innovations for green infrastructure, storm-water management, and other ways to strengthen a city's climate resilience?

The cities also have to figure out how to obtain the governance control, technical competencies, and financial resources they need to press on for the next decades. How can they, in other words, redesign and strengthen their underlying "operating systems" to more fully enable climate innovation?

These critical concerns live at the edge of urban climate innovation—where the lab cities' know-how and experience ends and additional experimentation begins. This emerging frontier is becoming fertile ground for change.

To highlight what's being learned about integrating climate innovations at multiple scales, we've drawn on examples from several innovation lab cities: Stockholm's low-carbon Royal Seaport district, one of the leading cases in the world; the Seattle Public Utilities' (SPU) water- and waste-management systems, which serve 1.4 million customers in the city and region; and Portland's comprehensive plan for the city's next twenty years of development, which incorporates extensive climate innovation into future land use.

A decarbonized district—a concentrated, bounded place—affects just a small slice of each city's land mass, built environment, and population. But new districts in Stockholm and other lab cities provide test-and-demonstration sites for the feasibility of integrated innovations and whether they sum to a product that people want. Working at neighborhood scale instead of at building-and-parcel scale, notes urban-policy journalist Emily Badger, allows district designers to "play with all the infrastructure that connects those parcels—the utility grid, the street network, the sidewalks." A big factor in the emergence of new districts is how much control a city has over land and other assets and decision-making processes. Stockholm, for instance, owns all the land on which the Royal Seaport is developing, and this gives it substantial authority over development. These districts also use principles for urban design that can be applied to other parts of the city over time. Creating low-carbon districts, says Lucia Athens, Austin's chief sustainability officer, helped the city "better articulate what Austin is trying to achieve at the neighborhood scale." The Royal Seaport "is becoming a role model for other developments in Stockholm," says Salmhofer. The district's development has influenced city policies on energy requirements, green-space standards, storm-water management, and traffic planning: "This project is waking up the whole development and building sector. In communities around Stockholm a lot of people are interested in the results."

Core city delivery systems—energy supply, transportation, buildings, water, solid waste, and others—blanket the entire city, encompassing many districts that may be quite different from each other. The many core systems in lab cities that are implementing a wide range of innovations tend to start with establishing a set of enabling conditions: The system's governing body sets bold climate-related goals for the system. It ensures that the system's managerial leadership is fully committed to these goals and has the skills to implement a change process sure to be long and complicated. These managers develop long-term strategies for developing and implementing innovations, detailed in multiyear and annual plans and budgets for actions and investments. They also muster customer and community support, while trying to safeguard the system's performance and affordability.

Citywide long-range plans address the urban whole. They provide an overlay of concepts, principles, and rules that will guide growth and development of districts and systems as well as major facilities—the many pieces of the whole. This urban-planning practice is made more complex in lab cities, because they have to take into account the way that numerous high-impact climate innovations are already changing the city's districts and systems. In 1980, when Portland adopted a comprehensive plan, climate change had not yet appeared on any community's radar screen. By 2016, though, it couldn't be missed. Even as Portland wrestled with other concerns that had emerged, it decreed the new planning goals of reducing carbon emissions and improving climate resilience.

Integration at these three scales is an essential step in a city's transformation, and experimentation is yielding some actionable insights.

CITY LIVABILITY IS THE PRIZE; CLIMATE ACTION IS A DRIVER

The point of integration isn't just to address climate change; it's to make the city better. The Royal Seaport, Salmhofer says, is attractive because of its location in the city, nearby natural amenities, and apartment size. In a 2016 survey of residents, she explains, "we had prepared possible answers for them in the survey, one of which was low carbon emissions. But that was just the respondents' ninth or tenth ranked priority. The highest priorities were proximity to the national park, larger apartments, and still being within the city." When it came to their living quarters, people wanted the benefits of immersion in nature, a sense of abundance, and easy access to the amenities of compact urban life.

Seattle Public Utilities has a carbon-neutrality goal, but its mission is to provide "efficient and forward-looking utility services that keep Seattle the best place to live." Its 2014 strategic plan contained twenty measurable targets for service levels and performance, including customer satisfaction and holding rate increases to no more than 4.6 percent.

Portland's comprehensive plan seeks to create "a future place that is equitable, healthy, prosperous and well connected." It emphasizes the city's general well-being, while elevating climate action as a new and critical element in making the city a better place for its citizens.

AGGRESSIVE PERFORMANCE EXPECTATIONS
CAN DRIVE INNOVATION

Setting clear targets without specifying how they should be reached will stimulate a diversity of creative responses. The Royal Seaport set high initial targets for energy efficiency in buildings and keeps increasing them. The city decided that the district's development would unfold in three stages, each bringing a new area into existence, and that performance targets would be raised for each stage. This was a way to drive developers and builders to innovate and perform better and better. "Most of the developers take lessons out of their experiences here," Salmhofer explains. "They learn, for instance, how to build a passive house that doesn't need energy, how to build green roofs. And they see that all these features are attractive to people." So far developers are meeting the city's standards, which were tougher than national standards.

In urban systems, stretch goals for decarbonization and climate resilience can be embedded in the system's short- and long-range plans, as well as in managers' performance expectations.

INTEGRATING AT URBAN SYSTEM SCALE

When Mami Hara started in 2016 as CEO of Seattle Public Utilities, appointed by the mayor, a strategic priority she inherited was to prepare the city's drainage, wastewater, and water systems for climate change and to make the utility as carbon neutral as possible. In other words, SPU should become carbon-free, hyperefficient, exceptionally green, and highly adaptive.

That is happening, says Hara, as the utility enhances some of its current practices and adopts a range of innovations and new goals. In the last year, SPU's drinking water, storm water, wastewater, and solid waste lines of business have made plans and investments around climate change. "Water managers have collaborated on utility and regional climate planning," Hara says, "as well as testing new approaches for increasing water storage. The drainage and wastewater team is developing an integrated management plan to manage future risks and maximize social and environmental benefits. Solid waste is taking first steps toward electrification of its fleet, part of utility-wide efforts to expand the use of electric vehicles and installation of charging stations."

The utility partners with the communities it serves to develop goals and design changes. For example, Seattle already had a high recycling rate, Hara explains, "but now our community is asking us to go well beyond recycling and get to zero waste." In 2017, Seattle banned disposable plastic utensils and straws, adding them to a prohibition of plastic grocery bags. The utility also has a history of holding down water consumption, even as the region's population increased significantly. "Conservation resonates with the ethos of the people here and was achieved through collaboration," Hara says, "and now we have to plan together again—this time for more potential variations in water supply" due to climate change.

The city's stewardship value resonates professionally and personally with Hara, who came to Seattle with a reputation as a creative manager after five years as chief of staff of Philadelphia's water utility, which aggressively implemented green infrastructure to contain storm-water runoff.

The SPU has embraced green infrastructure. "We're on our way to fully understanding how to make our infrastructure investments as sustainable as possible," says Hara. "Our staff are aware they need to put every decision through a 'green filter.' But we have to get beyond just green infrastructure projects. We have to figure out what the optimal system planning and design scale is. That's part of how you get maximum benefit from the investments you make."

Recognizing that climate change will bring increased extreme precipitation to Seattle, the utility intends to develop a citywide "cloudburst" resilience plan, much as Copenhagen has done, which will support Seattle's values for social and economic equity and public health.

INTEGRATION REQUIRES CHAMPIONS WITH THE POWER TO MAKE BIG CHANGES

It's a basic rule for making radical changes at any scale in the public or private sector: find and unleash skilled leaders, change agents who know when and how hard to push, and back them up when the going gets tough. Change managers have to break down the traditional silos in their systems. They have to establish cooperation and coordination within their systems and with other systems. "Systems change requires radical rethinking of the way cities do their work," notes Johanna Partin, director of the Carbon Neutral Cities Alliance. "Otherwise, everyone is siloed into their little boxes running their programs or regulations. That won't lead to systems change." Champions also have to challenge or bypass old thinking. They have to try new things and resist succumbing to incrementalism, just tweaking things a bit. It takes time, not just skill, to pull all of this off.

In the Royal Seaport, says Salmhofer, her sustainability team helps coordinate experts from city departments to decide what requirements the Seaport will place on developers of its land: "City planning, environment, waste management, traffic, climate, urban development—we are all working together."

Coordination among government systems is needed so investments form a coherent whole in a district, says Mami Hara. She points to the city's Duwamish Valley area, which includes the Georgetown and South Park neighborhoods, each of which contends with a variety of climate- and pollution-related risks. South Park is a flood-prone area with a diverse, low-income residential community that is adjacent to an industrial site and has experienced significant health problems. "It became clear to community members and the city that a siloed approach wouldn't work to address climate risks," Hara says. The utility's initial plans for coping with flooding and sewer backups include building storm-water conveyance, a pumping station, and a water-treatment plant at significant cost. Additional investments in protective structures to manage flood risks would probably also be needed. Other large investments by the city's department of transportation and other public agencies are also called for—amounting to hundreds of millions of dollars in total planned spending for the valley.

Given the low-lying topography of the area, the high economic value of industrial activities there, the relatively low value of many of the industrial buildings, and the critical need for "antidisplacement" measures such as safe, affordable housing and a healthy environment for community members, the city established ways for its departments to collaborate with community members and business owners, as well as tribal entities, to develop a more holistic and long-term approach. They are refocusing, Hara says, on an integrative question: "Could we reinvest in a way that creates a more twenty-first- and twenty-second-century area, by looking differently at the resources, future conditions, climate drivers, and land elevations in key areas? This might change investments that are focused on maintaining current activities for a short while and don't address the full range of community and business interests."

PRIVATE MARKETS CAN BE LEVERAGED TO GENERATE DESIRED CHANGES

In the Royal Seaport, the final product of integration—neighborhoods for residents and businesses—has to take into account what the real estate market wants. Developers have to believe they can make a profit, and potential buyers and renters have to believe they are getting their money's worth. The success of Portland's comprehensive plan also hinges in large part on how well it appeals to the interests of real estate developers and residents. "Ninety-five percent of the city will be built by the private sector," explains Mark Raggett, a senior planner for the city. "We have to find the right balance between the city's design and the development community." It's only in recent years, he says, that there has been significant demand for higher-density, compact neighborhoods.

Seattle Public Utilities, a provider of services, has to pay close attention to what it charges users, its key market. Holding down prices is built right into its strategic plan.

ONE DESIGN DOES NOT FIT ALL

Portland's comprehensive plan seeks to increase the density of the city, but it embraces variation in how this is achieved. "We're establishing our intent: here is the way the city intends to grow—all in the service of its neighborhoods," says Raggett. "Everywhere will see some growth and change, but everything does not end up looking the same. We're being strategic about density." The plan contains a half-dozen density scenarios for parts of the city, based on local conditions and the historic roles of areas. There is the large central city; several town centers anchored by a range of commercial and public services, with housing options and parks or public squares; and many smaller neighborhood centers that are hubs for local activities and gathering: "We're acknowledging that some of these areas are physically different and their residents may not value neighborhood assets in the same way. Some of the areas don't want to look like the inner city."

GUIDING CHANGE AT CITY SCALE

Portland's comprehensive plan for 2035 designs the evolution of the city's physical space to build on the city's assets: attractive neighborhoods, an active downtown, recreational waterfronts, a mix of historical buildings and districts, and an attractive natural setting of rivers and mountains. But it is also a plan for change that employs transformational ideas at city scale.

The 175-year-old city had grown rapidly around a dense central business district and waterfront before streetcar lines extending out from downtown enabled the development of a grid of streets and homes. After World War II, Portland redesigned for the automobile: freeways and high-volume roads were constructed; buildings in the center were razed to create parking lots. Further development in the twentieth century featured a typical suburban pattern of large tracts and privileging cars. Moving into the twenty-first century, the city had a number of neighborhoods that didn't meet the everyday needs of residents and weren't easily walked or biked. It had transportation corridors that discouraged walking and biking as mobility options. Most of its green spaces lay at the edges of the city and were unconnected to each other.

The Portland envisioned for 2035 will have moved a long way toward becoming carbon-free and more efficient and green—and the comprehensive plan holds one key for getting there. The city's "preferred growth scenario," explains the plan's Urban Design Direction, has several elements:

- Create "complete neighborhoods" in the form of more densely built-up and populated centers and corridors with "new mixed use and multi-story buildings on sites with the most redevelopment potential, such as surface parking lots, underutilized parcels and vacant lands."

- Improve, expand, and link natural areas, open spaces, and urban habitat areas using a citywide network of trails and park-like corridors that promote "active living, for both recreation and transportation, for people of all ages and abilities."

Portland Urban Design Direction: City of Portland Planning and Sustainability, "Urban Design Direction," accessed November 16, 2017, available for download at www.portlandoregon.gov/bps/65430, 14, 16, 31, 32.

> New urban habitat corridors, with native plants, tree plant-
> ings, vegetated storm-water facilities, and ecoroofs, will
> "green up" neighborhoods and business areas and help
> make the city more climate resilient.
>
> - Use mass-transit lines and greenways for biking and walk-
>   ing to support more Portlanders "by strengthening sense
>   of place, reducing reliance on cars, and encouraging active
>   healthy lifestyles." "Green Loop," a six-mile linear park in
>   the central city, would serve as a hub for the greenways net-
>   work while neighborhood greenways would be streets with
>   low volumes of cars and priority for bicycles.

Revising the Urban OS

In June 2016, 77 percent of voters in San Francisco—186,000
people—joined with voters in eight surrounding counties to approve
$500 million in new taxes to restore twenty thousand acres of wet-
lands of the San Francisco Bay and defend against rising sea levels.
The scientific analysis and case for restoration had been made years
earlier in a well-publicized process. The campaign to approve Measure AA, a $12 annual tax on land parcels in the region for twenty
years, tapped into the community's passionate love of the Bay and its
understanding of climate change.

It's remarkable any time such a large majority of voters agrees
to increase their taxes for any reason, but we highlight this development for a different purpose. It offers a version of the changing
urban operating system that is emerging in cities worldwide to
enable and sustain the innovations and radical transformations that
respond to the climate imperative. This climate-ready operating
system has three basic elements: new governance models, technical
capacities, and financial resources.

Innovation lab cities tend to develop the models and capacities
they need on the fly and just temporarily, and they try to work
around limitations on their governance authority over critical factors like regulation of buildings or investment in transportation
infrastructure. But patching things together that way won't work
over the long and complex run. What's needed is the development

of a next-generation urban operating system that fills gaps in cities' abilities to handle climate change. Like San Francisco, some climate innovation lab cities are already moving into this unmapped terrain.

DEVELOPING NEW GOVERNANCE MODELS

San Francisco's Measure AA characterizes a regional-collaboration approach—a temporary, focused alliance in which the city and eight county governments, several regional environmental and development authorities, and key nonprofit organizations in the Bay area aligned to design a ballot proposal and then organize a successful campaign that drew more than 1.1 million votes and established critical funding for two decades.

Regional alliances of this sort are particularly important in urban areas that have numerous local government jurisdictions. They bypass the more difficult task of restructuring governance into a single regional government, a model that has never been widely accepted in the US. Some cities—Toronto, Milan, and several cities in the United Kingdom—have recently moved toward a form of metropolitan-area government.

Other governance shifts are under way due to climate change. In Germany, the national government has been "remunicipalizing" the energy-supply sector, returning control to major cities' governments, partly to avoid national policy barriers to sufficient investment in decarbonization. "Decentralized and locally owned energy systems have played a positive role in facilitating the growth of renewable energy in Germany," reports Andrew Cumbers in *Can a City Be Sustainable?* In China, dozens of cities have received authorization from the national government to serve as pilot sites for innovations in use of green infrastructure, development of carbon-emissions markets, and other efforts to reduce energy consumption and GHG emissions.

What's apparent, then, is a scattering of power-sharing and power-shifting changes on the vertical axis of government levels— local up to national—and the horizontal axis of government jurisdictions within an area. (Note the counterexample of state governments in the US, some of which have prohibited certain actions by cities, such as the banning of plastic bags.) These efforts, Benjamin Barber points out, help cities align their authority with the things they now need to do, such as taking climate action. At the same time, he adds, because economic and political power have migrated to the global level, "cities must act together"—beyond just their local areas—"in order to assure the efficacy of what they try to do alone." Cooperation produces influence.

Various analysts contend that these trends will increase because cities are where problems like climate change mostly must be addressed and where people expect their leaders to deal with daily life concerns. Barber tells the story of when President Bill Clinton did a radio talk show in China with the mayor of Shanghai: "Two-thirds of the incoming calls were for the mayor. Reporters were surprised, but the former president, no stranger to local politics in Arkansas, got it: 'People were more interested in talking to the mayor about potholes and traffic jams,' he recalled."

The pattern seems to be that cities get more control or influence when other governments, horizontally or vertically, realize that they cannot solve a problem that they must solve for their own benefit. As climate disruptions increase, so will this driver of governance reinvention. The form that new governance arrangements take will likely be designed case by case rather than with a widely used model, because existing governance models vary so much worldwide.

DEVELOPING NEW TECHNICAL CAPACITIES

San Francisco, New York City, Boston, and other cities have established scientific advisory boards to help them understand and monitor what is happening in climate change and how it might impact the city. But this is just one of the new technical capacities, readily available expertise, that cities find they now need to be able to analyze, plan, design, and manage climate innovations in core urban systems. Most cities have little previous experience in understanding their energy-supply systems, much less figuring out how to reinvent them. Few cities knew much about designing bicycle networks that would appeal to potential riders. No city knew anything about setting up a charging infrastructure for electric vehicles.

To develop these capacities, city governments have hired, purchased, and partnered. Some have built up staffing in areas that appear to require long-term involvement, such as coastal management. A typical practice is to purchase consulting services, which can bring a city useful analytic tools and processes as well as experience from other cities. Some cities have been able to use funds from philanthropies to pay for short-term employees or consultants. Their employees attend conferences to get state-of-the-art know-how and attend training to become certified in new practices. They participate in city-to-city exchanges, using organizations like C40, 100 Resilient Cities, and the Urban Sustainability Directors Network, to find out what peers are doing and learning. They call on the private sector to join task forces and study groups, lend their expertise, and shape recommendations for action. They partner with nonprofit organizations and universities that have developed relevant specialized knowledge and may have designed tools for others to use. And they tap into the "indigenous knowledge" of community members, who bring lived experience and understanding to the table.

As individual cities scramble to get what they need, the growing demand for technical competence suggests that a new, organized, and sustained capacity to serve cities is needed in the climate-change era. Urban planning emerged as a widespread and organized practice in the twentieth century, not just something cities did every now and then. The design and management of decarbonized and resilient urban systems is an enormous technical challenge that will last for many decades. The response to this need so far has been rapid and significant but also makeshift and fragmented among many participants. While this may have been all that was possible to do in the short run, it does not yet involve the sort of intentional design and investment that could build a globally distributed, multidisciplinary, collaborative technical capacity that cities can use.

DEVELOPING NEW AND EXPANDED FINANCIAL RESOURCES

Innovative cities need risk capital to support the early stages of climate-innovation development that city budgets can't be asked to fund because taxpayers and elected officials have a low tolerance for the failure inherent in experimentation. That was the collective message of the mayors of Oslo, Rio de Janeiro, Sydney, and Vancouver during a workshop at C40's December 2016 summit in Mexico City. These cities belong to the CNCA, which has invested nearly

$2.5 million, provided by philanthropies, in two-dozen innovation projects developed by its twenty member-cities. "Even cities that have money for innovation have to justify what they spend it on," says CNCA's Partin. "Working with other CNCA cities lets them say that they have checked with other cities in the world that are intensely focused on becoming carbon neutral."

Risk capital for innovation is just one of the climate-driven capital challenges faced by cities during the next few decades. Even in small cities, decarbonizing urban energy, transportation, building, and waste systems may require billions of dollars for new equipment, infrastructure, and other hard assets, as well as more funds for operations. In 2016, C40 estimated that its city members had to spend $375 billion by 2020 and about $800 billion more between 2020 and 2050 to achieve carbon-reduction goals. Strengthening just the physical resilience of cities globally may require trillions of dollars.

Where will all this money come from? How much will be paid by governments, businesses, or property owners and other residents? How much of government's portion will be paid by local taxpayers, how much by users of water, transportation, and other public services, and how much by other levels of government? How much can cities borrow to cover large front-end costs of projects; how much will they have to pay as they go? Are there new sources of revenue that cities can tap to pay for investments and borrowing? What will cities do about the potential of investments in new infrastructure to generate financial and quality-of-life benefits for some residents in project areas while threatening to displace or disadvantage other residents? What can cities seeking private investment do to reduce the financial risks or increase the potential financial returns of private investors? How can cities persuade voters or customers of municipal services to accept increased costs?

Given the challenge of finding more money, cities are adopting policies requiring that future infrastructure projects that must happen—maintenance and upgrade of roads, streets, and water systems, for example—incorporate planning for climate adaptation. San Francisco, for instance, requires that future capital projects include plans for adapting to sea-level rise.

At the same time, innovations are emerging from a wide range of private investment entities and corporations; local, state, and national governments; development agencies like the World Bank; and philanthropies and wealthy individuals. For instance, carbon-trading markets run by nations or states already produce billions of dollars of revenue that can be invested in climate actions, and some cities are studying how to extend these markets to include auto emissions and carbon sequestration in soil. Washington, DC, issued a unique outcome-based green bond that provides investors with a lower rate of return if the green storm-water infrastructure that is installed does not perform as expected. The city also launched a green bank to use small amounts of public capital to leverage private funding for solar energy, energy efficiency, and other local projects. Copenhagen, New York City, and other cities have worked with engineering consulting firms to develop a credible methodology for calculating the social return on investment, the "business case," for local-government spending on green infrastructure. An initiative by Energy Efficiency for All, a local-state-national coalition of more than fifty environmental, affordable housing, and other advocacy nonprofits in the US, has generated more than $315 million in funding from energy utilities for retrofitting low-income multifamily housing.

These innovations are mostly promising pilots, and it's hard to discern patterns at this point that might unleash huge amounts of climate-focused capital. The inventions tend to focus on specific financial products, such as bonds or insurance. But that doesn't address what may be needed in the long run: an organized, "one-stop," permanent capacity that cities can use to assess their climate risks and opportunities; develop fundable projects, including at regional scale; design projects to achieve equitable outcomes; develop new revenue streams to pay for projects; effectively access various types of capital; and meet other critical needs.

Insistent Issues

Even as the world's most climate-smart cities succeed in applying transformational ideas—refining innovations, producing new ones, integrating innovations, and developing governance, technical, and financial capacities that support innovation for the long haul—they face a number of persistent questions about what they are doing and achieving, matters for which prevailing practices have not yet emerged.

WHICH RESIDENTS WILL BENEFIT?

In most if not every city, historic patterns of discrimination against races, ethnicities, religions, and economic classes have guided the distribution of benefits and costs and shaped socioeconomic disparities among groups of people and places in the city, including exposure to pollution; access to green space, public transportation, and services; and vulnerability to flooding and other extreme weather events. Will these patterns continue, or will they change? How far will cities go to acknowledge and address the social and economic harm that some residents have experienced? Will cities, in which the cost of living seems sure to rise in order to strengthen climate resilience, displace low-income populations and become havens solely for the affluent? Will they seek the "just distribution of the fruits of the earth" that Pope Francis called for?

Copenhagen Lord Mayor Frank Jensen insists that his city should be "a city for all." Cape Town is explicit about using innovations like transit-oriented development to repair the damage caused by years of apartheid. Shanghai contains thousands of rural migrants working in factories and living in dormitories or cheap shantytowns—part of a national economic pattern of low-wage urban employment. New York City Mayor Bill de Blasio linked his initiative for increasing energy efficiency in buildings with an agenda to increase the number of affordable housing units in the city. In most American lab cities, elected officials and community-based organizations advocate for "equity" in city decision-making processes and actions so the voices and interests of historically marginalized groups will be empowered.

WHAT ABOUT OTHER GHG EMISSIONS?

As innovative cities show how much they can do to reduce emissions within their borders, will they also develop broader efforts to cut emissions discharged elsewhere to make products and services used by people in cities—cars, food, and air travel, for example? A few cities are assessing their "consumption-based" emissions, but most cities focus only on locally released emissions. This understates the urban contribution to global warming and, perhaps, minimizes the creativity and influence cities may bring to the challenge.

WHAT ABOUT OTHER CITIES AND PLACES?

As innovative cities strengthen their economies and climate resilience, will they develop into an exclusive global network of wealthy, productive, and resilient urban areas at the expense of other cities and rural and agricultural areas? Will "the rich getting richer" be the favored pattern, or is a more widely shared urban-rural prosperity in the cards?

So many tough questions for cities to answer, so much more innovating to do to extend, spread, and deepen changes. Driven by climate change, the world's cities have entered a time of continuous urban reinvention that will certainly last through the twenty-first century. The framework of ideas that is replacing the modern city framework is still coming together.

13 A NEW URBAN FUTURE?

—

There is so much that can go wrong, even with ideas whose time has come.

—JEREMY RIFKIN

Nearly two centuries have passed between the birth of modern Melbourne along the Yarra River and the rise of Stockholm's Royal Seaport district next to the Baltic Sea, between Dean Stewart's song and Christina Salmhofer's story. That's a barely noticeable period on Gaia's lifeline of billions of years and only a small fraction of the time that humanity has been making cities. In that short span, the modern city emerged as a paradigm for economic, energetic, ecological, and social life and spread across the planet. More recently, though, the modern urban model has been losing its hold on imagination and action, because it cannot solve the climate problem it helped cause. New ideas are in play and a new model for urban development, a better paradigm, is forming.

Although we've examined the four transformational ideas separately, they are all of a piece. At heart, they respond to the challenge that climate change poses to modern ideas about our relationship with nature. We have polluted, overconsumed, wasted, overridden, separated from, and ignored nature. These destructive behaviors are so pervasive and their consequences so extreme that it's not enough to change just some of them; nearly everything about the way cities relate to nature has to change.

The ideas that serve this revolutionary purpose can be woven together into a new model for the development of cities, as we saw some innovation lab cities beginning to do at district, system, and citywide scales. Economic innovation based on renewable energy is compatible with zero waste and circularity, and these are compatible with realizing nature's full benefits, and all are compatible with developing a city's capacities to adapt in the future.

Edward O. Wilson offers a glimpse of some of this potential alignment when he asserts, in *Half-Earth*, that per-capita consumption will decline thanks to the free-market system: "The products that win competition today, and will continue to do so indefinitely, are those that cost less to manufacture and advertise, need less frequent repair and replacement, and give highest performance with a minimum amount of energy." A different kind of economic growth will emerge, he continues, based on increased performance instead of consumption, striving for quality of life in the context of environmental stability instead of accumulation of material wealth.

Wilson's future is more the stuff of vision than of practice—for now. But evidence is mounting that cities can evolve along the new lines we've examined. In just a few decades, we have seen the global rise of climate innovation lab cities, the spread of early adopter cities, the influential reach of swarms of allied urban climate rebels, and the emergence of market forces, professional standards, community and consumer demands, and government policies that are driving changes once unimagined.

In assessing the progress of the transition away from the modern city model, we are mindful that the transformational ideas we have identified must compete with other ideas. The contest can be thought of as a zero-sum, winner-take-all clash or a creative dialectic from which a new synthesis will emerge, as a natural transition between generations, or an evolutionary dynamic that can ascend to a new model, descend into chaos, or regress to a previous condition. But we also know that cities are living, evolving systems that, as urban planner Michael Batty says in *The New Science of Cities*, "can change abruptly and with surprising consequences."

Good News/Bad News

Change seems to have reached a fulcrum point at which advances and retreats fluctuate; good and bad developments appear in seemingly equal measure, so direction feels erratic.

The amount of global renewable energy is up, but so is the amount of fossil fuel being burned. Even though some nations, cities, and corporations are slowing their GHG emissions, the amount of CO_2 in the air increased in 2017. In 2017, Australia's emissions reached their highest level ever, even though the nation's amount of wind-generated electricity soared. Although Germany has mounted one of the world's most aggressive national efforts to decarbonize, it will not achieve its 2020 targets for GHG-emissions reduction.

The amount of recycled waste is up, but so is the total amount of waste—and global waste production is expected to increase for decades before peaking.

European nations have pledged to reduce consumption that results in deforestation—but that consumption has been increasing.

Even as China positions itself as an international leader in addressing climate change—developing the world's largest carbon-trading market and consumer market for electric vehicles—it remains the world's largest consumer of coal and builds coal-fired plants in other countries.

Oslo, the capital of Norway, is a world leader in tackling GHG emissions, but the nation continues to profit from pumping North Sea oil and gas. Miami is the poster child for inescapable, destructive sea-level rise, but property values in the city keep rising, and so does real estate development.

Companies that publicly support doing something about climate change also fund opposition to policy changes in America. As some automakers announce intentions to go all-electric, some of the same companies push for less stringent fuel-economy standards for vehicles in the US.

This vexing pattern of wins and losses shows that life-after-carbon change has momentum but is not yet at a "tipping point" that will overwhelm the old order and generate its own sustainable motion.

Expect Surprises

Technology developments for dealing with climate change are already bringing cities new options and risks, and more advances are likely. The arrival of autonomous vehicles (AVs) on city streets, a development some forty years in the making, raises questions about urban transportation systems that cities are just starting to wrestle with. Will the use of AVs boost or injure city efforts to reduce driving and vehicle-miles traveled? Developments in battery storage can be anticipated, with impacts on the design and performance of urban electricity systems. But again, how might they advance or hinder cities' climate-change efforts?

The biggest potentially disruptive technology application ahead is geoengineering, the use of biological and chemical methods to capture and sequester large amounts of atmospheric CO_2 or other methods to reflect solar radiation into space before it reaches earth and heats the atmosphere. Modeling and conceptualizing are under way, and in-the-field research has begun on several methods—but there are no rules, international laws, or agreements in place to guide or prevent a nation, company, or individual intent on initiating a geoengineering effort. If devastation from climate impacts increases and/or global GHG emissions keep rising, will someone act unilaterally? What would be the effects of geoengineering on GHG levels? What would be its environmental, economic, and social impacts? How would it affect the will of cities to keep innovating to reduce emissions or strengthen climate resilience?

Technology is just one source of potential surprise. Might the rise of nationalist politics in the US, Europe, and elsewhere erect policy walls that affect international cooperation on climate change? How much more or less aggressive will nations be in pursuing GHG reductions, given that the total of their pledges in Paris do not come close to meeting global targets for emissions reduction? Will climate-induced migration of millions of people, across national borders but also into cities from afflicted rural areas, overwhelm the resources of cities and end their openness to all comers? Will more people adopt "big-impact" ways to reduce carbon emissions, such as eating less meat—feasting instead on plant-based "burgers"—and having fewer children? Will more behavior-change campaigns and media about climate disasters prompt people to reduce consumption, as happened when Californians, inundated with drought news, cut water usage even before the state mandated water restrictions? Will a new data-driven "science of cities" help us to predict more about how cities evolve and to plan more effectively? Will more of the richest 1 percent of the world's population, who own half of global wealth, put their money and influence to work on behalf of climate action? Will climate disasters overwhelm cities and nations in a cascading, global environmental crisis that, along with other destructive forces, produces a severe economic and social collapse, much as earlier civilizations have fallen?

Although a climate-driven pathway has opened up for the evolution of cities, there will be twists and turns, potholes, roadblocks, and detours along the way. Arrival at an envisioned and desired future is far from guaranteed—but it cannot be ruled out.

Which Urban Future?

We live in "the century of the city," declared a 2008 report based on a global urban summit staged by the Rockefeller Foundation. "An urban future for mankind has dawned," the account continued. "The most massive population movement the world has ever seen," from rural to urban areas, will occupy cities with 70 percent of all people by 2050. This urban future is filled with vast challenges and startling opportunities, and it is urgent to act because the window of opportunity won't stay open forever: "There is no time to lose." Climate change was just one of many staggering urban problems the report identified, along with water, sanitation, shelter, health, inclusion, transportation, and the large gap in wealth between developed and developing cities.

As summit participants shared promising approaches with each other, they agreed that responses to these challenges had to be systemic, multisectoral, multidisciplinary, and workable at local, regional, and international scales. They said that the brightest and most creative minds would have to apply their skills and knowledge. Leaders everywhere had to join in a global movement to invest in ideas, institutions, and individuals making change.

This is precisely what climate innovation lab and other leading-edge cities have been doing, with their efforts reinforced, accelerated, and spread by other actors around the globe. Contained within their innovations are ideas that, even as they respond to climate change, have the power to alter the course our urbanizing planet is on. They do this by reshaping what we think a city is and by offering a better future city. "When I think about the personality of innovative cities," says CNCA's Johanna Partin, "there's a lot of pride about the local place, because it's innovative, risk taking. Everybody wants to be a city of the future, not a city of the past."

Imagine a city in which a critical mass of residents and workers understand that climate change is occurring; are motivated to act out of concern for their own well-being and that of others and future generations; realize that climate action can create economic opportunity, affordability, improved public health, and other significant benefits for the city; agree on investing in the strategies the city should use to decarbonize and build resilience; and are taking climate actions as individuals or in community groups, not just waiting for local government to act.

We took these specific characteristics from Boulder, where a set of community dialogues, focus groups, and surveys offer a picture of a highly aware, concerned, aligned, and action-oriented community. Boulder is an affluent city with a large highly educated, environment-friendly population, but this sort of widespread climate-based culture exists in other cities as well. It is most evident in the cities' political and institutional willingness to innovate and in the risk-taking leadership provided by their local governments, businesses, professionals, and community-based entities.

Austin Mayor Steve Adler has seen new ideas shape his city's culture since he settled there in the 1970s: "We were the 42nd largest city in the country, and today we're the eleventh." One of America's fastest-growing cities, Austin has more than nine hundred thousand people. "I think the reason Austin has grown so rapidly," Adler says, "why it has attracted the creative and entrepreneurial people, the forward lookers, the early adopters, is because of who we are culturally, because of the values that we have in the community. They are built around resilience and innovation. They are built around the environment. We try to demonstrate that an interest in the environment and sustainability does not come at an economic cost for the city. We're rated as one of the best cities in the country for the creation of new businesses. We create more middle-class jobs per capita than any city in the country. We don't do that *despite* the values that we have; it happens *because* those are our values."

In Austin, Boulder, and other cities, the many individuals and organizations working on GHG reduction and climate resilience are becoming highly networked and aligned in their purpose—forming a large and growing critical mass, an "innovation ecology," within each city's broader culture. They affect what the city is aware of and cares about, what it talks and thinks about, and what it wants done and is willing to do. They are changing modern urban culture, the way of feeling, thinking, and behaving that developed during the last two hundred years and became the prevailing urban norm.

As cities that are aggressively tackling climate change mature, the content of their local cultures increasingly embodies transformational ideas that express new desires and expectations and upend modern thinking and values. As these ideas and their innovations bring about real-world changes and the envisioned benefits, they win more hearts and minds. Being innovative, efficient, green, and adaptive becomes an explicit and important part of a city's emerging culture, a civic consensus about direction, a new normal, and a force that can sustain change through the next generations.

New ideas are taking hold in cities. They feed our needs and nourish our desires. They provide us with a new story about our future together. They fire our imaginations. They are transforming our cities.

EPILOGUE

—

Time Is Our Frenemy

*I have not seen a flaw in people as great as the flaw of
the able not reaching their potential.*

—IBN AL JAWZI

In the life of a modern city and society, thirty to eighty years—the
distance from now to 2050 or 2100—can bring many big changes.
Think back thirty years to 1990, when the world was just becoming
aware of global warming: half of today's global population wasn't
yet born, the Rio de Janeiro Earth Summit and Kyoto Protocol
hadn't occurred, no auto company was selling electric vehicles, solar
and wind power cost many times more than fossil-fuel power, and
no websites or smartphones existed. Think further back to 1940:
Europe was at war, parts of China were under Japanese control,
apartheid ruled South Africa, the US interstate highway system had
not been built, and the tallest building in Shanghai—and Asia—was
the twenty-two-floor Park Hotel.

The thirty years that will pass before we reach 2050 may sound
like a long time, but it is not. Some of then is being determined now.
Today's decisions about codes for new buildings and standards for
infrastructure—streets, roads, bridges, electricity grids, and more—
will live on for the rest of the century. Comprehensive plans for cities
that determine zoning and urban form will also have an enduring
impact. It can take decades to transition huge consumer markets,
such as for automobiles, because of the rate at which consumers
replace old products with new ones. A risk is that current trends

of consumption and infrastructure development will lock into place a high level of future emissions. If this happens, estimates a C40 report, "Deadline 2020," by 2050 as many as 1.3 billion people and assets worth $158 trillion would be put at risk from climate changes.

Thirty years is also the time span of a human generation—a cohort of people who are born in the same time period and experience similar significant events. Today, the Millennial generation is starting to occupy the seats of power that the Baby Boomer generation is relinquishing. Two to three decades from now, millennials will start exiting from the stage, to be replaced by members of Generation Z, born since 1995. So the next thirty years inevitably contain a passing of the torch between generations—not just to struggle with climate change but also to continue the evolution of cities.

Generational change was on Christiana Figueres's mind when she addressed college students at the University of Massachusetts–Boston about one hundred days after completing the difficult brokering of international negotiations that concluded in the UN's 2016 Paris climate accord. A seasoned Costa Rican diplomat and the mother of two adult children, Figueres began her twenty-minute presentation with a reminder that something unprecedented was under way: "We humans have managed to change the nature of nature. We are determining the evolution of the planet, for the first time in the history of the planet."

A little later, she spoke from the heart to the college students in the audience. "To the young generation who is here," she began, then paused, slightly nodding her head. "Let me say, you are the first generation"—she halted again—"that enters the productive economy in full knowledge that you are walking into a planet that is irreversibly changed. You are the first generation." After another pause, she wiped tears from her face. "Our generation had to learn, we didn't know. We inherited this. And we had to learn. We had to understand the impacts of climate change and we had to pull ourselves from our bootstraps and make sure that we did the best that we could. Frankly, we have not done enough."

Figueres did not end on this painfully candid note. "You have the cards in your hand to solve it, and you will," she said. "Our generation had the responsibility to understand. Your generation can turn that into the greatest opportunity that this planet has ever seen." There is an opportunity not just to address climate change, she continued, but, in the process, to create "a completely different society than we have right now."

That magnificent opportunity, it is clear, will live or die in our planet's cities. The need to change the fundamentals of city life—to have an earth that is urban, blue, and green in the age of climate change—is evident. A feasible vision for the next city is forming. Human ingenuity has been sparked into splendid motion; urban climate innovation, the motor of radical change, is humming. Different and better ideas for city building are rising, intensifying, and expanding. They show the way.

ACKNOWLEDGMENTS

—

It's knowing what can be done that gives people the
courage to fight.

—JANE GOODALL

On December 22, 2015, at the kickoff of the adventure that became this book, we consulted the *I Ching*, which advised us to "accept and welcome those who wish to join you, but do not pursue anyone who appears reluctant." Since then, many have joined and helped, sharing their expertise, experiences, and enthusiasm for our often vague or slow-moving project. (The oracle also counseled, "You have an eternity of lifetimes ahead of you in which to carry out your work." Sometimes it felt like a few of those lives might be needed.)

Our community of courageous urban climate rebels has encouraged and supported our commitment to figuring out and sharing what is known and can be done, so that others may follow and contribute.

First, a roll call of joiners, then a few call outs.

Thank you Jørgen Abildgaard, Richard Anderson, Susan Anderson, Michael Armstrong, Tim Beatley, Jessica Boehland, David Burdette, Christopher Chan, Amy Chester, Gary Cohen, Carl Costello, Lois DeBacker, Dong Peng, Marcia Ente, Fan Dongxing, Barbara Finamore, Adam Freed, Aaron Straus Garcia, Alan Greenberger, Guo Jianli (Jerry), Mami Hara, He Dongquan, Linda Holmstrom, Amos Hostetter, Eva Hsu, Bjorn Hugosson, Taj James, Frank Jensen, Håkon Jentoft, Kate Johnson, Sadhu Johnston, Roya Kazemi, Paul Kirshen, Bryan Koop, Jean Ku, Mette Søs Lassesen, John Lee, Robert Lempert, Mindy Lubber, Atyia Martin, Vincent Martinez, Ed Mazria, Fei Meng, Nils Moe, Steve Nicholas, Michael Northrop,

Melanie Nutter, Manuel Olivera, Donnie Oliveira, Henk Ovink, Johanna Partin, Mariella Puerto, Mark Raggett, Debbie Raphael, Trude Rauken, Graham Richard, Bud Ris, Mary Skelton Roberts, Gregor Robertson, Rodrigo Rosa, Christina Salmhofer, Eric Sanderson, Seth Schultz, Bernardo Baranda Sepúlveda, Neelima Shah, Brendan Shane, Ian Shears, Malcolm Shield, Kelly Shultz, Jill Simmons, Doug Smith, Dean Stewart, Dr. Susanna Sutherland, Brian Swett, Ken Thorp and family, Tian Zhan, Aisa Tobing, Maggie Ullman, Bill Updike, Mijo Vodopic, Sarah Ward, Morley Winograd, Darryl Young, Zang Ao Quan, and Joe Zehnder.

The Kresge Foundation provided a crucial grant, without which we would not have been able to undertake this project. Jessica Boehland, senior program officer for environment at Kresge, served as partner and sounding board, bringing her extensive knowledge and critical judgment to the project. The Summit Foundation provided additional funding for marketing the book, a hard-to-get resource in the nonprofit sector that we inhabit. Darryl Young, director of sustainable cities at Summit, offered wholehearted support when the book was just a two-page concept paper. Much thanks also to the Barr Foundation, which has been a lead funder of John Cleveland's work with the Boston Green Ribbon Commission.

To our publisher, Island Press, we offer thanks two ways. Thank you to the Island Press team—Heather Boyer, Milan Bozic, Kyler Geoffroy, Jamie Jennings, Julie Marshall, David Miller, Sharis Simonian, and Josh Wilkerson—for betting on the potential value of this book before it had been fully articulated and for ushering us through the manuscript development, book design, and production processes. (We weren't always easy to work with, we know.) And thank you, Island Press the organization, a nonprofit started in 1984 with a mission to communicate ideas for solving environmental problems. The Island Press canon, especially books concerning the built environment, was a fabulous resource for us. Time after time, books that provided important insights and examples turned out to be Island Press publications. We hope *Life after Carbon* adds to the written bounty.

People who know us well won't be surprised to learn that we have relied, once again, on the generosity and understanding of our families. Without their feedback and patient support, it would have been impossible to complete this project. Our gratitude is without limit.

In the preceding pages, we've treated cities as living entities and decision-making actors in the story we tell. How do you say thank you to your muse when it is several dozen cities? Other writers have explored the experience and meaning of cities in poems, songs, novels, histories, and journalism—offering their devotion and a portion of their lives. This book is our way of doing the same.

NOTES

—

All quotations that are not attributed in the text or in these end-notes are from interviews by the authors or from presentations attended by the authors.

Calvino quote: Italo Calvino, *Invisible Cities*, trans. William Weaver (New York: Harcourt, 1974), 44.

Margulis quote: from Lynn Margulis, "Gaia Is a Tough Bitch," in John Brockman, *The Third Culture: Beyond the Scientific Revolution* (New York: Simon & Schuster, 1995).

Kuhn quote: Cited in Lisa Bennett, "10 Things You Want to Know about Human Nature If You're Fighting Climate Change," *Grist*, June 10, 2015, http://grist.org/climate-energy/10-things-you-want-to-know-about-human-nature-if-youre-fighting-climate-change/.

Prologue: Creation Stories

Aboriginal guided tour of Melbourne: Dean Stewart owns and operates Aboriginal Tours and Education Melbourne. The guided walk of Melbourne on which this account is based occurred on July 9, 2017, with members of the Carbon Neutral Cities Alliance. For more on Stewart and the inspiring walks he leads, see https://www.youtube.com/watch?v=fkMhehS-iqo, https://www.youtube.com/watch?v=_UlUHjQ1QyA, and http://www.theage.com.au/news/national/dreamtime-a-reality/2008/01/10/1199554822371.html?page=fullpage. For a cultural landscape map Stewart helped produce, see http://www.portphillip.vic.gov.au/Ngargee_to_Nerm_DL_V12.pdf.

Introduction

Monbiot quote: George Monbiot, "Neoliberalism: The Deep Story That Lies beneath Donald Trump's Triumph," *Guardian*, November 14, 2016, https://www.theguardian.com/commentisfree/2016/nov/14/neoliberalsim-donald-trump-george-monbiot.

Travis quote: Will Travis, "Shoreline of the Future: Permanently Temporary," *Meeting of the Minds*, August 3, 2017, http://meetingoftheminds.org/the-shoreline-of-the-future-permanently-temporary-13099?.

Where an estimated . . . live today: For the US estimate, see Mark Crowell et al., "How Many People Live in Coastal Areas?," *Journal of Coastal Research* 23, no. 5 (2007), http://www.jcronline.org/doi/full/10.2112/07A-0017.1. Note that 30 percent of the US population would be more than one hundred million people; for China's estimate, see Henry Gass, "More Chinese on the Coast, Less Fish in the Sea," *Scientific American*, August 8, 2014, https://www.scientificamerican.com/article/more-chinese-on-the-coast-less-fish-in-the-sea/.

Their climate innovations are generating . . . energy costs: See C40 Cities and LSE Cities, "Co-benefits of Urban Climate Action: A Framework for Cities," September 2016, http://www.c40.org/researches/c40-lse-cobenefits.

Glaeser quote: Edward Glaeser, *Triumph of the City: How Our Greatest Invention Makes Us Richer, Smarter, Greener, Healthier, and Happier* (New York: Penguin, 2011), 1.

Mumford quote: Lewis Mumford, *The City in History: Its Origins, Its Transformations, and Its Prospects* (New York: Harcourt, 1989), 34, 35.

Just a few cities . . . as one million residents: Only six other cities are believed by demographers to have reached this size before the eighteenth century: Alexandria in Egypt; Rome in the centuries before and after Christ; Chang'an, Kaifeng, and Hangzou in China between AD 700 and 1200; and Ayutthaya in Thailand, destroyed militarily in 1767.

Worldwide, more than five hundred . . . ten million people each: United Nations, "The World's Cities in 2016: Data Booklet," accessed September 5, 2017, http://www.un.org/en/

development/desa/population/publications/pdf/urbanization/
the_worlds_cities_in_2016_data_booklet.pdf.

A single megacity ... lifetimes ago: "Megacity," *Wikipedia*, accessed January 21, 2018, https://en.wikipedia.org/wiki/Megacity.

By 2050, the United Nations ... dwell in cities: United Nations, "World's Population Increasingly Urban with More than Half Living in Urban Areas," July 10, 2014, http://www.un.org/en/development/desa/news/population/world-urbanization-prospects-2014.html.

Shepard quote: Wade Shepard, *Ghost Cities of China: The Story of Cities without People in the World's Most Populated Country* (London: Zed, 2015), 44–45.

Rohter quote: Larry Rohter, "Rio: The War of the Favelas," *New York Review of Books*, May 12, 2016, 62.

Chapter 1: Innovation Proliferation

Hidalgo quote: Compact of Mayors, "Climate Leaders from around the World Show Support for Compact of Mayors and Covenant of Mayors Merger," *Medium*, June 22, 2016, https://medium.com/compact-of-mayors/climate-leaders-from-around-the-world-show-support-for-compact-of-mayors-covenant-of-mayors-92d4b42ec42e.

The $60-million Living Breakwaters ... Hurricane Sandy: Governor's Office of Storm Recovery, "Learn More about the Living Breakwaters Project," https://stormrecovery.ny.gov/learn-more-about-living-breakwaters-project; and Rebuild By Design, "Living Breakwaters," http://www.rebuildbydesign.org/our-work/all-proposals/winning-projects/ny-living-breakwaters, both accessed September 10, 2017.

Living Breakwaters project designers' quote: Buckminster Fuller Institute, "Living Breakwaters," accessed September 10, 2017, https://www.bfi.org/ideaindex/projects/2014/living-breakwaters.

Hayes quote: Sadhu Aufochs Johnson, Steven S. Nicholas, and Julia Parzen, *The Guide to Greening Cities* (Washington, DC: Island Press, 2013), 46.

In Minneapolis ... forty thousand riders each weekday: Wikipedia contributors, "Metro Green Line (Minnesota)," accessed

January 21, 2018, https://en.wikipedia.org/wiki/Metro_Green _Line_(Minnesota).

The first African . . . change strategy: City of Cape Town, "Energy Futures Report: Cape Town," September 2015, http://samset project.net/wp-content/uploads/2016/02/Cape-Town-decision -makers-report-2015.pdf.

Johnston quote: Peter Plastrik et al., *Connecting to Change the World: Harnessing the Power of Networks for Social Impact* (Washington, DC: Island Press, 2014), 14.

Bloomberg quote: C40 Cities, "C40 Forum, Paris 2015," video, 2:04:05, filmed December 4, 2015, Paris, France, http://www .c40.org/events/c40-forum.

UN quote: UN-Habitat, "Hot Cities: Battle-ground for Climate Change," release with "Cities and Climate Change: Global Report on Human Settlements 2011," accessed September 17, 2017, http://mirror.unhabitat.org/downloads/docs/E_Hot _Cities.pdf.

Ban Ki-Moon quote: United Nations, "'Our Struggle for Global Sustainability Will Be Won or Lost in Cities,' Says Secretary-General, at New York Event," press release, April 12, 2012, http://www.un.org/press/en/2012/sgsm14249.doc.htm.

Membership in the Global Covenant . . . this century: Global Covenant of Mayors for Climate and Energy, accessed July 26, 2017, http://www.globalcovenantofmayors.org.

The 100 Resilient Cities . . . urban population: 100 Resilient Cities, accessed July 26, 2017, http://www.100resilientcities.org.

Urban CO$_2$ Reduction Project: Around 1990, thirteen municipalities in North America, Europe, and Turkey launched a two-year experiment to see what could be planned at the city level to reduce emissions. The thirteen cities were: Ankara, Turkey; Bologna, Italy; Copenhagen, Denmark; Saarbrücken and Hannover, Germany; Helsinki, Finland; Toronto, Canada; Denver, Miami/Dade County, Minneapolis, Portland, St. Paul, and San Jose, United States. See Jeb Brugmann and Philip Jessup, "Cities for Climate Protection: An International Campaign to Reduce Urban Emissions of Greenhouse Gases," International Council for Local Environmental Initiatives (ICLEI), Urban CO2 Reduction Project, February 15, 1993, http://archive.iclei

.org/fileadmin/user_upload/documents/Global/Progams/CCP/ CCP_Reports/ICLEI_TheBirthofCCP_1993.pdf.

Ovink quote: Michael Kimmelman, "The Dutch Have Solutions to Rising Seas. The World Is Watching," *New York Times*, June 15, 2017, https://www.nytimes.com/interactive/2017/06/15/ world/europe/100000005162197.mobile.html?_r=0.

C40 Cities . . . $10 million each: C40 Cities and Arup, "Climate Action in Megacities 3.0," December 2015, http://www.cam3 .c40.org/images/C40ClimateActionInMegacities3.pdf.

Researchers looking . . . climate changes: Lucien Georgeson et al., "Adaptation Responses to Climate Change Differ between Global Megacities," *Nature Climate Change* 6 (2016): 584–88, http://www.nature.com/nclimate/journal/vaop/ncurrent/full/ nclimate2944.html. The ten cities are London, Paris, New York, Mexico City, São Paulo, Beijing, Mumbai, Jakarta, Lagos, and Addis Ababa.

A year earlier . . . LED streetlights: Urban Sustainability Directors Network, "USDN Member Impact Survey," April 2016, https://www .usdn.org/uploads/cms/documents/usdn_2016_member_impact _survey_report_-_may_2016.pdf?source=http%3a%2f%2fusdn .org%2fuploads%2fcms%2fdocuments%2fusdn_2016_member _impact_survey_report_-_may_2016.pdf.

In China . . . low-carbon development: Compact of Mayors, "The Compact of Mayors, Alliance of Peaking Pioneer Cities Sign MOU," press release, June 7, 2016, https://www.compactofmayors.org/ press/the-compact-of-mayors-alliance-of-peaking-pioneer-cities -sign-mou-2/.

And 189 cities . . . disclosure system: See CDP, "Citywide Emissions 2016, Map," accessed November 11, 2017, https://data.cdp.net/ Cities/Citywide-Emissions-2016-Map/iqbu-zjaj.

When the Carbon Neutral Cities . . . energy-efficiency projects: Examples drawn from materials distributed at the Carbon Neutral Cities Alliance annual meeting in Melbourne, July 10, 2017.

Chapter 2: Urban Climate Innovation Laboratories

Andersson quote: Åke Andersson et al., "Creative People Need Creative Cities," *Regional Science and Urban Economics* 47 (2014): 128–37.

Barber quote: Benjamin Barber, *If Mayors Ruled the World: Dysfunctional Nations, Rising Cities* (New Haven, CT: Yale University Press, 2014), 88–89.

Aboutaleb quote: City of Rotterdam, "Rotterdam: Climate Change Adaptation Strategy," October 2013, http://www.rotterdam climateinitiative.nl/documents/2015-en-ouder/Documenten/ 20121210_RAS_EN_lr_versie_4.pdf, 2.

Walsh quote: City of Boston, "Climate Ready Boston: Final Report," December 2016, https://www.boston.gov/sites/default/ files/20161207_climate_ready_boston_digital2.pdf, 2.

De Lille quote: City of Cape Town, "Moving Mountains: Cape Town's Action Plan for Energy and Climate Change," November 2011, http://resource.capetown.gov.za/documentcentre/ Documents/Graphics%20and%20educational%20material/ Moving_Mountains_Energy+CC_booklet_2011-11.pdf, 7.

Hydropower that produces relatively low GHG emissions: For discussion of emissions produced by hydropower, see Bobby Magill, "Hydropower May Be Huge Source of Methane Emissions," *Climate Central*, October 29, 2014, http://www.climatecentral .org/news/hydropower-as-major-methane-emitter-18246; and Chris Mooney, "Reservoirs Are a Major Source of Greenhouse Gases, Scientists Say," *Washington Post*, September 28, 2016, https://www.washingtonpost.com/news/energy-environment/ wp/2016/09/28/scientists-just-found-yet-another-way-that -humans-are-creating-greenhouse-gases/?utm_term =.7c0cf31f4a8c.

In Cape Town . . . household income: For low-income users of transport, the average cost is 45 percent of monthly household income. See City of Cape Town Transport and Urban Development Authority, "What We Do," accessed March 24, 2018, https:// tdacontenthubfunctions.azurewebsites.net/Document/907.

Cape Town went . . . electricity: Patricia De Lille, "Cape Town Taking Control of Its Energy Future," statement issued, *PoliticsWeb*, November 2, 2016, http://www.politicsweb .co.za/news-and-analysis/cape-town-taking-control-of-its -energy-future--pat.

Chapter 3: Goals, Systems, Clusters, and Waves

SimCity quote: SimCity, game info, accessed August 5, 2017, http://www2.ea.com/sim-city.

Vancouver . . . renewable sources by 2050: City of Vancouver, "Renewable City Strategy: 2015–2050," 2015, http://vancouver.ca/files/cov/renewable-city-strategy-booklet-2015.pdf.

Cape Town . . . by 37 percent: City of Cape Town, "Report to the Mayoral Committee and Council: Cape Town's Energy2040 Vision and Commitment to the Associated Energy and Carbon Emissions Targets For 2020," Cape Town Energy, Environment, and Spatial Planning draft memorandum provided to authors.

Boston's adaptation plan quote: City of Boston, "Climate Ready Boston: Final Report," December 2016, https://www.boston.gov/sites/default/files/20161207_climate_ready_boston_digital2.pdf, 74.

Rotterdam quote: City of Rotterdam, "Rotterdam: Climate Change Adaptation Strategy," October 2013, http://www.rotterdamclimateinitiative.nl/documents/2015-en-ouder/Documenten/20121210_RAS_EN_lr_versie_4.pdf, 7.

Boston's storm-water . . . flooding in parts of the city: City of Boston, "Climate Ready Boston," 18.

In New York City . . . peak month: Emma G. Fitzsimmons and Winnie Hu, "The Downside of Ride-Hailing: More New York City Gridlock," *New York Times*, March 6, 2017, https://www.nytimes.com/2017/03/06/nyregion/uber-ride-hailing-new-york-transportation.html?smprod=nytcore-iphone&smid=nytcore-iphone-share&_r=0.

Boulder, with about 108,000 residents . . . 650,000 trees: City of Boulder, website, accessed December 18, 2016, https://bouldercolorado.gov.

DC Water . . . $600 million a year in revenue: District of Columbia Water and Sewer Authority, "Executive Budget Summary: Approved FY 2018, Adopted December 1, 2016," 2016, https://www.dcwater.com/sites/default/files/documents/executive_budget_summary.pdf.

Shanghai's port . . . containers: "Shanghai Keeps Lead as World's Busiest Port," *World Maritime News*, January 20, 2015, http://

worldmaritimenews.com/archives/149917/shanghai
-keeps-lead-as-worlds-busiest-container-port/.

New York City's property is worth more than $1 trillion: Javier
David, "NYC Total Property Value Surges over $1 Trillion,
Setting a Record," *CNBC*, January 16, 2016, https://www.cnbc
.com/2016/01/16/nyc-total-property-value-surges-over-1-trillion
-setting-a-record.html.

Williams quote: Peter Williams, "Protecting Cities' Critical Assets,"
Meeting of the Minds, August 31, 2017, http://meetingoftheminds
.org/protecting-cities-critical-assets-22507.

2015 report by C40 Cities . . . act directly on its own: C40 Cities,
"Climate Action in Megacities 3.0," December 2015, http://cam3
.c40.org/images/C40ClimateActionInMegacities3.pdf, 19, 32.

Portland assessment quote: City of Portland, Letter of Intent to
Carbon Neutral Cities Alliance Innovation Fund, April 13,
2017. Not publicly available; for related information, see Urban
Sustainability Directors Network, "CNCA Kicks off Research
around Autonomous Vehicles in Pacific Northwest," January
2018, https://www.usdn.org/uploads/cms/documents/usdn
_innovation_report-citesandavs-1-2018.pdf.

C40 Cities report quote: C40 Cities and Arup, "Deadline 2020: How
Cities Will Get the Job Done," December 2016, http://www.c40
.org/researches/deadline-2020, 79.

In 2011, Boulder's voters . . . serving the city: Alex Burness, "Plu-
rality of Voters Backs Boulder Municipalization—but Support Has Waned, Daily Camera Poll Finds," *Daily Camera*,
December 5, 2016, http://www.dailycamera.com/news/boulder/
ci_30628398/boulder-municipalization-poll.

When Sidewalk Labs . . . intense community conversation: Ian
Austen, "City of the Future? Humans, Not Technology, Are
the Challenge in Toronto," *New York Times*, December 29, 2107,
https://www.nytimes.com/2017/12/29/world/canada/google
-toronto-city-future.html?_r=0.

1.2 billion automobiles and trucks: John Voelcker, "1.2 Billion Vehicles on World's Roads Now, 2 Billion By 2035: Report," *Green
Car Reports*, July 29, 2014, http://www.greencarreports.com/
news/1093560_1-2-billion-vehicles-on-worlds-roads-now-2
-billion-by-2035-report.

Seventy million new vehicles sold annually: Statista, "Number of Cars Sold Worldwide from 1990 to 2018 (in Million Units)," accessed December 27, 2017, http://www.statista.com/statistics/200002/international-car-sales-since-1990/.

Worldwide, transportation systems . . . 14 percent of all GHG emissions: US Environmental Protection Agency, "Global Greenhouse Gas Emissions," accessed September 15, 2017, https://www.epa.gov/ghgemissions/global-greenhouse-gas-emissions-data.

London had the largest electric bus fleet in Europe: Gunjan Parik, "Cities are Leading an Electric Bus Revolution," C40 Cities, accessed March 28, 2018, http://www.c40.org/blog_posts/cities-are-leading-an-electric-bus-revolution.

In 2015, San Francisco tested . . . use the renewable fuel: Rachel Matsuoka, "San Francisco Switches City Vehicles to Biodiesel," *SFBay*, July 21, 2015, https://sfbay.ca/2015/07/21/san-francisco-switches-city-vehicles-to-biodiesel/.

The city also started . . . a technology that is only beginning to reach the market: Tina Casey, "Land and Sea: San Francisco Doubles Down on Hydrogen Fuel Cell EVs," *Gas2*, May 23, 2016, http://gas2.org/2016/05/23/land-sea-san-francisco-doubles-hydrogen-fuel-cell-evs/.

In the US, cities . . . thirty-five thousand public charging stations by 2016: US Department of Energy data cited in Greg Gardner, "The Self-Driving Revolution Will Be Mostly Electric," *Detroit Free Press*, September 18, 2016, http://www.freep.com/story/money/cars/2016/09/18/self-driving-revolution-mostly-electric/90410520/. The US also had about 150,000 gas stations, each with between six and twelve pumps.

Shanghai had about 3,500 . . . add twenty-eight thousand more by 2020: Dale Hall, Marissa Moultak, and Nic Lutsey, "Electric Vehicle Capitals of the World: Demonstrating the Path to Electric Drive," International Council on Clean Transportation, March 2017, http://www.theicct.org/sites/default/files/publications/Global-EV-Capitals_White-Paper_06032017_vF.pdf.

San Francisco opened . . . licensed diesel vehicles: US Environmental Protection Agency, "San Francisco Opens First Biodiesel Fueling Station—Trucks Running on Waste Oil from

City Restaurants," accessed January 21, 2018, https://www3
.epa.gov/region9/waste/biodiesel/ca/sf-first-station.html.

Half of the world's . . . contain innovation lab cities: Hall et al.,
"Electric Vehicle Capitals."

The city provides . . . buses and taxis: Sture Portvik, "Oslo—the
EV Capital of the World" (presentation, Annual Meeting of
Carbon Neutral Cities Alliance, Oslo, Norway, June 22, 2016).

Shanghai . . . new car license plates: Hall et al., "Electric Vehicle
Capitals."

San Francisco 2004 climate action plan: San Francisco Department
of Environment and San Francisco Public Utilities Commission, "Climate Action Plan for San Francisco: Local Actions to
Reduce Greenhouse Gas Emissions," September 2004, https://sf
environment.org/sites/default/files/fliers/files/climateactionplan.pdf.

Vancouver, for instance, decided . . . 60 percent in 2008: City of
Vancouver, "Transportation 2040 Plan," accessed November 12,
2017, http://vancouver.ca/files/cov/Transportation_2040_Plan
_as_adopted_by_Council.pdf.

The Xinzhuang Metro Station . . . shopping mall: Arup, "A Mini-
City Well Connected by Various Rail and Road Networks,"
accessed January 22, 2018, http://www.arup.com/projects/
xinzhuang_todtown.

In 2016, transit-oriented development . . . jobs in the city: See Brett
Herron, "A New Approach to Transportation Planning—
Cape Town," *PoliticsWeb*, March 15, 2016, http://www
.politicsweb.co.za/news-and-analysis/a-new-approach-to
-transport-planning--cape-town; and Cape Town Green Map,
"Cape Town a Finalist in 2016 C40 Cities Awards," September 26, 2016, http://www.capetowngreenmap.co.za/blog/
cape-town-finalist-2016-c40-cities-awards.

Mexico City . . . BRT system: "Mexico City's Metrobus Cel-
ebrates 10 Years of Service," World Resources Institute, June 23, 2015, http://www.wrirosscities.org/news/
mexico-city's-metrobus-celebrates-10-years-service.

Plans for connecting overcrowded . . . cities every day: Adam
Minter, "How Big Can China's Cities Get?," *Bloomberg
View*, August 25, 2016, https://www.bloomberg.com/view/
articles/2016-08-25/how-big-can-china-s-cities-get.

Minneapolis initiated . . . bicycles into the fleet: Janet Moore,
"Dockless Bike Sharing: Coming Soon to the Twin Cities,"
Star Tribune, November 6, 2017, http://www.startribune.com/
coming-soon-to-the-twin-cities-dockless-bike-sharing/
455456513/.

Singapore . . . the city's tropical downpours: D'Artagnan Consulting,
"Singapore Will Have World's First GNSS Urban Congestion
Pricing Scheme By 2020," March 18, 2016, http://roadpricing.blog
spot.com/2016/03/singapore-will-have-worlds-first-gnss.html.

In an effort to reduce driving . . . $485 million in annual fees:
Christina Anderson et al., "3 Far-Flung Cities Offer Clues to
Unsnarling Manhattan's Streets," *New York Times*, February 26,
2018, https://www.nytimes.com/2018/02/26/nyregion/congestion
-pricing-new-york.html.

The Obama effect: One Gear, Two Legs and Fourteen Islands, "The
Obama Effect," accessed August 22, 2017, http://www.fourteen
islands.com/2032/the-obama-effect/.

During the presidential visit . . . the inner city: Frida Sundkvist,
"Nätjubel Över Ren Luft i Stockholm," *Metro*, September 5,
2013, http://www.metro.se/stockholm/obamaeffekten-mindre
-giftgas-i-luften/EVHmie!XtgWjaeiHh4Q2/.

A commenter . . . keep our city clean?:"New Obama Effect after Stockholm Visit," Kalmstrom.com, September 10, 2013, http://blog
.kalmstrom.com/2013/09/new-obama-effect-after-stockholm
-visit.html.

Montgomery quote: Charles Montgomery, *Happy City: Transforming Our Lives through Urban Design* (New York: Farrar, Straus,
and Giroux, 2013), 8.

When Paris . . . along the Seine River: Kim Willsher, "Paris's First
Attempt at Car-Free Day Brings Big Drop in Air and Noise
Pollution," *Guardian*, October 3, 2015, http://www.theguardian
.com/world/2015/oct/03/pariss-first-attempt-at-car-free-day
-brings-big-drop-in-air-and-noise-pollution.

Sadik-Khan quote: Janette Sadik-Khan, "C40 Mayors Summit—
Day 2: Beyond Cars: Walking, Cycling and Mass Transit"
(presentation at C40 Mayors Summit 2016, Mexico City,
Mexico, December 22, 2016), https://www.youtube.com/
watch?v=HEI7KwQdLH4.

Chapter 4: Making a Better City

Geddes quote: Cited in Michael Batty, *The New Science of Cities* (Cambridge, MA: MIT Press, 2013), 1.

A big change in . . . eight thousand residents, plus shops and businesses: See CBC News, "Vancouver Viaducts to Be Removed, Votes Council," October 28, 2015, http://www.cbc.ca/news/canada/british-columbia/vancouver-viaducts-vote-remove-1.3291781; and Frances Bula, "Vancouver Prepares for Life after Viaducts," *Globe and Mail*, November 20, 2015, http://www.vancouversun.com/vancouver+unveils+million+plan+remove+georgia+dunsmuir+viaducts/11418320/story.html.

Riise quote: Bakken Riise, "Green, Alive and Car Free" (presentation, Annual Meeting of Carbon Neutral Cities Alliance, Oslo, Norway, June 2016).

China Development Bank guidelines: China Development Bank Capital, "12 Green Guidelines: CDBC's Green and Smart Urban Development Guidelines," Draft for Comment, October 2015, http://energyinnovation.org/wp-content/uploads/2015/12/12-Green-Guidelines.pdf.

The shift toward . . . the air we breathe cleaner: C40 Cities, "Our Commitment to Green and Healthy Streets," accessed January 22, 2018, http://www.c40.org/other/fossil-fuel-free-streets-declaration.

C40 Cities identified . . . quality of life: London School of Economics and C40, "Co-benefits of Urban Climate Action: A Framework for Cities," September 2016, http://www.c40.org/researches/c40-lse-cobenefits.

China Development Bank quote: China Development Bank Capital, "12 Green Guidelines."

Seattle plan quote: City of Seattle, "Seattle Climate Action Plan," June 2013, http://www.seattle.gov/Documents/Departments/OSE/2013_CAP_20130612.pdf, 16.

London School of Economics quote: LSE Cities, "Copenhagen: Green Economy Leader," https://lsecities.net/publications/reports/copenhagen/, 34.

The city's per-capita . . . 1991 and 2012: LSE Cities, 34.

29 percent . . . taken on bicycles: City of Copenhagen, "Copenhagen City of Cyclists: The Bicycle Account 2016," September 2017,

PDF downloaded at http://kk.sites.itera.dk/apps/kk_pub2/
index.asp?mode=detalje&id=1698.

Since 2014, it has built ten bridges in the harbor area: City of
Copenhagen, "Copenhagen City of Cyclists."

Chapter 5: The Rebel Alliance

Barber quote: Benjamin Barber, *If Mayors Ruled the World: Dysfunctional Nations, Rising Cities* (New Haven, CT: Yale University Press, 2014).

Clover Moore ... 750 stations around London: C40 Cities, "2015
C40 Forum," video, 2:04:05, filmed December 4, 2015, Paris,
France, http://www.c40.org/events/c40-forum.

Workshop, "China: Towards a Zero Carbon Built Environment":
Architecture 2030, "Net Zero Carbon Professional Training
Program," September 28, 2017, http://architecture2030.org/
china_znc_training/.

More than $17 million ... work: Nils Moe, email to authors,
August 31, 2017.

USDN's annual meeting: The development of the Urban Sustainability Directors Network is described in Peter Plastrik et al.,
*Connecting to Change the World: Harnessing the Power of Net-
works for Social Impact* (Washington, DC: Island Press, 2014).

Chapter 6: The Power of Transformational Ideas

Goethe quote: Johann Wolfgang von Goethe, source unknown,
Goodreads, accessed March 30, 2018, https://www.goodreads
.com/quotes/tag/ideas.

The design and use of ... open to all: Joan DeJean, *How Paris
Became Paris: The Invention of the Modern City* (New York:
Bloomsbury, 2014), 22, 26.

Kotkin quote: Joel Kotkin, *The City: A Global History* (New York:
Modern Library, 2005), 7.

Bennett quote: Lisa Bennett, "10 Things You Want to Know about
Human Nature If You're Fighting Climate Change," *Grist*, June
10, 2015, http://grist.org/climate-energy/10-things-you-want-to
-know-about-human-nature-if-youre-fighting-climate-change/.

Shanghai's stunning . . . a century ago: Wikipedia contributors, "List of Tallest Buildings in Shanghai," *Wikipedia*, accessed March 30, 2016, https://en.wikipedia.org/wiki/List_of_tallest _buildings_in_Shanghai.

Zoom in on London: Drawn from several sources: H. W. Brands, *The First American: The Life and Times of Benjamin Franklin* (New York: Anchor, 2000), 60–63; Clive Emsley, Tim Hitchcock, and Robert Shoemaker, "London History—Material London," *The Proceedings of the Old Bailey*, https://www.old baileyonline.org/static/Material-london.jsp; and Julie L. Horan, *The Porcelain God: A Social History of the Toilet* (New York: Citadel Press, 2000), 64, 73–74. See more at http://www.bl.uk/ georgian-britain/articles/the-rise-of-cities-in-the-18th-century #sthash.Iy1JZIoY.dpuf.

Kearney quote: Richard Kearney, *The Wake of Imagination* (Minneapolis: University of Minnesota Press, 1988), 156.

Hughes quote: Robert Hughes, *The Shock of the New and the Century of Change* (London: BBC Publications, 1980), 11. Cited in Kearney, *Wake of Imagination*, 22.

Rifkin quotes: Jeremy Rifkin, *The Third Industrial Revolution: How Lateral Power Is Transforming Energy, the Economy, and the World* (New York: St. Martin's Press, 2011), see chapter 7, "Retiring Adam Smith," 193–228.

Barry quote: John M. Barry, *Rising Tide: The Great Mississippi Flood of 1927 and How It Changed America* (New York: Simon and Schuster, 1997), 21.

Adams quote: Henry Adams, *The Education of Henry Adams* (Digireads.com, 2009), 233–34.

Trentmann quote (What the department store . . .): Frank Trentmann, *Empire of Things: How We Became a World of Consumers, from the Fifteenth Century to the Twenty-First* (New York: Harper Perennial, 2016), 192–94.

Trentmann quote (Cities were battle zones . . .): Trentmann, 207.

Trentmann quote (Across the world . . .): Trentmann, 207.

Steinberg quotes: Ted Steinberg, *Down to Earth: Nature's Role in American History* (Oxford: Oxford University Press, 2002), see chapter 10, "Death of the Organic City."

General Motors . . . Futurama: See Wikipedia contributors, "New York World's Fair," September 19, 2017, https://en.wikipedia .org/wiki/Futurama_(New_York_World%27s_Fair). A film made in 1939 about the General Motors pavilion can be seen at https://www.wired.com/2007/11/ff-futurama-original/.

Brook quote: Daniel Brook, *A History of Future Cities* (New York: W. W. Norton, 2013), 7–8.

Hall quote: Peter Hall, *Cities of Tomorrow*, 3rd ed. (Malden, MA: Blackwell, 2002), 347.

Car ownership and driving . . . city planning: Hall, 347–48. Peter Newman and Jeffrey Kenworthy note, in *The End of Automobile Dependence: How Cities Are Moving beyond Car-Based Planning* (Washington, DC: Island Press, 2015), chapter 1, that it wasn't until the last decade of the twentieth century that growth of vehicle-kilometers-traveled plateaued in European cities in their Global Cities Database.

A 2016 ranking . . . congested city in the US: TomTom, "TomTom Traffic Index 2016—the Results Are In! Mexico City Takes Crown of 'Most Traffic Congested City' in World from Istanbul," press release, March 22, 2016, http://corporate.tomtom .com/releasedetail.cfm?ReleaseID=961546.

Shepard quote: Wade Shepard, *Ghost Cities of China: The Story of Cities without People in the World's Most Populated Country* (London: Zed, 2015), 119–20.

Malm quote: Andreas Malm, *Fossil Capital: The Rise of Steam Power and the Roots of Global Warming* (London: Verso, 2016), 300.

Florida quote: Richard Florida, *The Rise of the Creative Class*, 10th anniversary ed. (New York: Basic, 2012), e-book location 5919.

Wilson quote: E. O. Wilson, foreword to Timothy Beatley, *Biophilic Cities: Integrating Nature into Urban Design and Planning* (Washington, DC: Island Press, 2011), xv.

Connell quote: David J. Connell, "Planning and Its Orientation to the Future," *International Planning Studies* 14, no. 1 (February 2009): 85–98, accessed September 27, 2017, http://www.tandf online.com/doi/abs/10.1080/13563470902741609.

Janareen quote: Yosef Janareen, *The Risk City: Cities Countering Climate Change—Emerging Planning Theories and Practices*

around the World (Dordrecht, Netherlands: Springer Netherlands, 2015), 3, 8.

Peñalosa quote: Neil Peirce and Gregory Scruggs, "Bogotá Mayor
Enrique Peñalosa on Making Better Cities," *Citiscope*, October
7, 2016, http://citiscope.org/story/2016/bogota-mayor
-enrique-penalosa-making-better-cities?.

Chapter 7: Carbon-Free Advantage

Jacobs quote: Jane Jacobs, conversation with authors, November 25,
1999.

Sixty-one thousand vehicles: Guo Jianli, email to authors, January
12, 2018.

**The one hundred thousand residents of Boulder . . . decarboniza-
tion goal**: City of Boulder, "Energy Future," accessed September 7, 2017, https://bouldercolorado.gov/energy-future/
budget-funding.

Went to court . . . monopoly: Zara Nicholson, "Cape Town Taking
Control of Its Energy Future—Patricia De Lille," *PoliticsWeb*,
November 2, 2016, http://www.politicsweb.co.za/news-and
-analysis/cape-town-taking-control-of-its-energy-future--pat.

Renewable energy has . . . the US alone: Advanced Energy Economy, "Advanced Energy Now 2016 Market Report," accessed
September 19, 2017, http://info.aee.net/aen-2016-market-report.

Ørsted Energy: On November 1, 2017, DONG Energy changed
its name to Ørsted, after Danish physicist and chemist Charles
Hans Ørsted, who in 1820 found that electric current produces
magnetic fields.

Shanghai has negotiated with Tesla: Bloomberg News, "Auto
Suppliers Jump on Report Tesla to Fully Own China Plant,"
Bloomberg, October 22, 2017, https://www.bloomberg.com/
news/articles/2017-10-22/tesla-shanghai-reach-deal-on-wholly
-owned-facility-wsj-says.

The city was where . . . in EV development: Keith Bradsher,
"China Will Lead an Electric Car Future, Ford's Chairman
Says," *New York Times*, December 5, 2017, https://www
.nytimes.com/2017/12/05/business/ford-china-electric-cars.html
?hp&action=click&pgtype=Homepage&clickSource=story

-heading&module=second-column-region&region=top-news
&WT.nav=top-news.

In Cape Town . . . about 25 percent: City of Cape Town, "Frequently
Asked Questions," accessed February 7, 2018, http://saving
electricity.org.za/pages/faqs.php#pfaqs.

In South Africa . . . charged to supply cities: Chris Yelland, "Cape
Town Takes Govt to Court in Bid to Buy Electricity from
IPPs," *Fin24*, August 7, 2017, https://www.fin24.com/Economy/
Eskom/cape-town-takes-govt-to-court-in-bid-to-buy-electricity
-from-ipps-20170807.

Around 1800, Berlin . . . a century earlier: Alexandra Richie, *Faust's
Metropolis: A History of Berlin* (New York: Carroll and Grad,
1998), 143–52.

Mumford quote: Lewis Mumford, *The City in History: Its Origins,
Its Transformations, and Its Prospects* (New York: Harcourt,
1989), 458.

About half of the residents . . . where they lived: Andrew Lees, *The
City: A World History* (Oxford: Oxford University Press, 2015), 67.

Cities developed . . . conditions of industrial work: Andreas Malm,
*Fossil Capital: The Rise of Steam Power and the Roots of Global
Warming* (London: Verso, 2016), 149.

Rifkin quote: Jeremy Rifkin, *The Third Industrial Revolution: How
Lateral Power Is Transforming Energy, the Economy, and the
World* (New York: St. Martin's Press, 2011), 108.

The new towers allowed . . . beacon of commerce: Jason M. Barr,
"Asia Dreams in Skyscrapers," *New York Times*, October 11,
2017, https://www.nytimes.com/2017/10/11/opinion/china-asia
-skyscrapers.html?_r=0.

Florida quote (The economic importance . . .): Richard Florida,
The Rise of the Creative Class, 10th anniversary ed. (New York:
Basic, 2012), e-book location 3090.

Florida quote (Cities are not . . .): Florida, e-book location 3074.

Florida quote (The clustering force . . .): Richard Florida, *Who's
Your City?: How the Creative Economy Is Making Where to Live
the Most Important Decision of Your Life* (New York: Basic,
2008), e-book location 164.

Porter quote: Eduardo Porter, "Why Big Cities Thrive, and
Smaller Ones Are Being Left Behind," *New York Times*,

October 10, 2017, https://www.nytimes.com/2017/10/10/business/economy/big-cities.html?_r=0.

Storper quote: Emily Badger, "What Happens When the Richest U.S. Cities Turn to the World?," *New York Times*, December 22, 2017, https://www.nytimes.com/2017/12/22/upshot/the-great-disconnect-megacities-go-global-but-lose-local-links.html.

Rifkin quote: Rifkin, *Third Industrial Revolution*, see chapter 2, "A New Narrative," 33–36.

Rifkin quote (boutique, high-tech . . .): Rifkin, 264.

Education levels . . . complexity of its systems: Rifkin, 127.

Global energy consumption . . . the entire year: Hannah Ritchie and Max Roser, "Energy Production and Changing Energy Sources," Our World in Data, accessed September 17, 2017, https://ourworldindata.org/energy-production-and-changing-energy-sources/.

Cities were left . . . more energy efficient: ICLEI, "Cities for Climate Protection Campaign 1993," February 15, 1993, http://archive.iclei.org/fileadmin/user_upload/documents/Global/Progams/CCP/CCP_Reports/ICLEI_TheBirthofCCP_1993.pdf.

Thanks to lowering costs . . . global electricity: Damian Carrington, "'Spectacular' Drop in Renewable Energy Costs Leads to Record Global Boost," *Guardian*, June 6, 2017, https://www.theguardian.com/environment/2017/jun/06/spectacular-drop-in-renewable-energy-costs-leads-to-record-global-boost.

Even at these modest . . . four million in China: Paul Horn, "U.S. Renewable Energy Jobs Employ 800,000+ People and Rising: In Charts," *InsideClimate News*, May 30, 2017, https://insideclimatenews.org/news/26052017/infographic-renewable-energy-jobs-worldwide-solar-wind-trump.

A 2016 US government report . . . than in fossil fuels: James B. Stewart, "Electric Vehicle Tax Credit Survives, but G. M. and Tesla Aren't Cheering," *New York Times*, January 11, 2018, https://www.nytimes.com/2018/01/11/business/electric-vehicles-taxes-tesla-gm.html?_r=0.

The world's expenditure . . . on electricity: "World Energy Expenditures Have More than Doubled in 20 Years," *Enerdata*, November 28, 2011, https://www.enerdata.net/publications/executive-briefing/world-energy-expenditures.html.

Stockholm is phasing out . . . the city's electricity: Jesper Starn, "Stockholm Power Goes Green as Biomass Ousts Coal," *Bloomberg*, February 9, 2015, http://www.renewableenergyworld .com/news/2015/02/stockholm-power-goes-green-as-biomass -ousts-coal.html.

Rio de Janeiro . . . resilience officer: Frances Bula, "At 'Renewable Cities' Forum, Envisioning a City That Produces More Energy than It Uses," *Citiscope*, May 19, 2017, http://citiscope.org/ story/2017/renewable-cities-forum-envisioning-city-produces -more-energy-it-uses.

Peduto quote: Anne Hidalgo and William Peduto, "The Mayors of Pittsburgh and Paris: We Have Our Own Climate Deal," *New York Times*, June 7, 2017, https://www.nytimes.com/2017/06/07/ opinion/the-mayors-of-pittsburgh-and-paris-we-have-our-own -climate-deal.html.

Full electrification of transportation . . . 56 percent: The Brattle Group, "Transportation and Heating Electrification Could Aid in Increasing Utility Sales and Reducing Carbon Emissions, According to Brattle Economists," January 24, 2017, http://www.brattle .com/news-and-knowledge/news/transportation-and-heating -electrification-could-aid-in-increasing-utility-sales-and-reducing -carbon-emissions-according-to-brattle-economists.

By 2020, there will be more than twelve million EV charging stations: "Global EV Charging Stations to Skyrocket by 2020, IHS Report Says," IHS Markit, May 28, 2015, http://news .ihsmarkit.com/press-release/automotive/global-ev-charging -stations-skyrocket-2020-ihs-report-says.

In September 2017 . . . two thousand charging stations: Steve Hanley, "40% of New Cars in Oslo = Fully Electric Cars, 20% = Plug-In Hybrids," *Clean Technica*, October 3, 2017, https://clean technica.com/2017/10/03/40-new-cars-oslo-fully-electric-cars -20-plug-hybrids-hot/.

London, Portland, San Francisco . . . any city in the world: Dale Hall, Marissa Moultak, and Nic Lutsey, "Electric Vehicle Capitals of the World Demonstrating the Path to Electric Drive," International Council on Clean Transportation, March 2017, https:// www.theicct.org/sites/default/files/publications/Global-EV -Capitals_White-Paper_06032017_vF.pdf.

Rifkin quote: Rifkin, *Third Industrial Revolution*, 36.

In the last decade . . . start-up companies: Nick Wingfield, "Next Big Tech Corridor? Between Seattle and Vancouver, Planners Hope," *New York Times*, October 2, 2016, https://www.nytimes .com/2016/10/03/technology/next-big-tech-corridor-between -seattle-and-vancouver-planners-hope.html.

Vancouver also provides . . . innovative products: Bryan Buggey, "Cities as Innovation Platform for Green Economic Development," *Meeting of the Minds*, May 15, 2017, http://meetingofthe minds.org/cities-innovation-platform-green-economic -development-21356?utm_source=Meeting+of+the+Minds +Newsletter+List&utm_campaign=dd3317f066-RSS_EMAIL _CAMPAIGN&utm_medium=email&utm_term=0 _cdb70a5ce7-dd3317f066-53205189&mc_cid=dd3317f066&mc _eid=cb375934cd.

Redevelopment-district promoters quote: London Sustainable Development Commission, "Better Future: A Route Map to Creating a Cleantech Cluster in London," accessed March 30, 2018, http://www.londonsdc.org.uk/documents/LSDC_Better Future_March2016_FINAL.pdf.

In 2017, Mayor Sadiq Khan . . . one hundred business start-ups: Natasha Lomas, "London's Mayor Announces £1.6M Clean Tech Incubator," *TechCrunch*, June 12, 2017, https://techcrunch .com/2017/06/12/londons-mayor-announces-1-6m-clean -tech-incubator/.

Boulder 2017 climate action-plan quote: City of Boulder, "Boulder's Climate Commitment: Rising to the Climate Challenge, Powering a Vibrant Future," May 2017, https://bouldercolorado .gov/climate/climate-commitment.

In 1979, the first wind turbine . . . produced offshore: "A World-Leader in Wind Energy," Denmark, official website, November 2015, http://denmark.dk/en/green-living/wind-energy/.

Copenhagen Cleantech Cluster: Cleantech, "Copenhagen's Cleantech Cluster Wins Best-Practice Award," *Copenhagen Capacity*, October 19, 2016, http://www.copcap.com/newslist/2016/ copenhagens-cleantech-cluster-wins-best-practice-award.

In 2015, Danish companies' . . . the nation's exports: "World-Leader," Denmark, official website.

In 2017, China . . . offshore wind power: Teis Jensen, "China to Call on Denmark to Help Build Offshore Wind Farm," *Reuters*, September 4, 2017, https://www.reuters.com/article/us-denmark-windpower-china/china-to-call-on-denmark-to-help-build-offshore-wind-farm-idUSKCN1BF1DX.

In October 2017, the US government . . . for Danish companies: "US to Tap Into Denmark's Offshore Wind Know-How," *Offshore Wind*, October 27, 2017, https://www.offshorewind.biz/2017/10/27/us-to-tap-into-denmarks-offshore-wind-know-how/.

Nordhavn district: Dan Howis Lauritsen, "Copenhagen's Northern Harbour to Serve as Lab and Showroom for Danish Energy Technology," *State of Green*, January 5, 2015, https://stateofgreen.com/en/profiles/state-of-green/news/copenhagen-s-northern-harbour-to-serve-as-lab-and-showroom-for-danish-energy-technology.

The city also declared . . . capacities in the city: "Hitachi Opens Big Data Laboratory in Copenhagen," *Copenhagen Capacity*, accessed October 4, 2017, http://www.copcap.com/invest-in-greater-copenhagen/case-stories/hitachi-opens-big-data-laboratory-in-copenhagen.

Jacobs quote: Jane Jacobs, *Cities and the Wealth of Nations: Principles of Economic Life* (New York: Random House, 1984), 35, 39.

Washington, DC. . . . and six US states: Carbon Neutral Cities Alliance, "Washington D.C. Residents, Businesses and Local Government Spend $1.8 Billion on Fossil Fuels Every Year," accessed October 11, 2017, https://www.usdn.org/uploads/cms/documents/cnca_infographic_-_washingtondc.pdf.

Boulder 2017 climate plan quote: City of Boulder, "Boulder's Climate Commitment."

In Australia . . . cost them to produce the electricity: Michael Slezak, "From Solar Boom to Bill Shock: Australians Face Loss of Rooftop Payments," *Guardian*, July 31, 2016, https://www.theguardian.com/environment/2016/jul/31/australia-residents-solar-rooftop-lose-payments.

Pacific Gas and Electricity: Pacific Gas and Electricity, "PG&E Launches Distributed Energy Resource Projects Testing Technology to Unlock Benefits of the Grid," news release, July 12, 2016, https://www.pge.com/en/about/newsroom/newsdetails/index.page?title=20160712.

In New York State . . . energy-storage industry alone: Leslie Kaufman, "How New York Is Building the Renewable Energy Grid of the Future," *InsideClimate News*, May 25, 2017, https://inside climatenews.org/news/24052017/new-york-renewable-energy -electrical-grid-solar-wind-energy-coal-natural-gas.

In Germany . . . government financial incentives: Richard Heinberg and David Fridley, *Our Renewable Future: Laying the Path for One Hundred Percent Clean Energy* (Washington, DC: Island Press, 2016), 77.

Cumbers quote: Andrew Cumbers, "Remunicipalization, the Low-Carbon Transition, and Energy Democracy," in Worldwatch Institute, *Can a City Be Sustainable?* (Washington, DC: Island Press, 2016), 281.

C40 Cities quote: C40 Cities and Arup, "Deadline 2020: How Cities Will Get the Job Done," December 2016, http://www.c40 .org/researches/deadline-2020, 65.

In 2016 Rio de Janeiro . . . reliability of hydropower: Rio Renewables, "Energy Toolkit for Buildings," accessed January 8, 2018, https://riorenewables.com/why-renewables.

The resilience of microgrids . . . will double: Erica Gies, "Microgrids Keep These Cities Going When the Power Goes," *InsideClimate News*, December 4, 2017, https://insideclimatenews .org/news/04122017/microgrid-emergency-power-backup -renewable-energy-cities-electric-grid.

The number of solar installations . . . in 2011: Kaya Laterman, "Is New York Ready for Solar Power?," *New York Times*, September 30, 2016, https://www.nytimes.com/2016/10/02/realestate/ is-new-york-ready-for-solar-power.html.

In Hamburg . . . city's boundaries: Andrew Cumbers, "Remunicipalization," 284.

Rotterdam's vision quote: TIR Consulting Group, "The Third Industrial Revolution Roadmap Next Economy for the Metropolitan Region of Rotterdam and the Hague," November 4, 2016, https://roadmapnedteconomy.com/wp-content/uploads/2017/ 12/The-Third-Industrial-Revolution, 227.

Kraemer quote: Stanley Reed, "A Small Firm in Germany Has Big Ambitions in Green Energy," *New York Times*, October 17, 2017, https://www.nytimes.com/2017/10/17/business/energy -environment/germany-renewable-energy-solar-wind.html.

Oslo's FutureBuilt program . . . manage energy use: Clayton Moore, "Beneath the Futuristic Architecture, Oslo Really Is as Smart as It Looks," *Digital Trends*, July 10, 2017, https://www.digital trends.com/home/oslo-norway-smart-city-technology/.

A scenario developed for Shanghai: Natural Resources Defense Council, "The Potential of Grid Integration of Electric Vehicles in Shanghai," obtained from Natural Resources Defense Council, September 2016, 3.

This also could earn money . . . the 2016 report: Barbara Finamore, "Uncovering the Full Potential of Electric Vehicles in China," Natural Resources Defense Council, August 10, 2016, https:// www.nrdc.org/experts/barbara-finamore/uncovering -full-potential-electric-vehicles-china.

In Puerto Rico . . . cheaper way of restoring service: Emma Foehringer Merchant, "Puerto Rico Energy Commission Lays Out Rules for a Future Microgrid Landscape," *Green Tech Media*, January 8, 2018, https://www.greentechmedia.com/articles/read/ puerto-rico-energy-commission-island-microgrid.

Some companies in Germany . . . these businesses: Reed, "Small Firm in Germany."

Baum quote: "Written Evidence of Edgar Baum, Brand Finance (Canada) Inc.," accessed October 12, 2017, http://vancouver.ca/ files/cov/Evidence-Edgar-Baum-Vancouver-brand-valuation .pdf. Brand scores for each city: Vancouver, seventy-seven; Singapore, sixty-nine; San Francisco, sixty-four; Sydney, sixty-two; Hong Kong, forty-six; Shanghai, forty-four.

City website quote: City of Vancouver, "Be Part of Vancouver's Story," accessed October 12, 2017, http://vancouver.ca/news -calendar/brand.aspx.

Sustainable Sydney 2030 quote: City of Sydney, "Sustainable Sydney 2030: Green. Global. Connected," accessed October 5, 2017, http:// www.cityofsydney.nsw.gov.au/vision/sustainable-sydney-2030.

Co-Create Copenhagen quote: City of Copenhagen Technical and Environmental Administration, "Co-Create Copenhagen: Vision for 2025," accessed August 11, 2017, https://urbandevelopmentcph .kk.dk/artikel/co-create-copenhagen.

Boulder climate-plan quote: City of Boulder, "Boulder's Climate Commitment."

Ljungkvist quote: Karen Ljungkvist, *The Global City 2.0: From Strategic Site to Global Actor* (New York: Routledge, 2016), 20.

Florida quote: Florida, *Who's Your City?*, e-book location 117.

University of Virginia report: Demographics Research Group, "The Changing Shape of American Cities," Weldon Cooper Center for Public Service, University of Virginia, February 25, 2015, http://demographics.coopercenter.org/files/2016/12/Changing Shape-AmericanCities_UVA-CooperCenter_February2015.pdf.

Amazon Request for Proposals quote: Amazon, "Amazon HQ2 RFP," accessed November 12, 2017, https://images-na.ssl -images-amazon.com/images/G/01/Anything/test/images/usa/ RFP_3._V516043504_.pdf.

Zhu Dajiang quote: Zhang Chun, "Shanghai Must Target Heavy Industry to Peak Emissions," *ClimateChange News*, April 29, 2016, http://www.climatechangenews.com/2016/04/29/ shanghai-must-target-heavy-industry-to-peak-emissions/.

Chapter 8: Efficient Abundance

Montgomery quote: Charles Montgomery, *Happy City: Transforming Our Lives through Urban Design* (New York: Farrar, Straus and Giroux, 2013), 42.

60 percent from natural gas and fuel oils: New York City Mayor's Office of Sustainability, "Inventory of New York City Greenhouse Gas Emissions in 2015," April 2017, http://www.dec .ny.gov/docs/administration_pdf/nycghg.pdf.

Three-quarters of its power from carbon-emitting sources: US Energy Information Administration, "New York: Profile Overview," accessed October 11, 2017, https://www.eia.gov/ state/?sid=NY.

De Blasio report quotation: New York City Mayor's Office of Long-Term Planning and Sustainability, "One City: Built to Last," 2014, http://www.nyc.gov/html/builttolast/assets/downloads/ pdf/OneCity.pdf, 12.

So began the global rise . . . a new height: Katie Medlock, "Worldwide Fossil Fuel Consumption Set a New Record In 2015," *Inhabitat*, June 10, 2016, http://inhabitat.com/worldwide-fossil -fuel-consumption-set-a-new-record-in-2015/. In 2015, coal production declined, but petroleum and natural gas production increased more than the amount of that decline.

Trentmann quote: Frank Trentmann, *Empire of Things: How We Became a World of Consumers, from the Fifteenth Century to the Twenty-First* (New York: Harper Perennial, 2016), 118.

History of consumption quote: Neva Goodwin et al., "Consumption and the Consumer Society," Global Development and Environment Institute, Tufts University, accessed September 11, 2017, http://www.ase.tufts.edu/gdae/education_materials/ modules/Consumption_and_the_Consumer_Society.pdf, 5.

Trentmann quote: Trentmann, *Empire of Things*, 147.

McDonough and Braungart quote: William McDonough and Michael Braungart, *The Upcycle: Beyond Sustainability— Designing for Abundance* (New York: North Point Press, 2013), e-book location 157.

Heinberg quote: Richard Heinberg, "Think Resilience," Post Carbon Institute, series of twenty-two video lectures, available by subscription. Transcript available at https://education.resilience .org/wp-content/uploads/2017/02/Ch07Transcript.pdf.

Dickinson quote: Elizabeth Dickinson, "GDP: A Brief History: One Stat to Rule Them All," *Foreign Policy*, January 3, 2011, http://foreignpolicy.com/2011/01/03/gdp-a-brief-history/.

Trentmann quote: Trentmann, *Empire of Things*, 175.

Electric streetcars . . . ridership: Samuel I. Schwartz and William Rosen, *Street Smart: The Rise of Cities and the Fall of Cars* (New York: Public Affairs, 2015), 6–7.

Cohen quote: Deborah Cohen, "More Is More," *New York Review of Books*, May 25, 2017, 43.

With consumption patterns . . . and transit facilities: David W. Dunlap, "Zoning Arrived 100 Years Ago. It Changed New York City Forever," *New York Times*, July 25, 2016, https://www.nytimes .com/2016/07/26/nyregion/new-yorks-first-zoning-resolution -which-brought-order-to-a-chaotic-building-boom-turns-100 .html.

Barnett and Beasley quote: Jonathan Barnett and Larry Beasley, *Ecodesign for Cities and Suburbs* (Washington, DC: Island Press, 2015), 97–98.

Re-use and recycling . . . 1812 fire: Trentmann, *Empire of Things*, 628.

Hanchao Lu quote: Hanchao Lu, *Beyond the Neon Lights: Everyday Shanghai in the Early Twentieth Century* (Berkeley: University of California Press, 1999). See chapter 6, "Beyond Stone Portals."

"Smellbourne": Julie L. Horan, *The Porcelain God: A Social History of the Toilet* (New York: Citadel Press, 2000), 79.

By the beginning of the twenty-first century . . . three million tons every day: Perinaz Bhada-Tata and Daniel Hoornweg, "Solid Waste and Climate Change," in Worldwatch Institute, *Can a City Be Sustainable?* (Washington, DC: Island Press, 2016), 241.

Stockholm per capita annual disposal: City of Stockholm, "Waste Management Plan for Stockholm, 2017–2020," April 3, 2017, http://www.stockholmvattenochavfall.se/globalassets/pdf1/riktlinjer/avfall/avfallsplan/sva072-avfallsplan_en.pdf, 8.

New York City . . . demolition of buildings: City of New York, "PlaNYC: New York City's Pathways to Deep Carbon Reductions," December 2013, https://www.foet.org/about/tir-consulting -group/cover-third-industrial-revolution-rne/, 100.

Wenar quote: Leif Wenar, "Is Humanity Getting Better?," *New York Times*, February 15, 2016, https://opinionator.blogs .nytimes.com/2016/02/15/is-humanity-getting-better/?_r=1.

Kristof quote: Nicholas Kristof, "Why 2017 Was the Best Year in Human History," *New York Times*, January 6, 2018, https:// www.nytimes.com/2018/01/06/opinion/sunday/2017-progress -illiteracy-poverty.html.

Global Footprint Network quote: Global Footprint Network, "Ecological Footprint," accessed October 15, 2017, http://www.foot printnetwork.org/our-work/ecological-footprint/.

Calgary footprint: Global Footprint Network, "Calgary," April 10, 2015, https://www.footprintnetwork.org/2015/04/10/calgary/.

McDonough and Braungart quote: McDonough and Braungart, *The Upcycle*, e-book location 156.

Yangtze River plastic pollution: Russell McLendon, "10 Rivers May Deliver Bulk of Ocean Plastic," *Mother Nature Network*, October 13, 2017, https://www.mnn.com/earth-matters/wilderness-resources/blogs/ocean-plastic-rivers.

Costanza quote: Robert Costanza et al., *An Introduction to Ecological Economics*, 2nd ed. (Boca Raton, FL: CRC Press, 2015), 21.

Calthorpe quote: Peter Calthorpe, "Urbanism and Global Sprawl," in Worldwatch Institute, *Can a City Be Sustainable?* (Washington, DC: Island Press, 2016), 92.

Brundtland report: "Report of the World Commission on Environment and Development: Our Common Future," United Nations, April 1987, http://www.un-documents.net/our -common-future.pdf.

McDonough and Braungart quote (the item is designed . . .): McDonough and Braungart, *The Upcycle*, e-book location 156.

McDonough and Braungart quote (If human beings . . .): McDonough and Braungart, e-book location 146.

Brynjolfsson and McAfee quote: Erik Brynjolfsson and Andrew McAfee, *The Second Machine Age: Work, Progress, and Prosperity in a Time of Brilliant Technologies* (New York: W. W. Norton, 2016), 165.

Heinberg quote: Richard Heinberg, "Think Resilience," Post Carbon Institute, series of twenty-two video lectures, available by subscription. Transcript available at https://education.resilience .org/wp-content/uploads/2017/02/Ch12Transcript.pdf.

Costanza quote: Costanza, *Introduction*, 1.

Florida quote: Richard Florida, *The Rise of the Creative Class*, 10th anniversary ed. (New York: Basic, 2012), e-book location 5962.

Murray quote: City of Seattle, "Seattle Equity Agenda," accessed November 12, 2017, https://www.seattle.gov/Documents/ Departments/OSE/SeattleEquityAgenda.pdf, 1.

Movement Generation collaborators quote: Movement Generation, "Redefining Resilience: Principles, Practices and Pathways," in Movement Strategy Center, "Pathways to Resilience: Transforming Cities in a Changing Climate," January 2015, 25, http:// pathways-2-resilience.org/ebook/prt-ii-redefining-resilience/.

Boston resilience-plan quote: City of Boston, "The Blueprint: A Preview of the Principles & Framework for Boston's Resilience Strategy," November 19, 2016, https://www.boston.gov/sites/ default/files/document-file-11-2016/skd_100rc_boston _theblueprint_v4.pdf.

Austin . . . elsewhere in the city: Philip Jankowski, "Austin Affordability Plan Shows Incentives to Build Taller, Denser,"

Austin-American Statesman, June 16, 2017, http://www
.mystatesman.com/news/local/austin-affordability-plan
-shows-incentives-build-taller-denser/NaSBkLVF6dxe
VeXN3PJv3J/.

When New York City . . . empowered to act: Urban Sustainability Directors Network, "Marketing for Action Guidebook,"
download available at https://www.usdn.org/public/page/130/
Marketing-for-Action-Guidebook, 24.

Efficiency gains in . . . Energy-Efficient Economy: American Council for an Energy-Efficient Economy, "The Greatest Energy
Story You Haven't Heard," accessed December 12, 2017, http://
aceee.org/sites/default/files/publications/researchreports/u1604
.pdf, 8.

Top ten US cities for energy efficiency: American Council for an
Energy-Efficient Economy, "Cities Boost Efforts to Reduce
Energy Waste: Here's How They Rank," May 10, 2017, http://
aceee.org/press/2017/05/cities-boost-efforts-reduce-energy. The
top ten cities were, in order: Boston, New York City, Seattle,
Los Angeles, Portland, Austin, Chicago, Washington, DC,
Denver, and San Francisco.

The average building energy . . . about 15 percent: Gregory H.
Kats, "Energy Efficiency in Buildings: A Crisis of Opportunity," in Worldwatch Institute, *Can a City Be Sustainable?*, 144.

In September 2017 . . . to make GHG reductions: William Neu-
man, "De Blasio Vows to Cut Emissions in New York's Larger
Buildings," *New York Times*, September 14, 2017, https://www
.nytimes.com/2017/09/14/nyregion/de-blasio-mayor-environment
-buildings-emissions.html.

Vancouver Net Zero Emissions: Stefan Labbé, "Vancouver to Eliminate New Greenhouse Gas Building Emissions by 2030," *CBC
News*, July 13, 2016, http://www.cbc.ca/news/canada/british
-columbia/vancouver-to-eliminate-new-building-emissions-by
-2030-1.3676517.

Pander quote: City of Vancouver, Green Building Manager, "Zero
Emissions Building Plan," policy report to Vancouver City
Council, July 5, 2016, http://council.vancouver.ca/20160712/
documents/rr2.pdf.

An analysis prepared . . . have been upgraded: Architecture 2030, "Achieving Zero: Emissions Reduction in the Built Environment," accessed November 15, 2017, http://architecture2030 .org/initiatives/achieving-zero/, 5.

In New York . . . 45 percent of citywide energy use: New York City Mayor's Office of Long-Term Planning and Sustainability, "One City: Built to Last," 31.

San Francisco quote: Bay Area Air Quality Management District, "Consumption-based GHG Emissions Inventory," January 6, 2016, http://www.baaqmd.gov/research-and-data/ emission-inventory/consumption-based-ghg-emissions-inventory.

Oslo bus company announcement: Nancy Bazilchuk, "Food Waste Recycling Not Always the Best Idea," *Gemini*, January 12, 2016, https://geminiresearchnews.com/2016/01/food-waste-recycling -not-always-the-best-idea/.

San Francisco "zero waste" goal: San Francisco Environment, "Zero Waste," accessed December 18, 2017, https://sfenvironment.org/ zero-waste-in-SF-is-recycling-composting-and-reuse.

Rifkin quote: TIR Consulting Group, "The Third Industrial Revolution Roadmap Next Economy for the Metropolitan Region of Rotterdam and The Hague," November 4, 2016, https://www .foet.org/about/tir-consulting-group/cover-third-industrial -revolution-rne/, 250.

In Europe . . . used only 35–50 percent of the time: Ellen MacArthur Foundation, "Cities in the Circular Economy: An Initial Exploration," accessed October 15, 2017, https://www.ellen macarthurfoundation.org/assets/downloads/publications/Cities -in-the-CE_An-Initial-Exploration.pdf, 5.

European Commission study: World Economic Forum, "Toward the Circular Economy: Accelerating the Scale-up across Global Supply Chains," January 2014, http://www3.weforum.org/docs/ WEF_ENV_TowardsCircularEconomy_Report_2014.pdf.

But by 2016 . . . unused capacity: Håkon Jentoft, "Circular Bio-Resources: Treatment of Food Waste, Garden Waste, and Sludge from Wastewater," Eurocities 2017, accessed September 19, 2017, http://www.eurocities2017.eu/files/uploads/files/Oslo_Circular %20economy%20case%20study.pdf.

Owen quote: David Owen, *Green Metropolis: Why Living Smaller, Living Closer, and Driving Less Are the Keys to Sustainability* (New York: Riverhead, 2009), 7–9.

Research shows that . . . economic productivity: Ellen MacArthur Foundation, "Cities," 5.

In Seattle . . . traffic in 2014: Editorial Board, "Waking Up to Shorter Commutes," *New York Times*, October 29, 2016, https://www.nytimes.com/2016/10/30/opinion/sunday/waking-up-to-shorter-commutes.html?smprod=nytcore-iphone&smid=nytcore-iphone-share.

Calthorpe quote (Mixed use, walkable . . .): Calthorpe, "Urbanism and Global Sprawl," 91.

Calthorpe quote (Single-use residential . . .): Calthorpe, 94.

Energy Foundation China quote: Energy Foundation China, "Shaping China's Sustainable Future through Cities: Could China's Early Peaking Cities Play a Role?," Draft for discussion, September 2016, 3.

Street design guide for Shanghai quote: Deng Han and Huang Runjie, "Taking Back the Streets of Shanghai," *Citiscope*, October 12, 2017, http://citiscope.org/partner/2017/taking-back-streets-shanghai-0?utm_source=Citiscope&utm_campaign=98641ea575-Mailchimp_2017_10_13&utm_medium=email&utm_term=0_ce992dbfef-98641ea575-118053529.

Portland long-range comprehensive plan quote: City of Portland, "2035 Comprehensive Plan," accessed September 15, 2017, https://www.portlandoregon.gov/bps/57352, 6.

Chapter 9: Nature's Benefits

Aboriginal saying: City of Melbourne and Monash University, "Caring for Country: An Urban Application—the Possibilities for Melbourne," accessed August 20, 2017, https://www.nespurban.edu.au/resources/CaringforCountryReport_Apr2016.pdf, 8.

History of city's forest quote: City of Melbourne, "Urban Forest Strategy: Making a Great City Greener, 2012–2032," accessed August 15, 2017, http://www.melbourne.vic.gov.au/SiteCollectionDocuments/urban-forest-strategy.pdf, 18.

Annual rainfall . . . 2002 and 2009: Dave Kendal and Jess Baumann, "The City of Melbourne's Future Urban Forest: Identifying Vulnerability to Future Temperatures," June 2016, https://www.nespurban.edu.au/publications-resources/research-reports/CAULRR02_CoMFutureUrbanForest_Nov2016.pdf, 7.

Residents adapted . . . over mountains: Brittany Patterson, "What Australia Can Teach the World about Surviving Drought," *Scientific American*, May 28, 2015, https://www.scientificamerican.com/article/what-australia-can-teach-the-world-about-surviving-drought/.

Since 2012 . . . three thousand trees a year: City of Melbourne, "Climate Change Adaptation Strategy Refresh 2017," accessed December 12, 2017, http://www.melbourne.vic.gov.au/site collectiondocuments/climate-change-adaptation-strategy-refresh-2017.pdf, 24.

Urban Forest Fund: City of Melbourne, untitled draft media release, obtained July 11, 2017; and City of Melbourne, "$1.2 Million Fund for New Green Projects in Melbourne," media release, May 31, 2017.

Brechin quote: Gray Brechin, *Imperial San Francisco: Urban Power, Earthly Ruin* (Berkeley: University of California Press, 2001), xxiv.

Brundtland report: "Report of the World Commission on Environment and Development: Our Common Future," United Nations, April 1987, http://www.un-documents.net/our-common-future.pdf.

Especially in Western society . . . human agency: See Richard Kearney, *The Wake of Imagination* (Minneapolis: University of Minnesota Press, 1988) for an excellent explanation of this development in thinking.

Register quote: Richard Register, *Ecocities: Rebuilding Cities in Balance with Nature*, rev. ed. (Gabriola Island, BC: New Society, 2006), 80–81.

Sanderson quote: Eric Sanderson, *Mannahatta: A Natural History of New York City* (New York: Abrams, 2009), 13.

Barnett and Beasley quote: Jonathan Barnett and Larry Beasley, *Ecodesign for Cities and Suburbs* (Washington, DC: Island Press, 2015), 96–97.

Today, nearly 15 percent . . . protected status: World Bank, "Terrestrial Protected Areas (% of Total Land Area)," accessed September 11, 2017, http://data.worldbank.org/indicator/ER.LND .PTLD.ZS?page=5.

National Geographic **reports:** "How Green Buildings Could Save Our Cities," *National Geographic*, January 24, 2017, http://www .nationalgeographic.com/environment/urban-expeditions/ green-buildings/benefits-of-green-buildings-human-health -economics-environment/.

The US Environmental Protection Agency website: US Environmental Protection Agency, "Green Infrastructure," accessed August 7, 2017, https://www.epa.gov/green-infrastructure.

Rotterdam adaptation plan quote: City of Rotterdam, "Rotterdam: Climate Change Adaptation Strategy," October 2013, http:// www.rotterdamclimateinitiative.nl/documents/2015-en-ouder/ Documenten/20121210_RAS_EN_lr_versie_4.pdf, 100.

The Zoho . . . a giant rainwater collector: Vittoria Zanuso, "Water Management and Multi-benefit Solutions: The Rotterdam Exchange," 100 Resilient Cities, February 23, 2016, http:// www.100resilientcities.org/blog/entry/rotterdam-exchange.

Especially important is . . . enables urban development: Victoria State Government, "Yarra River Protection (Birrarung): Discussion Paper Summary," 2016, https://www.planning.vic .gov.au/__data/assets/pdf_file/0033/18996/Protecting-the -Yarra-River-Birrarung-discussion-paper-summary.pdf.

Kay quote: Jane Kay, "How the Bay Area Is Restoring Nature's Delicate Balance," *National Geographic*, June 13, 2017, http://news .nationalgeographic.com/2016/12/estuaries-california/.

In 2015 Vancouver . . . outside the city's borders: City of Vancouver, "Greenest City: 2020 Action Plan, Part Two: 2015–2020," accessed November 6, 2017, http://vancouver.ca/files/cov/ greenest-city-2020-action-plan-2015-2020.pdf, 39–55.

Wilson quote: Edward O. Wilson, *Half-Earth: Our Planet's Fight for Life* (New York: Liveright, 2016), 106.

City Biodiversity Index: Singapore Government National Parks, "Singapore Index on Cities' Biodiversity," accessed September 1, 2017, https://www.nparks.gov.sg/biodiversity/urban -biodiversity/the-singapore-index-on-cities-biodiversity.

United Kingdom's Future of Cities project quote: Joe Ravetz, "The Future of the Urban Environment and Ecosystem Services in the UK," October 2015, UK Government Office for Science, 8.

TNC report quote: The Nature Conservancy, "Assessing the Return on Investment in Watershed Conservation," September 16, 2017, https://thought-leadership-production .s3.amazonaws.com/2017/08/11/16/44/32/9d6885b2-3679-4512 -845c-408ae9cb6519/BrazilWaterROI_2.pdf.

Plan to protect the Yarra River quote: Victoria State Government, "Yarra River Protection (Birrarung)," 10.

"Caring for Country" initiative quote: City of Melbourne, "Nature in the City: Thriving Biodiversity and Healthy Ecosystems," accessed October 1, 2017, https://www.melbourne.vic.gov.au/ SiteCollectionDocuments/nature-in-the-city-strategy.pdf, 25.

Caring for Country quote (is a practice of resource use . . .): City of Melbourne and Monash University, "Caring for Country," 7, 12.

New York City . . . building filtration plants: Alice Kenny, "Ecosystem Services in the New York City Watershed," Ecosystem Market-place, accessed September 20, 2017, http://www.ecosystem marketplace.com/articles/ecosystem-services-in-the-new-york -city-watershed-1969-12-31-2/.

They are among the twenty-four . . . daily lives: Timothy Beatley, in email communication to authors on August 15, 2017, iden-tified twenty-four cities that were either original partner cities, newly joined cities that have gone through the protocol process, or cities in some stage of joining the Biophilic Cities Network.

Biophilic projects in cities: For eight city case studies, see Timothy Beatley, *Handbook of Biophilic City Planning and Design* (Wash-ington, DC: Island Press, 2016), part 2, "Creating Biophilic Cities: Emerging Global Practice," 49–138.

Beatley quote: Christopher Swope, "What's a 'Biophilic City'? Let Tim Beatley Explain," *Citiscope*, January 23, 2015, http://citiscope.org/ story/2015/whats-biophilic-city-let-timothy-beatley-explain.

Chapter 10: Adaptive Futures

Hoffer quote: Quote from Eric Hoffer, *Reflections on the Human Condition* (Titusville, NJ: Hopewell, 2006); cited in "Eric

Hoffer," *Goodreads*, https://www.goodreads.com/quotes/146081
-in-a-time-of-drastic-change-it-is-the-learners.

A ton of carbon per passenger: Carbon emissions calculated for a one-
person, one-way flight between Boston and Shanghai, at Carbon Neutral®, accessed December 1, 2017, http://www.carbon
neutralcalculator.com/flightcalculator.aspx.

A 2013 study . . . inundate 30 percent of the city: Casey Ross, "Rising Water Levels Threaten Boston's Waterfront," *Boston Globe*,
August 4, 2013, https://www.bostonglobe.com/business/
2013/08/03/water-threatening-waterfront-development/
b4eCLXFdwk5d8hUHcYdIeI/story.html.

***Boston Globe* quote**: David Abel and Tim Logan, "Floods Seen as
Warning of Boston's Future," *Boston Globe*, January 6, 2018,
https://www.bostonglobe.com/metro/2018/01/05/threat-rising
-sea-levels-hits-home/kRSnmY2avJ2kLbvcYEYRbP/story.html.

The US opened . . . and a freeze: Kendra Pierre-Louis, "These Billion-
Dollar Natural Disasters Set a U.S. Record in 2017," *New York
Times*, January 8, 2018, https://www.nytimes.com/2018/01/08/
climate/2017-weather-disasters.html?nytapp=true&_r=0.

Bernstein quote: Peter L. Bernstein, *Against the Gods: The Remarkable Story of Risk* (New York: Wiley and Sons, 1998), 1–2.

Connell quote: David J. Connell, "Planning and Its Orientation to
the Future," *International Planning Studies* 14, no. 1 (February
2009): 93, http://www.tandfonline.com/doi/abs/10.1080/
13563470902741609.

Connell quote: Connell, 95.

An assessment of the state of climate adaptation in the US: Susanne
Moser, Joyce Coffee, and Aleka Seville, "A Review and Critical
Assessment of the State of the US Climate Adaptation Field,"
December 2017, https://kresge.org/content/rising-challenge
-together, 7.

Ovink was working . . . Indonesia: Architecture Workroom Brus-
sels, "Water as Leverage for Resilient Cities: Asia," November
10, 2017, http://www.architectureworkroom.eu.

Actions to prevent . . . over several decades: Abel and Logan,
"Floods."

Room for the River initiative: Ruimte voor de Rivier, "Fact Sheet:
Dutch Water Programme—Room for the River," May 14, 2011,

https://issuu.com/ruimtevoorderivier/docs/factsheet_english
_room_for_the_river.

Living Breakwaters: New York Governor's Office of Storm
Recovery, "Learn More about the Living Breakwaters Project," accessed February 7, 2018, https://stormrecovery.ny.gov/
learn-more-about-living-breakwaters-project.

Charles River Water Association model: Charles River Watershed
Association, *Transformation: Water Infrastructure for a Sustainable Future* (self-pub., Kindle, 2016). Also see https://www.crwa
.org/transformation.

Lempert and Knopman quote: Debra Knopman and Robert J.
Lempert, *Urban Responses to Climate Change: Framework for
Decisionmaking and Supporting Indicators* (Santa Monica, CA:
RAND Corporation, 2016), 21.

In Boston . . . and limited English proficiency: City of Boston,
"Climate Ready Boston," 2016, https://www.boston.gov/
departments/environment/climate-ready-boston.

USDN Racial Equity Toolkit Guide: Urban Sustainability Directors
Network, "USDN Innovation Products on Social Equity," May
2017, https://www.usdn.org/public/page/18/Climate-Change
-Preparedness#GuideClimate.

Publication (coedited by Taj James) quote: Movement Strategy
Center, "Executive Summary," *Pathways to Resilience: Transforming Cities in a Changing Climate*, accessed January 3, 2018,
http://pathways-2-resilience.org/ebook/executive-summary/.

Rodin quote: Judith Rodin, *The Resilience Dividend: Being Strong in a
World Where Things Go Wrong* (New York: Public Affairs, 2014), 7.

Kostof quote: Spiro Kostof, *The City Assembled: The Elements of Human
Form through History* (London: Thames and Hudson, 1992), 298.

Chapter 11: New Thinking Spreads

Mandela quote: Quote Investigator, "It Always Seems Impossible
until It's Done," January 5, 2016, https://quoteinvestigator
.com/2016/01/05/done/. Quote attributed to Mandela in 2001.

"Cultural creative" values: Wikipedia contributors, "The Cultural Creatives," *Wikipedia*, https://en.wikipedia.org/wiki/
The_Cultural_Creatives.

Strauss and Howe: William Strauss and Neil Howe, *The Fourth Turning: An American Prophecy* (New York: Three Rivers Press, 1997).

LEED standards: "Better Buildings Are Our Legacy," US Green Building Council, accessed December 21, 2017, https://new .usgbc.org/leed.

Boston Green Ribbon Commission: Coauthor John Cleveland serves as executive director of the Boston Green Ribbon Commission.

Boston Properties: "About," Boston Properties, accessed February 6, 2018, http://www.bostonproperties.com/pages/about.

Carbon pricing incentives: Jennifer Gallé, "The Price Is Right for a Corporate Carbon Tax," November 29, 2017, https://www .greenbiz.com/article/price-right-corporate-carbon-tax. The High-Level Commission on Carbon Prices acknowledged in 2017 that 85 percent of global emissions of greenhouse gases are currently not priced, and about three-quarters of the emissions that are covered by a carbon price are priced below $10 per ton of carbon dioxide–equivalent.

Half the coal plants . . . phased out: Michael R. Bloomberg and Jerry Brown, "The U.S. Is Tackling Global Warming, Even If Trump Isn't," *New York Times*, November 14, 2017, https://www.nytimes .com/2017/11/14/opinion/global-warming-paris-climate-agreement .html?action=click&pgtype=Homepage&clickSource=story -heading&module=opinion-c-col-left-region&region=opinion -c-col-left-region&WT.nav=opinion-c-col-left-region&_r=0.

McKibben quote: Bill McKibben, "Cashing Out from the Climate Casino," *New York Times*, December 15, 2017, https://www .nytimes.com/2017/12/15/opinion/finance-global-warming .html.

Bain and Company quote: Aaron Denman, Arnaud Leroi, and Hubert Shen, "How Utilities Can Make the Most of Distributed Energy Resources," Bain and Company, February 1, 2017, http:// www.bain.com/publications/articles/how-utilities-can-make -the-most-of-distributed-energy-resources.aspx.

In March 2018 . . . forecasted local demand: Robert Walton, "Efficiency, DERs Saving $2.6B in Avoided Transmission Costs, CAISO Says," *Utility Dive*, March 26, 2018, https://www.utility dive.com/news/efficiency-ders-saving-26b-in-avoided-transmission -costs-caiso-says/519935/.

China had more EV sales: Keith Bradsher, "China Hastens the World toward an Electric-Car Future," *New York Times*, October 9, 2017, https://www.nytimes.com/2017/10/09/business/china -hastens-the-world-toward-an-electric-car-future.html?_r=0.

Norway ... alternative fuels: Amie Tsang and Henrik Pryser Libell, "In Norway, Electric and Hybrid Cars Outsell Conventional Models," *New York Times*, January 4, 2018, https://www .nytimes.com/2018/01/04/business/energy-environment/ norway-electric-hybrid-cars.html?_r=0.

Germany's highest administrative court ... air pollution: Melissa Eddy, "German Court Rules Cities Can Ban Vehicles to Tackle Air Pollution," *New York Times*, February 27, 2018, https:// www.nytimes.com/2018/02/27/business/energy-environment/ germany-diesel-air-pollution.html.

Royal Dutch purchase: Matt Egan, "Oil Giant Shell Bets on Electric Cars," *CNN Money*, October 12, 2017, http://money.cnn .com/2017/10/12/investing/shell-oil-buys-electric-car-charging/ index.html.

LEED standards ... ninety-two thousand projects: US Green Building Council, "Better Buildings Are Our Legacy," accessed December 12, 2017, https://new.usgbc.org/leed.

Zero-net-carbon building code: "Zero Net Carbon (ZNC): A Definition," Architecture 2030, July 11, 2016, http://www.architecture 2030.org/zero-net-carbon-a-new-definition/.

Choho quote: Abdeluheb Choho, "How Cities Are Transitioning to a Circular Economy," *Cities Today*, September 22, 2017, https://cities-today.com/how-cities-are-transitioning-to-a -circular-economy/.

About 80 percent ... disposed in the US every year: "Ikea U.S. Introduces National Mattress Recycling Program," Ikea Corporate News, October 2, 2017, http://www.ikea.com/us/en/about_ikea/ newsitem/100217_IKEA_US_mattress_recycling_program.

European Environment Agency quote: European Environment Agency, "Urban Adaptation to Climate Change in Europe 2016—Transforming Cities in a Changing Climate," August 18, 2016, https://www.eea.europa.eu/publications/urban-adaptation -2016, 36.

In a prod for US cities . . . climate changes: Moody's Investors Services, "Climate Change Forecast to Heighten US Exposure to Economic Loss Placing Short- and Long-Term Credit Pressure on US States and Local Governments," announcement, November 28, 2017, https://www.moodys.com/research/Moodys -Climate-change-is-forecast-to-heighten-US-exposure-to --PR_376056.

Swiss foundation issued a new standard quote: Global Infrastructure Basel, "The Standard for Sustainable and Resilient Infrastructure," accessed January 6, 2018, http://www.gib-foundation.org/ sure-standard/.

Arup quotation: Arup, "Cities Alive—Rethinking Green Infrastructure" (London: Arup, 2014), https://www.arup.com/perspectives/ themes/cities/cities-alive-rethinking-green-infrastructure, 9.

Illman quotation: Arup, 5.

European . . . to varying degrees: The Australian government in 2016 issued a plan for working with cities to set goals for each decade leading to 2050 to increase urban tree canopies; see Nicole Hasham, "Turnbull Government's Plan to Make Cities Cooler and Greener," *Sydney Morning Herald*, January 18, 2016, http://www.smh.com.au/federal-politics/political-news/turnbull -governments-plan-to-make-cities-cooler-and-greener-20160118 -gm8fdz.html. In the US, the Environmental Protection Agency issued a guidebook for cities to increase green infrastructure, including green streets, rainwater harvesting, and retrofitting storm-water systems; see US Environmental Protection Agency, "Green Infrastructure," accessed December 28, 2017, https:// www.epa.gov/green-infrastructure/policy-guides. The 2015 green guidelines of the equity-investment arm of China Development Bank, the national government–founded bank for development, called for 20 to 40 percent of new construction to be publicly accessible and usable green space and more for residential areas; see China Development Bank Capital, "12 Green Guidelines: CDBC's Green and Smart Urban Development Guidelines," October 2015, http://energyinnovation.org/wp -content/uploads/2015/12/12-Green-Guidelines.pdf.

Chapter 12: Continuous Innovation

Wilde quote: From Oscar Wilde, "The Soul of Man under Socialism," an essay published in 1891; quote found at *Goodreads*, https://www.goodreads.com/quotes/150705-a-map-of-the-world-that-does-not-include-utopia.

Moore quote: Kenneth R. Wise, "Vancouver's Green Dream," *Science* 352, no. 6288 (May 20, 2016): 921.

Sanderson quote: Eric W. Sanderson, *Mannahatta: A Natural History of New York City* (New York: Abrams, 2009), 237–43.

Van Begin quote: Gino van Begin, "How to Globalize the Sustainable City," *Citiscope*, July 4, 2016, http://citiscope.org/habitatIII/commentary/2016/07/how-globalize-sustainable-city.

$2.6 billion for streets, parks, and other infrastructure: Christina Salmhofer, email to authors, January 8, 2018.

When the city . . . to plot new investments: Mark Sutton, "Copenhagen Crowd Maps Cycling Infrastructure Needs as It Shoots for 50+% Modal Share," *Cycling Industry News*, October 19, 2017, https://cyclingindustry.news/copenhagen-crowd-maps-cycling-infratrustructure-needs-as-it-shoots-for-50-modal-share/.

Some research shows . . . thirty feet tall: Matthew Gordy, "High-Performance Urban Forestry for Green Infrastructure," Boston Society of Architects, April 4, 2011, https://www.architects.org/news/high-performance-urban-forestry-green-infrastructure.

A 2015 assessment . . . condition impacted this performance: Carter H. Strickland Jr., "Green Infrastructure Performance in NYC" (presentation, Rutgers University, Newark, NJ, January 8, 2015), http://www.state.nj.us/dep/dwq/pdf/cso-ppt-green-infra-perform-nyc.pdf.

Shanghai and fifteen . . . water shortages: Asit K. Biswas and Kris Hartley, "China's 'Sponge Cities' Aim to Re-use 70% of Rainwater," *CNN*, September 17, 2017, http://www.cnn.com/2017/09/17/asia/china-sponge-cities/index.html.

Sydney, Melbourne . . . international best practices: Carbon Neutral Cities Alliance, "A Blueprint for Development Approval of Hydrogen Re-fuelling Stations," accessed October 18, 2017, https://www.usdn.org/public/page/91/CNCA-Innovation-Fund-Products#REALIZE.

Badger quote: Emily Badger, "Google's Founders Wanted to Shape a City. Toronto Is Their Chance," *New York Times*, October 10, 2018, https://www.nytimes.com/2017/10/18/upshot/taxibots -sensors-and-self-driving-shuttles-a-glimpse-at-an-internet -city-in-toronto.html.

Seattle Public Utilities goal quote: Seattle Public Utilities, "Strategic Business Plan," accessed November 12, 2017, http://www.seattle .gov/util/aboutus/.

Its 2014 strategic plan . . . 4.6 percent: Seattle Public Utilities, "Progress Report to Council: Second Quarter, 2017," accessed November 12, 2017, http://www.seattle.gov/util/cs/groups/public/ @spu/@diroff/documents/webcontent/1_065561.pdf.

Portland's comprehensive plan quote: City of Portland Planning and Sustainability, "Urban Design Direction," https://www.portland oregon.gov/bps/65430, 38.

San Francisco's Proposition . . . for two decades: "San Francisco Bay Restoration Authority 'Clean and Healthy Bay' Parcel Tax, Measure AA (June 2016)," Ballotpedia, November 11, 2017, https://ballotpedia.org/San_Francisco_Bay_Restoration _Authority_"Clean_and_Healthy_Bay"_Parcel_Tax,_Measure _AA_(June_2016).

Cumbers quote: Andrew Cumbers, "Remunicipalization, the Low-Carbon Transition, and Energy Democracy," in Worldwatch Institute, *Can a City Be Sustainable?* (Washington, DC: Island Press, 2016), 276.

Barber quote: Benjamin R. Barber, *If Mayors Ruled the World: Dysfunctional Nations, Rising Cities* (New Haven, CT: Yale University Press, 2014), xvi.

Barber quote, President Clinton story: Barber, 84–85.

In 2016, C40 estimated . . . reduction goals: C40 and Arup, "Deadline 2020," December 2016, http://www.c40.org/other/deadline _2020, 47.

The city also launched . . . other local projects: Washington, DC, Department of Energy and Environment, "DC Green Bank," accessed January 8, 2018, https://doee.dc.gov/greenbank.

Chapter 13: A New Urban Future?

Rifkin quote: Rifkin quoted in Jeff Beer, "Will the Third Industrial Revolution Create an Economic Boom That Saves the Planet?," *Fast Company*, April 26, 2017, https://www.fastcompany.com/40410329/will-the-third-industrial-revolution-create-an-economic-boom-that-saves-the-planet.

Wilson quote: Edward O. Wilson, *Half-Earth: Our Planet's Fight for Life* (New York: Liveright, 2016), 192.

Batty quote: Michael Batty, *The New Science of Cities* (Cambridge, MA: MIT Press, 2013), 245.

The amount of CO_2 in the air increased in 2017: Craig Welch, "Carbon Emissions Had Leveled Off. Now They're Rising Again," *National Geographic*, November 13, 2017, https://news.nationalgeographic.com/2017/11/climate-change-carbon-emissions-rising-environment/.

Australia's emissions . . . electricity soared: Michael Slezak, "Australia's Greenhouse Gas Emissions Highest on Record," *Guardian*, December 10, 2017, https://www.theguardian.com/environment/2017/dec/11/australias-transport-emissions-in-past-year-the-highest-on-record.

Although Germany . . . GHG-emissions reduction: Megan Darby, "Germany Set to Abandon 2020 Climate Target: Reports," *Climate Home News*, August 1, 2017, http://www.climatechangenews.com/2018/01/08/germany-set-abandon-2020-climate-target-reports/.

Oslo . . . North Sea oil and gas: Anca Gurzu, "The Norwegians Who Would Slay Golden Energy Goose," *Politico*, September 5, 2017, https://www.politico.eu/article/norway-election-could-promote-oil-and-gas-skeptics/.

Companies that . . . changes in America: Rachel Leven, "These Companies Support Climate Action, So Why Are They Funding Opposition to It?," *Center for Public Integrity*, September 19, 2017, https://www.publicintegrity.org/2017/09/19/21168/these-companies-support-climate-action-so-why-are-they-funding-opposition-it.

Geoengineering: See Alister Doyle, "Scientists Dim Sunlight, Suck up Carbon Dioxide to Cool Planet," *Reuters*, July 26, 2017,

http://www.reuters.com/article/us-climatechange-geoengineering/
scientists-dim-sunlight-suck-up-carbon-dioxide-to-cool-planet
-idUSKBN1AB0J3; John Flakla, "Should We Change Earth to
Halt Warming? Scientists Say Maybe," *E&E News*, July 11, 2017,
https://www.eenews.net/stories/1060057162; and Laurie Goer-
ing, "Carbon-sucking Technology Needed by 2030s, Scientists
Warn," *Thompson Reuters Foundation News*, October 10, 2017,
http://news.trust.org/item/20171010175429-zazqr/.

"Big-impact" ways: Damian Carrington, "Want to Fight Climate
Change? Have Fewer Children," *Guardian*, July 12, 2017,
https://www.theguardian.com/environment/2017/jul/12/
want-to-fight-climate-change-have-fewer-children.

When Californians . . . mandated water restrictions: Karen Kaplan,
"More Ink, Less Water: News Coverage of the Drought
Prompted Californians to Conserve, Study Suggests," *Los Angeles Times*, October 27, 2017, http://www.latimes.com/science/
sciencenow/la-sci-sn-drought-media-coverage-20171026-story
.html.

"Science of cities": See Batty, *New Science*, 245.

"The century of the City" report: Neil R. Peirce, Curtis Johnson,
and Farley M. Peters, *Century of the City: No Time to Lose*
(New York: Rockefeller Foundation, 2008), 18.

**We took these . . . concerned, aligned, and action-oriented commu-
nity**: City of Boulder, "Boulder's Climate Commitment: Rising
to the Climate Challenge, Powering a Vibrant Future," May
2017, https://bouldercolorado.gov/climate/climate-commitment.
Details from the city's data include the following:

> *Awareness*. Most residents and workers in the community—
> 94 percent in Boulder—understand that climate change is
> occurring.
> *Caring*. "Boulder residents and workers consistently cited
> concern for the well-being of themselves, others and future
> generations as the primary value motivating action on
> climate change." A bigger picture: "The good news is that
> the actions that help reduce climate impacts can also bring
> significant local benefits including supporting energy secu-
> rity and ownership, expanding access to affordable living

and clean, accessible mobility, capitalizing on economic opportunity and improving environmental health and biodiversity."

Agreement. Community members support key climate-change actions.

Action. Nearly 91 percent of Boulder residents and workers surveyed are already taking climate action, and so are community groups.

Epilogue: Time Is Our Frenemy

Ibn al Jawzi quote: Cited in Sam Knight, "Sadiq Khan Takes on Brexit and Terror," *New Yorker*, July 29, 2017, https://www.newyorker.com/magazine/2017/07/31/sadiq-khan-takes-on-brexit-and-terror. Knight quotes Sadiq Khan, mayor of London, quoting Ibn Al Jawzi.

Half of today's global population wasn't yet born: In July 2016, the median age of the world population was 30.1 years, per "World Demographics Profile 2018," Index Mundi, June 5, 2017, http://www.indexmundi.com/world/demographics_profile.html.

If this happens . . . at risk from climate changes: C40 Cities and Arup, "Deadline 2020: How Cities Will Get the Job Done," December 2016, http://www.c40.org/researches/deadline-2020.

Figueres quotes: Christiana Figueres, "Climate at a Crossroads" (speech, UMass Boston Speaker Series, University of Massachusetts–Boston, Boston, MA, April 6, 2016), https://www.youtube.com/watch?v=RGl3LSWwVS4&feature=youtu.be.

Acknowledgments

Goodall quote: In Melena Ryzik, "Jane Goodall's Unparalleled Life, in Never-Before-Seen Footage," *New York Times*, October 20, 2017, https://www.nytimes.com/2017/10/20/movies/jane-goodall-documentary-marriage.html?_r=0.

ABOUT THE AUTHORS

—

Peter Plastrik was born in Paris, grew up in New York City, and lived in four cities in Michigan. He is cofounder and vice president of the Innovation Network for Communities (INC), established in 2007. Along with John Cleveland, he was a founding consultant to the Carbon Neutral Cities Alliance and helped it develop its strategic plan and Innovation Fund. He also consulted closely with the Urban Sustainability Directors Network (USDN) and managed USDN's Innovation Fund. Pete has been the lead author on several INC reports about cities and climate change, including "Essential Capacities for Urban Climate Adaptation," supported by the Summit Foundation, and "Leadership by US Cities: Innovations in Climate Action," supported by Bloomberg Philanthropies. He is coauthor with John Cleveland and Madeleine Taylor of *Connecting to Change the World: Harnessing the Power of Networks for Social Impact* (2014). He coauthored two books with David Osborne: *Banishing Bureaucracy: The Five Strategies* (1997) and *The Reinventor's Fieldbook: Tools for Transforming Your Government* (2000). He lives on Beaver Island in Lake Michigan with his wife, Deb, and their pugs.

John Cleveland was born in Alexandria, Virginia, and spent the first twelve years of his life living in small Athabaskan villages on the Yukon River in Alaska that are now "ground zero" for climate-change impacts. Living in remote wilderness gave him an appreciation for the power of Mother Nature and the truth of the admonition "Don't mess with Mama!" Since Alaska, he has lived outside of Boston and in several cities in Michigan, where he worked first in state-government economic development and then as a strategy consultant to small and medium-sized manufacturing companies, most of them automotive suppliers. Along with Pete Plastrik, he is a cofounder of the Innovation Network for Communities, and he has worked with Pete in supporting the growth of the

Urban Sustainability Directors Network and the launch of the Carbon Neutral Cities Alliance. He is coauthor with Pete Plastrik and Madeleine Taylor of *Connecting to Change the World: Harnessing the Power of Networks for Social Impact* (2014). He serves as the executive director of the Boston Green Ribbon Commission, a CEO network that is supporting the development and implementation of the city of Boston's Climate Action Plan. The Commission work has given him a deep appreciation for the nuts and bolts of city-based climate mitigation and adaptation strategies. John lives with wife, Michelle, in Tamworth, New Hampshire, where he greatly enjoys hiking, skiing, biking, and building stone walls.

INDEX
